KIDS ♥ ~~WITHDRAWN~~ MARYLAND

Your Family Travel Guide to Exploring "Kid-Friendly" Maryland

600 Fun Stops & Unique Spots

Michele Darrall Zavatsky

Dedicated to the Families of Maryland

In a Hundred Years…It will not matter, The size of my bank account…The kind of house that I lived in, the kind of car that I drove…But what will matter is…That the world may be different…Because I was important in the life of a child.

- *author unknown*

For the latest major updates corresponding to the pages in this book visit our website:

www.KidsLoveTravel.com

Although the authors have exhaustively researched all sources to ensure accuracy and completeness of the information contained in this book, we assume no responsibility for errors, inaccuracies, omissions or any other inconsistency herein. Any slights against any entries or organizations are unintentional.

- *__REMEMBER__: Museum exhibits change frequently. Check the site's website before you visit to note any changes. Also, HOURS and ADMISSIONS are subject to change at the owner's discretion. If you are tight on time or money, check the attraction's website or call before you visit.*

- *__INTERNET PRECAUTION__: All websites mentioned in KIDS LOVE MARYLAND have been checked for appropriate content. However, due to the fast-changing nature of the Internet, we strongly urge parents to preview any recommended sites and to always supervise their children when on-line.*

- *__EDUCATORS__: There are suggestions for finding FREE lessons plans embedded in many listings as helpful notes for educators.*

KIDS ♥ Maryland ™   Kids Love Publications, LLC

TABLE OF CONTENTS

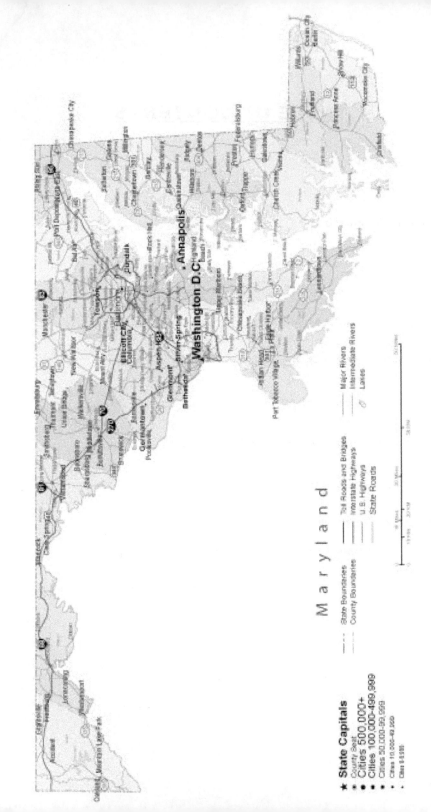

Chapter Area Map

(Chapters arranged alphabetically by chapter name)

HOW TO USE THIS BOOK

(a few hints to make your adventures run smoothly:)

BEFORE YOU LEAVE:

- ☐ Each chapter represents a two hour radius area of the state or a Day Trip. The chapter begins with an introduction and Quick Tour of favorites within the chapter. The listings are by City and then alphabetical by name, numeric by zip code. Each listing has tons of important details (pricing, hours, website, etc.) and a review noting the most engaging aspects of the place. Our popular Activity Index in back is helpful if you want to focus on a particular type of attraction (i.e. History, Tours, Outdoor Exploring, Animals & Farms, etc.).

- ☐ Begin by assigning each family member a different colored highlighter (for example: Daniel gets blue, Jenny gets pink, Mommy gets yellow and Daddy gets green). At your leisure, begin to read each review and put a highlighter "check" mark next to the sites that most interest each family member or highlight the features you most want to see. Now, when you go to plan a quick trip - or a long van ride - you can easily choose different stops in one day to please everyone.

- ☐ Know directions and parking. Use a GPS system or print off directions from websites.

- ☐ Most attractions are closed major holidays unless noted.

- ☐ When children are in tow, it is better to make your lodging reservations ahead of time. Every time we've tried to "wing it", we've always ended up at a place that was overpriced, in a unsafe area, or not super clean. We've never been satisfied when we didn't make a reservation ahead of time.

- ☐ If you have a large family, or are traveling with extended family or friends, most places offer group discounts. Check out the company's website for details.

- ☐ For the latest critical updates corresponding to the pages in this book, visit our website: www.kidslovetravel.com. Click on *Updates*.

ON THE ROAD:

- ☐ Consider the child's age before you stop at an exit. Some attractions and restaurants, even hotels, are too formal for young ones or not enough of an adventure for teens. Read our trusted reviews first.

- ☐ Estimate the duration of the trip and how many stops you can afford to make. From our experience, it is best to stop every two hours to stretch your legs or eat/snack or maybe visit an inexpensive attraction.

- ☐ Bring along travel books and games for "quiet time" in the van. (see tested travel products on www.kidslovetravel.com) As an added bonus, these "enriching" games also stimulate conversation - you may get to know your family better and create memorable life lessons.

- In between meals, we offer the family snacks like: pretzels, whole grain chips, nuts, water bottles, bite-size (dark) chocolates, grapes and apples. None of these are messy and all are healthy.
- Plan picnics along the way. Many Historical sites and State Parks are scattered along the highway. Allow time for a rest stop or a scenic byway to take advantage of these free picnic facilities.

WHEN YOU GET HOME:

- Make a family "treasure chest". Decorate a big box or use an old popcorn tin. Store memorabilia from a fun outing, journals, pictures, brochures and souvenirs. Once a year, look through the "treasure chest" and reminisce.

WAYS TO SAVE MONEY:

- Memberships - many children's museums, science centers, zoos and aquariums are members of associations that provide FREE or Discounted reciprocity to other such museums across the country. AAA Auto Club cards offer discounts to many of the activities and hotels in this book. If grandparents are along for the ride, they can use their AARP card and get discounts. Be sure to carry your member cards with you as proof to receive the discounts.
- Supermarket Customer Cards - national and local supermarkets often offer good discounted tickets to major attractions in the area.
- Internet Hotel Reservations - if you're traveling with kids, don't take the risk of being spontaneous with lodging. Make reservations ahead of time. We don't use non-refundable, deep discount hotel "scouting" websites (ex. Hotwire) unless we're traveling on business - just adults. You can't cancel your reservation, or change them, and you can't be guaranteed the type of room you want (ex. non-smoking, two beds). Instead, stick with a national hotel chain you trust and join their rewards program (ex. Choice Privileges) to accumulate points towards FREE night stays.
- State Travel Centers - as you enter a new state, their welcome centers offer many current promotions.
- Hotel Lobbies - often have a display of discount coupons to area shops and restaurants. When you check in, ask the clerk for discount pizza coupons they may have at the front desk.
- Attraction Online Coupons - check the websites listed with each review for possible printable coupons or discounted online tickets good towards the attraction.

AIRPORTS - All children love to visit the airport! Why not take a tour and understand all the jobs it takes to run an airport? Tour the terminal, baggage claim, gates and security / currency exchange. Maybe you'll even get to board a plane.

ANIMAL SHELTERS - Great for the would-be pet owner. Not only will you see many cats and dogs available for adoption, but a guide will show you the clinic and explain the needs of a pet. Be prepared to have the children "fall in love" with one of the animals while they are there!

BANKS - Take a "behind the scenes" look at automated teller machines, bank vaults and drive-thru window chutes. You may want to take this tour and then open a savings account for your child.

CITY HALLS - Halls of Fame, City Council Chambers & Meeting Room, Mayor's Office and famous statues.

ELECTRIC COMPANY / POWER PLANTS - Modern science has created many ways to generate electricity today, but what really goes on with the "flip of a switch". Because coal can be dirty, wear old, comfortable clothes. Coal furnaces heat water, which produces steam, that propels turbines, that drives generators, that make electricity.

FIRE STATIONS - Many Open Houses in October, Fire Prevention Month. Take a look into the life of the firefighters servicing your area and try on their gear. See where they hang out, sleep and eat. Hop aboard a real-life fire engine truck and learn fire safety too.

HOSPITALS - Some Children's Hospitals offer pre-surgery and general tours.

NEWSPAPERS - You'll be amazed at all the new technology. See monster printers and robotics. See samples in the layout department and maybe try to put together your own page. After seeing a newspaper made, most companies give you a free copy (dated that day) as your souvenir. National Newspaper Week is in October.

PETCO - Various stores. Contact each store manager to see if they participate. The Fur, Feathers & Fins™ program allows children to learn about the characteristics and habitats of fish, reptiles, birds, and small animals. At your local Petco, lessons in science, math and geography come to life through this hands-on field trip. As students develop a respect for animals, they will also develop a greater sense of responsibility.

PIZZA HUT & PAPA JOHN'S - Participating locations. Telephone the store manager. Best days are Monday, Tuesday and Wednesday mid-afternoon. Minimum of 10 people. Small charge per person. All children love pizza – especially when they can create their own! As the children tour the kitchen, they learn how to make a pizza, bake it, and then eat it. The admission charge generally includes lots of creatively made pizzas, beverage and coloring book.

KRISPY KREME DONUTS - Participating locations. Get an "inside look" and learn the techniques that make these donuts some of our favorites! Watch the dough being made in "giant" mixers, being formed into donuts and taking a "trip" through the fryer. Seeing them being iced and topped with colorful sprinkles is always a favorite with the kids. Contact your local store manager. They prefer Monday or Tuesday. Free.

SUPERMARKETS - Kids are fascinated to go behind the scenes of the same store where Mom and Dad shop. Usually you will see them grind meat, walk into large freezer rooms, watch cakes and bread bake and receive free samples along the way. Maybe you'll even get to pet a live lobster!

TV / RADIO STATIONS - Studios, newsrooms, Fox kids clubs. Why do weathermen never wear blue/green clothes on TV? What makes a "DJ's" voice sound so deep and smooth?

WATER TREATMENT PLANTS - A giant science experiment! You can watch seven stages of water treatment. The favorite is usually the wall of bright buttons flashing as workers monitor the different processes.

U.S. MAIN POST OFFICES - Did you know Ben Franklin was the first Postmaster General (over 200 years ago)? Most interesting is the high-speed automated mail processing equipment. Learn how to address envelopes so they will be sent quicker (there are secrets). To make your tour more interesting, have your children write a letter to themselves and address it with colorful markers. Mail it earlier that day and they will stay interested trying to locate their letter in all the high-speed machinery.

General State Agency & Recreational Information

Call *(or visit websites)* for the services of interest. Request to be added to their mailing lists.

- ▢ MARYLAND TOURISM: www.visitmaryland.org
- ▢ State Park Camping & Cabin Reservations: (888) 432-CAMP or ▢ http://reservations.dnr.state.md.us.

- ▢ Maryland Association Of Campgrounds: (301) 271-7012. www.gocampingamerica.com/stateOverview.aspx?id=MD&state=Maryland

- ▢ Maryland Department Of Natural Resources: (877) 620-8DNR. www.dnr.state.md.us.

- ▢ Maryland Bicycle Maps And Publications: (410) 545-5656 or www.sha.state.md.us/SHAservices/mapsbrochures/maps/oppe/maps.asp

- ▢ Maryland Scenic Byways: (877) 632-9929 or www.sha.state.md.us/exploremd/oed/scenicbyways/scenicbyways.asp

- ▢ U.S. Fish & Wildlife Service, Maryland Fishery Resources Office: (410) 263-2604 or http://marylandfisheries.fws.gov

- ▢ Chesapeake Bay Gateways Network: (866) BAY WAYS or www.baygateways.net

- ▢ Maryland's Underground Railroad: www.visitmaryland.org/BrochuresandMaps/UndergroundRailroad.pdf

- ▢ **CAPITAL** - Tourism Council Of Frederick County: (800) 999-3613 or www.fredericktourism.org

- ▢ **CENTRAL** - Annapolis & Anne Arundel County CVB: (888) 302-2852 or www.visitannapolis.org

- ▢ **CENTRAL** - Baltimore Area CVB: (800) 343-3468 or www.baltimore.org and Harborpass - www.baltimore.org/harborpass

- ▢ **CENTRAL** - Havre de Grace Tourism: (800) 851-7756. www.havredegracemd.com

- ▢ **CENTRAL** - Howard County Tourism / Ellicott City: (800) 288-TRIP or www.howardcountymd.gov/hct/hct_homepage.htm

- ▢ **EASTERN SHORE** - Ocean City Department: (800) OC-OCEAN or www.ococean.com

- ▢ **EASTERN SHORE** - Wicomico County CVB: www.wicomicotourism.org

- ▢ **SOUTHERN** - Calvery County Tourism: (800) 331-9771 or www.ecalvert.com

- ▢ **SOUTHERN** - St. Mary's County Tourism: www.stmarysmd.com/tourism

- ▢ **WESTERN** - Deep Creek Lake / Garrett County Chamber: www.garrettchamber.com

- ▢ **WESTERN** - Hagerstown CVB: (888) 257-2600 or www.marylandmemories.com

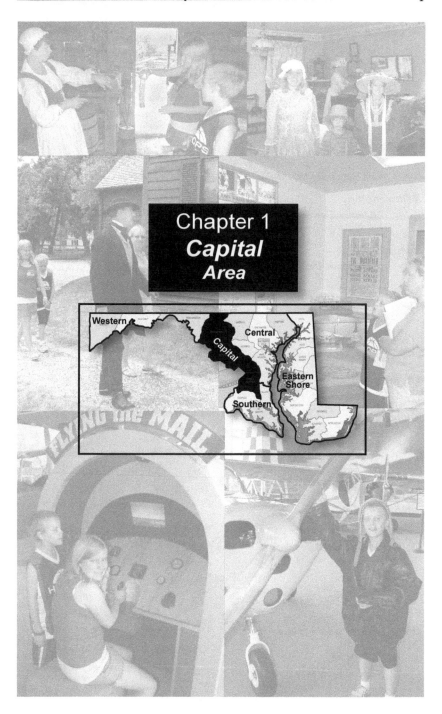

Chapter 1
Capital
Area

Accokeek
- National Colonial Farm In Piscataway Park

Bethesda
- Imagination Bethesda

Bowie
- Bowie Baysox

Boyds
- King Barn Dairy Mooseum

Brunswick
- Brunswick Railroad Museum / C & O Canal Visitors Center

Camp Springs
- Andrews Air Show

Chevy Chase
- Audubon Naturalist Society, Woodend Sanctuary

Clinton
- Surratt House Museum

Colesville
- National Capital Trolley Museum

College Park
- College Park Aviation Museum & Airport

Derwood
- Go Ape Treetop Adventure

Dickerson
- White's Ferry

Fort Washington
- Fort Washington Park

Frederick
- Roger Brooke Taney House
- Rose Hill Manor Park / Children's & Farm Museum

Frederick (cont.)
- Way Off Broadway Dinner Theater & Children's Theater

- Sleep Inn - Frederick
- Hampton Inn & Suites
- Monocacy National Battlefield
- National Museum Of Civil War Medicine
- Frederick's 4th – An Independence Day Celebration
- Great Frederick Fair
- Maze At Crumland Farms
- Oktoberfest
- Summers Farm Adventure

Frederick (New Market)
- Adventure Park USA

Gaithersburg
- Seneca Creek State Park
- Sugarloaf Crafts Festival

Germantown
- Butler's Orchard

Glen Echo
- Clara Barton National Historic Site

Glenn Dale
- Marietta House Museum

Greenbelt
- NASA Goddard Space Flight Center

Landover
- Washington Redskins Football

Largo
- Radisson Hotel Largo
- Six Flags America

Laurel
- National Wildlife Visitor Center
- Montpelier Mansion Holiday Tours

Oxon Hill
- Oxon Hill Farm At Oxon Cove Park

Potomac
- C & O Canal National Historical Park

Riverdale Park
- War Of 1812 Encampment
- Riverdale House Winter Evenings

Rockville
- Rockville Science Day

Suitland
- Airmen Memorial Museum

Thurmont
- Cotoctin Wildlife Preserve/Zoo

Thurmont (cont.)
- Cunningham Falls State Park/ Catoctin Furnace / Gambrill

State Park
- Lawyers Moonlight Maze

Upper Marlboro
- Merkle Wildlife Sanctuary & Visitors Center
- Watkins Regional Park
- Capital Challenge Horse Show/ Washington International
- Gingerbread House Contest And Show
- Hansel & Gretel Tea Party

Walkersville
- Walkersville Southern Railroad

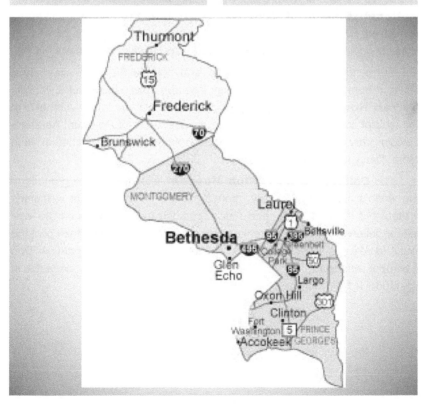

A Quick Tour of our Hand-Picked Favorites Around...

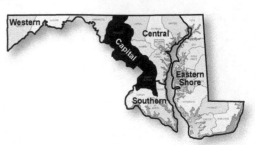

Capital Maryland

Frederick County, Maryland is less than one hour from Washington, DC, Baltimore and nearby Gettysburg, **Antietam** and Harpers Ferry. Today Frederick tells the story of a town divided and the healing provided by this hospital center. Tour **Monocacy National Battlefield** with its new interactive stations or learn about Frederick's healing role in the War at the **National Museum of Civil War Medicine**. **Frederick**'s beautifully revitalized, 50-block downtown area shows off intriguing shops and sites linked to celebrated "locals" like Francis Scott Key & Civil War heroine Barbara Fritchie.

Surrounding the DC area are several notable historical sites, quite different from DC attractions and away from the hussle-bussle of town. The **Surratt House** explores the impact of the Civil War era family entangled in the web of conspiracy surrounding the assassination of President Abraham Lincoln. Very entertaining costumed guides share engaging stories in each room. Can you find the hidden rifle?

The **College Park Aviation Museum** is located on the grounds of the world's oldest continuously operating airport. Wilbur Wright welcomes visitors but the kids don't need much prodding to start exploring the vast indoor gallery of planes. Create your own Air Mail postcard and then pilot the plane to deliver it, work the controls, and test the drag and lift, or airflow. Don a bomber jackets and cap and hop into the Imagination Plane or take a ride in the Model B flight simulator.

Sites and attractions are listed in order by City, Zip Code, and Name. Symbols indicated represent: 🍴 Restaurants   🛏 Lodging

NATIONAL COLONIAL FARM IN PISCATAWAY PARK

Accokeek - *3400 Bryan Point Road (I-95 exit 3A to Rte. 210S to right on Bryan Point) 20607. Phone: (301) 283-2113.   www.accokeek.org.   Hours: Tuesday-Sunday 10:00am-4:00pm (mid-March thru mid-December). Weekends only (rest of year). Park open dawn to dusk. Admission: FREE. Tours: Guided tours at 1:00pm. Note: Weekend visitors may see sewing, cooking, spinning, dyeing, candlemaking, gardening, woodworking and colonial games. Best to plan a visit during a seasonal festival weekend as there is more going on to occupy the kids interest.*

PISCATAWAY PARK, a national park, is on the shore of the Potomac River directly across from George Washington's home, "Mount Vernon". Visitors enjoy the fishing pier; picnic areas; hiking trails; and open spaces. You can check out an excellent view of Mount Vernon from the fishing pier. At the NATIONAL COLONIAL FARM, costumed interpreters offer visitors a glimpse into the lives of middle-class colonial farmers, their animals, and their agriculture. The farm depicts life for an ordinary tobacco planting family in the 1770s. Check out the farm, barn, and smokehouse. A costumed character is usually stationed out in the kitchen, cooking something.

Learning about "farm life"

Historic varieties of field crops such as Virginia Gourdseed corn and Red May wheat are cultivated on a seasonal basis. The Museum Garden crops typify plants grown from different immigrants to the area (ex. Okra from Africa, planted in a circle vs. rows). The Livestock area contains live animals like the milking Devon Cattle or Hog Island Sheep. A modern ecosystem farm near the property demonstrates sustainable, organic farming practices of service to the community co-op program.

WINTER'S EVE CELEBRATION

Accokeek - *National Colonial Farm In Piscataway Park. The farm will celebrate the beginning of the winter season with a cup of colonial cranberry tea, cookies, popcorn, and carols by the fire. Features special musical entertainment and a gift shop. FREE. (December)*

PUBLIC FIELD DAY

Beltsville (Powder) - *Beltsville Agricultural Research Center. View research exhibits, guided tour hay rides, dairy tour, animal petting area, farm equipment on display. (first Saturday in June)*

IMAGINATION BETHESDA

Bethesda - *Woodmont Ave & Elm Street. Children's street festival featuring performers, giveaways and hands-on activities. www.bethesda.org/bethesda/imagination-bethesda. (first Saturday in June)*

BOWIE BAYSOX

Bowie - *Prince George's Stadium, Crain Hwy NE 20716. www.baysox.com. Phone: (301) 803-6000.*

Hot dogs, popcorn and peanuts for the entire family. The Baysox are a AA farm team for the Baltimore Orioles. Season runs April through September and features endless special promotions and special appearances. Also, fireworks, a kids' play area and carousel.

JULY 4TH CELEBRATION

Bowie - *Allen Pond Park. www.cityofbowie.org. One of the biggest July 4th celebrations in the country. Fireworks celebration at dark, food, live entertainment. Baysox play the annual baseball game. FREE for celebration, FEE for baseball game. (July 4th)*

KING BARN DAIRY MOOSEUM

Boyds - *18028 Central Park Circle (South Germantown Recreational Park, I-270 exit Rte 118) 20876. Phone: (301) 528-6530. http://MOOseum.com. Hours: Saturdays 10:00am-3:00pm (May - October) as well as the fourth Sunday of each month (1:00-4:00pm). Admission: FREE.*

This farm is a dairy heritage site dedicated to interpreting the history of farms, families and businesses related to farm products. The stories are told through a permanent collection featuring interactive exhibits and educational programs PLUS seeing the milking stations. Fun on the farm with a recreational park (with playsets) surrounding it.

BRUNSWICK RAILROAD MUSEUM / C&O CANAL VISITORS CENTER

Brunswick - *40 W. Potomac Street   21716. Phone: (301) 834-7100.   www. brunswickmuseum.org.   Hours: Friday 10:00am-2:00pm, Saturday 10:00am-4:00pm, Sunday 1:00-4:00pm. Admission: $7.00 adult, $4.00 youth (6-12). Regular admission is charged whenever a guest would like to view Museum Exhibits. Visitors may however visit the National Park Service's C&O Canal Visitor center and browse the Museum Store without a fee. Note: Nearby towns have Canal related aqueducts: Catoctin Aqueduct (catoctinaqueduct.org) is on Lander Road in Jefferson and Monocacy Aqueduct is at the mouth of Monocacy Road off Rte. 28 near the Frederick/Montgomery County Line.*

Have fun pretending to be a "local"...

The museum offers a giant interactive HO scale model railroad layout, which depicts the B&O Railroad's "Metropolitan Subdivision" from Washington DC's Union Station platforms to Brunswick's large rail yards. The big display takes up an entire floor and has many sight-and-sound push buttons that create smoke or move a carrousel. On the second floor, you will find the exhibits about Brunswick and the people and society located here in 1900. Try on some Victorian era clothing for a picture or use a computer to transmit Morse Code to the conductor down the line. They opened a "Hands on History" Children's entertainment center for the kids (loads of trains to play with). This, and the C&O CANAL VISITOR CENTER are located on the first floor. This visitor center, one of only 6 along the C&O Canal, shows a basic history of Brunswick, as well as showing the competition between the C&O canal and B&O railroad in the 1830s and beyond.

BRUNSWICK RAILROAD DAYS

Brunswick - *East and West Potomac Streets, Railroad Square, Fire Hall. Craft, car, motorcycle, and train show, carnival, pony and MARC train rides, live entertainment. (first weekend in October)*

ANDREWS AIR SHOW

Camp Springs - *Andrews Air Force Base. The Joint Services Open House and Air Show is the largest military open house in the United States. The Open House features vintage and state-of-the-art aircraft, demos, displays, food and refreshments, and a dazzling air show. This is the only event of its kind in the Washington metro area. ID required for each guest age 16+. www.facebook.com/andrewsairshow. FREE. (September weekend)*

AUDUBON NATURALIST SOCIETY, WOODEND SANCTUARY

Chevy Chase - *8940 Jones Mill Road (I-495 exit Connecticut Ave, exit 33 toward Chevy Chase. Left on Manor Rd., right on Jones Bridge, and left on Jones Mill Road)   20815.   www.audubonnaturalist.org/index.php/sanctuaries/woodend-chevy-chase-md   Phone: (301) 652-9188.*

Enjoy the serenity of a wildflower meadow, hike meandering trails, explore the aquatic life of a pond at the 40-acre nature sanctuary, minutes from our nation's capital. Classes feature outdoor, hands-on experiences which build on children's natural curiosity. Open daylight hours. FREE admission.

SURRATT HOUSE MUSEUM

Clinton - *9118 Brandywine Road (Beltway exit 7A, Branch Ave. South (MD 5), right onto Woodyard Rd. (Rte.223W), left on Brandywine) 20735. Phone: (301) 868-1121. www.surrattmuseum.org.   Hours: Wednesday-Friday 11:00am-3:00pm, Saturdays and Sundays Noon-4:00pm (January thru mid-December). Closed Easter Sunday and 4th of July. Last tour of the day begins one-half hour before closing. Admission: $5.00 adult, $4.00 senior and groups, $2.00 child (5-18).*

The 1800s middle-class farm home, tavern and post office with special emphasis on the crucial years from 1840 to 1865. It explores the impact of

this period on our national history as well as on the family of John and Mary Surratt who became entangled in the web of conspiracy surrounding the assassination of President Abraham Lincoln. Today, much of the structure of the House & Tavern is original. Very engaging, entertaining costumed guides share little stories in every room. On a tour, you can see a reproduction of the original attic of the kitchen wing and look down a shaft where a rifle was hidden by Lloyd after Booth and Herold left the premises. The museum's permanent exhibit displays family artifacts, such as Surratt's wire-rim spectacles, pocket watch and a handkerchief with the family name embroidered on it. Want to follow the trail John Wilkes Booth followed to escape being caught? The visitors center map is a great start. The kids really liked this tour and the guides, especially.

JOHN WILKES BOOTH ESCAPE ROUTE TOUR (SPRING)

Clinton - Surratt House Museum. Narrated bus tour on the trail of President Lincoln's assassin. Advance reservations required, sells out quickly. Admission. (two Saturdays in April)

Probably not a coincidence that a rifle was hidden in the wall...

JOHN WILKES BOOTH ESCAPE ROUTE TOUR (FALL)

Clinton - Surratt House Museum. Narrated bus tour on the trail of President Lincoln's assassin; advance reservations required. Admission. (second and fourth Saturday in September)

VICTORIAN YULETIDE BY CANDLELIGHT

Clinton - Holiday tours, period greens, antique dolls and toys, 19th century cards and ornaments, refreshments. Admission. (weekend in December)

NATIONAL CAPITAL TROLLEY MUSEUM

Colesville - *1313 Bonifant Road (New Hampshire Avenue North (Route 650) and go for 5.7 miles to Bonifant Road) 20905. www.dctrolley.org. Phone: (301) 384-6088.   Hours: Saturday & Sunday Noon-5:00pm. Admission: One day museum admission and unlimited rides: $5.00-$7.00.   Educators: Lesson Plans for a variety of subjects: www.dctrolley.org/trips.html#lessonplans.*

The collections consist of 17 streetcars from Washington D.C. and other cities. Many of these are operated on a one-mile demonstration railway. Check out the O-scale model layout representing a Washington streetscape from the 1930s, a video or various street railway artifacts. Trolley rides.

HOLLY TROLLEYFEST

Colesville - Northwest Branch Park. Ride with Santa aboard a trolley and see toy trains in operation. Admission. (first three weekends in December)

COLLEGE PARK AVIATION MUSEUM & AIRPORT

College Park - *1985 Corporal Frank Scott Drive 20740. Phone: (301) 864-6029. www.collegeparkaviationmuseum.com. Hours: Daily 10:00am-5:00pm. Closed major holidays. Admission: $2.00-$5.00 per person. Educators: www. collegeparkaviationmuseum.com/For_Educators/School_Tours.htm Teachers guides for activities and worksheets.*

> The airport was founded in 1909 for the Wright Brothers' instruction of the first military aviators.

The College Park Aviation Museum is located on the grounds of the world's oldest continuously operating airport. The Museum tells the story of flight from the Wright Brothers to today.

Ananimatronic Wilbur Wright welcomes visitors to the exhibits. The museum gallery contains historic and reproduction aircraft associated with the history of the airfield, as well as hands-on activities and experimentation areas for children. Create your own Air Mail postcard using rubbings and stamps. Be an Air Mail pilot, work the controls, test the drag and lift, or air flow. While you're a test pilot, look the part and try on some bomber jackets and caps. Now, hop into the Imagination Plane

and pretend you're the pilot of a 1939 Taylorcraft Airplane...a real plane. Next, write a short story about your "first flight." For the little guys, there is a mini-airport outside with small planes the kids can sit on and ride. The newer 1911 Model B Flight Simulator allows a visitor to fly over the airport with cockpit hand controls and state-of-the-art visuals (the 3-minute "ride" is $1.00 additional). The airport runway is just outside the glass windows of the museum - be sure to watch for a take-off or landing as today's pilots fly. One of the best aviation museums for kids.

HOLIDAY TRAINS AND PLANE

College Park - *College Park Aviation Museum. The museum is all decked out in the Yuletide spirit complete with an encore exhibit. Miniature trains, villages, tunnels and depots bring history to life. Santa fly-in first weekend. Admission. (Saturdays in Dec)*

GO APE TREETOP ADVENTURE

Derwood - *Rock Creek Regional Park, 6129 Needwood Lake Drive (I-270 north exit 8) 20855. Phone: (888) 520-7322. www.goape.com.*

Fun on ziplines, obstacles and Tarzan swings on the most elaborate ropes course you've ever seen. Go Ape's course is centered around the beautiful 75-acre Lake Needwood and is surrounded by hiking trails through forests and along lakeshores, includes picnic areas, boat rentals, fishing and the beginning of the 12 mile Rock Creek hiker/biker trail into Washington DC. The treetop adventure course is made up of numerous rope ladders, 34 crossings to include the Giants Leap and Cacapon Crossing, 2 Tarzan swings and 5 zip lines. Season runs Spring thru Fall. $58.00 adult, $38.00 child (age 10-15).

WHITE'S FERRY

Dickerson - *24801 White's Ferry Road, US 107 (from I-270 & Route 28) 20842. Phone: (301) 349-5200. www.facebook.com/WhitesFerry*

There used to be 100 ferries operating on the Potomac, This is the last one and it's still pretty busy. Vehicles line up and fill up the barge ferry. The ferry follows a wire cable to the other side. It runs continuously, year round, from 5:00am-11:00pm. $5.00 one way or $8.00 round trip.

FORT WASHINGTON PARK

Fort Washington - *13551 Fort Washington Road (I-495 exit 3. Indian Head Hwy south 4 miles to Fort Washington Rd) 20744. www.nps.gov/fowa/. Phone: (301) 763-4600. Hours: Daily 9:00am-4:30pm. Admission: $5.00 per vehicle. Note: Civil War artillery demonstrations, first Sunday of the month from April to October.*

Picturesque Fort Washington sits on high ground overlooking the Potomac River and offers a grand view of Washington and the Virginia shoreline. Today, only one silent gun stands behind the masonry wall-the last armament of the powerful fort that once guarded the water approach to our Nation's Capital. The old fort is one of the few U.S. seacoast fortifications still in its original form - although repairs for the crumbling structure occur often. Exhibits inside the Visitors Center include information and artifacts describing the history of Fort Washington as the Capital's Guardian.

FORT WASHINGTON PARK (cont.)

The old **FORT FOOTE** is just down the road in Oxon Hill. (301-763-4600 or www.nps.gov/fofo) Open 10:00am to dark, the fort was designed in the 1860s to protect the river entrance to the surrounding sea ports. The National Park Service has cleared paths around the ruins of what is considered the best preserved Civil War fort in the region.

ROGER BROOKE TANEY HOUSE

Frederick - 121 S. Bentz Street 21701. www.frederickhistory.org/taney/index. htm Phone: (301) 228-2828. Hours: Saturday 10:00-4:00pm, Sunday 1:00-4:00pm (April - mid-December). Admission: $3.00-$6.00 (ages 12+).

Built in 1799, the site, including the house, detached kitchen, root cellar, smokehouse and slaves' quarters interprets the life of Taney and various aspects of life in early nineteenth century Frederick County. The docents are full of fun and interesting stories and the house creaks and groans as you climb the worn stairs to the top floor. Through guided tours, exhibits and special events, the lifestyle of Frederick's "middling class" is presented to visitors. It contains personal items of the Chief Justice Taney and the Key families (his wife was Francis Scott Key's sister). Taney is best remembered as the author of the majority opinion in Dred Scott v. Sandford (1857), overturning all restrictions on the spread of slavery into the territories, and declared that no African American, either slave or free, could ever be counted as a citizen under the Constitution of the United States. Francis Scott Key is the author of the Star Spangled Banner.

ROSE HILL MANOR PARK / CHILDREN'S & FARM MUSEUM

Frederick - 1611 North Market Street, downtown (US 15, take the Motter Avenue exit; left on 14th Street, left on N. Market St.) 21701. www.rosehillmuseum.com. Phone: (301) 694-1646. Hours: Monday-Saturday 11:00am-4:00pm, Sunday 1:00-4:00pm (April-September). Weekends only in October & November. Admission: $4.00-$5.00 per person (ages 3+). Tours: Reservations are required for groups of 10 or more. No tours between Noon-12:30pm. Educators: Lesson plans and activities are on the Teachers & Parents click thru online.

This living history museum specializes in early American life, historic tours and events designed for children and their adults. The tours focus on the early 1800s, the manor's owners, and their lifestyles. The Farm and Family Exhibit Building houses the following exhibit themes and displays:

The Farm Family Kitchen; The Farmer's Carpentry Shop; The Farmer's Broom Shop; On the Farm Pork Butchering; a Rumly Steam Tractor; and a Wheat Thrashing Machine. All of these spaces have interactive exhibits. The Bank Barn houses The Planting and Harvesting exhibit which includes a large collection of agricultural hand tools and machinery. The Carriage Museum exhibits a variety of restored carriages and sleighs. During the tour, children can card wool, weave on a table loom, play with replicas of old toys, dress up in period costumes, and experience old-fashioned daily chores. For the adult visitor, interpretation of architecture, furnishings, and site history is also included.

FARM MUSEUM FAMILY FESTIVAL

Frederick - *Rose Hill Manor Park. Family festival with hayrides, tractor pull, lawn games, crafts and activity relating to agricultural heritage. Admission. (last weekend in April)*

CIVIL WAR ENCAMPMENT

Frederick - *Rose Hill Manor Park. Civil War living history encampment; demos, skirmish, food concessions, manor tours, and children's activities. Admission. (second weekend in July)*

FARM MUSEUM FALL FESTIVAL

Frederick - *Rose Hill Manor Park. Family festival; demos and activities relating to the agricultural heritage of the area. Admission. (first weekend in October)*

HOLIDAY MAGIC

Frederick - *Rose Hill Manor Park. Holiday programming for children and their families; hands-on activities, snacks, magic shows. Admission. (first Saturday in December)*

WAY OFF BROADWAY DINNER THEATER & CHILDREN'S THEATER

Frederick - *5 Willowdale Drive (Rte. 40 West at Willowtree Plaza) 21702. Phone: (301) 662-6600. www.wayoffbroadway.com. Performances: Children's Theater: Performances every Saturday afternoon and the 2nd and 4th Sunday of each month. Mainstage performances are on: Select Thursday Evenings throughout the month; Friday Evenings; Saturday Evenings; Matinees on Saturday and Sunday. Admission: $18.00 for everyone (Children's). Everyone gets a choice of an individual cheese pizza, a hot dog, or a peanut butter & jelly sandwich. All are served with chips. There's a choice of sodas or lemonade to drink. And for dessert there's ice cream. Mainstage serve a deluxe buffet $32.00-$42.00 per person.*

Broadway musicals with live orchestra, comedies, mysteries, dramas, and Children's Theater lunch matinees (ex. Cinderella, Wizard of Oz). Every production includes a delicious buffet featuring bakery items.

SLEEP INN

Frederick - 5361 Spectrum Drive (I-270 exit 31A or I-70 exit 54 south) 21703. Phone: (301) 668-2003. www.sleepinn.com/hotel-frederick-maryland-MD125. This property has a super friendly staff and is located in the middle of a large shopping and dining complex. Clean rooms and breakfast area. Comfortable beds and spacious. Microwaves and refrigerators available. Their free deluxe continental breakfast lasts 4-5 hours each morning and features fresh pastries, hard-boiled eggs, cereals, juices, fruits, etc. Again, clean and fresh. Nice place to base from while visiting the many favorite historic attractions in Frederick. Often rooms under $75.

HAMPTON INN & SUITES

Frederick - 5311 Buckeystown Pike off I - 270 at Route 85, Exit 31B, three miles from historic downtown 21704. (301) 698-2500. http://hamptoninn.hilton.com/en/hp/hotels/index.jhtml?ctyhocn=FDRMDHX. Complimentary fresh, hot breakfast. Comfy new beds & linens.

MONOCACY NATIONAL BATTLEFIELD

Frederick - 4801 Urbana Pike (I-70 exit 54. Proceed south on SR 355, just past the Monocacy River bridge) 21704. Phone: (301) 662-3515. www.nps.gov/mono/. Hours: Open Daily 8:30am-5:00pm. Closed Thanksgiving, Christmas and New Years. Admission: FREE. Tours: Ranger conducted programs and caravan tours of the battlefield are available on weekends during the summer months.

On Saturday, July 9, 1864, along the banks of the Monocacy River, two armies clashed in a desperate battle for time. Confederates (led by General Jubal Early and his army of 15,000) were on the march towards overtaking Washington D.C. (the Federal Capital). At this battleground, they encountered Union Major General Lew Wallace, with only 5,800 troops, blocking the road to try to save advancement on the Nation's Capital. Greatly outnumbered, Wallace's Union forces lost the battle, but did cost the Confederates time allowing reinforcements to arrive in the Capital, saving Washington from capture.

The center provides interpretive exhibits, an electric map orientation program (outlining the battle sequences) and an interactive computer program. The electric map is really engaging and the kids understand the strategy of the battle and why it was a win AND loss situation. Brochures are available for the self-guided auto tour (this can be boring for kids, we recommend the short trail instead). Two trails are offered within the park: a one-half mile boardwalk loop trail near the visitor center and a six-mile trail on a historic farm within the battlefield.

NATIONAL MUSEUM OF CIVIL WAR MEDICINE

Frederick - *48 E. Patrick Street, downtown (I-70 exit 56, Route 144 west - E. Patrick Street) 21705. Phone: (301) 695-186. Hours: Monday-Saturday 10:00am-5:00pm, Sunday 11:00am-5:00pm. Closed New Years, Easter, Thanksgiving and Christmastime. Admission: $9.50 adult, $8.50 senior (60+), $7.00 student (10-16).*

Immediately following the battles of Antietam and Gettysburg, Frederick was transformed into a hospital center. The town's "clustered spire" churches were used as makeshift infirmaries where as many as 8,000 soldiers were treated at one time. This museum is dedicated to telling the real story of medicine in the Civil War. Major advances changed medicine forever. Two floors of exhibit space cover topics such as: medical schools of the time; men enlisting with chronic diseases; the impact of infectious diseases, poor sanitation and diet on soldiers in camp (more died from illness than wounds); and transporting wounded and field stations. Do you know what the difference is between a Field hospital and a pavilion hospital? Most areas feature immersion exhibits that bring the visitor into a setting vividly illustrating different aspects of Civil War medicine. Walk thru a battlefield or hospital train, identify bones, or feed horses. While you're touring, look for the doctor's final exam, handmade paper chess board and fragrant pine. Each are significant. What an interesting place to study the medical side of a war! Every exhibit solicits conversation and questions - well done!

FREDERICK'S 4TH – AN INDEPENDENCE DAY CELEBRATION

Frederick - *Baker Park. www.celebratefrederick.com. Annual celebration with fireworks, food, four stages of entertainment, boat rides, children's activities and more. (July 4th)*

GREAT FREDERICK FAIR

Frederick - *Frederick Fairgrounds. www.thegreatfrederickfair.com. Agricultural fair, large midway, top musical entertainment. Admission. (third full weekend in September)*

MAZE AT CRUMLAND FARMS

Frederick - *Cumberland Farms. www.crumland.com. 6 acres of twisty-turny joy in the middle of a real working cornfield, truly an a-Maze-ing way to get lost in the fun. Admission. (late September thru October)*

OKTOBERFEST

Frederick - *Frederick Fairgrounds. www.frederickoktoberfest.com. German oompah bands, dancers, food, crafters, children's area, polka, contests. Admission. (first weekend in October)*

SUMMERS FARM ADVENTURE

Frederick - *5614 Butterfly Lane. www.summersfarm.com. Pumpkin patch, hayrides, giant slides, five-acre corn maze, hayloft jumping, farm animals, pumpkin train, pony rides and concession. Admission. (weekends in October)*

ADVENTURE PARK USA

Frederick (New Market) - *11113 W. Baldwin Road (I-70 East. Take Exit 62 – Rte. 75 (Libertytown/Hyattstown). Make a right off the exit ramp. Make first right. At intersection go straight) 21774. www.adventureparkusa.com. Phone: (301) 865-6800. Hours: Sunday-Thursday 11:00am-7:30pm, Friday 11:00am-9:30pm, and Saturday 10:00am-9:30pm. Remember outdoor park attractions may be closed due to cold or inclement weather. Admission: Parking and entrance is FREE. Choose the attractions you like best and purchase a Fun Pass and use it just like a debit card on all rides and attractions. Most cost $2.00-$6.00 per ride.*

This Wild Western themed Family Entertainment Center features Go-Karts, Ropes course, Mini Coaster, Bumper Boats, Miniature Golf, Paint Ball arena, Laser Tag, Arcade, Kiddie-rides, and a café.

SENECA CREEK STATE PARK

Gaithersburg - *11950 Clopper Road (I-270 north towards Frederick, Maryland. Take Exit 10, Clopper Road (Route 117) 20878. Phone: (301) 924-2127. www.dnr. state.md.us/publiclands/Pages/central/seneca.aspx Admission: Day use charge of $2.00-$3.00/person on weekends and holidays (April-October).*

The park extends along 14 scenic miles of Seneca Creek, as it winds its way to the Potomac River. The Clopper Day-Use Area contains many scenic areas, including the 90-acre Clopper Lake, surrounded by forests and fields. Picnicking, boat rentals, trails and a tire playground are just some of its recreational opportunities. A restored 19th century cabin and a self-guided path interpret the history of the area. Traces of the Black Rock and Clopper

Mills are still present today. Black Rock Mill has been stabilized and ou exhibits interpret its operation. The Seneca Sandstone Quarries historic site is near the Potomac River and contains a number of buildings, including the Seneca Stone Cutting Mill and the Seneca Schoolhouse, which is open to the public. The red sandstone was used in the construction of the C&O Canal and the original Smithsonian Institution "Castle." Nearby, the Schaeffer Farm Trail Area offers 12 miles of marked trails for hiking and mountain biking. Water activities include: boat rental, fishing, flatwater canoeing and kayaking.

SHAKER FOREST FESTIVAL

Gaithersburg - Seneca Creek State Park. Observe craftspeople dressed in Shaker-period attire, demonstrating their skills and offering their wares for sale. Shop amid a canopy of trees and mulched pathways for quality handcrafted items and artwork and enjoy performances by entertainers. At the Shaker kitchen, sample selections from delicious foods. Admission. www.shakerforest.org. (second and third weekend in September)

DECEMBERWINTER LIGHTS

Gaithersburg - Seneca Creek State Park. 3 1/2 mile drive through a winter wonderland light display; 350 displays, 60 of them animated. Large capacity vehicles welcome. Admission. www.gaithersburgmd.gov. (Thanksgiving thru end of December)

SUGARLOAF CRAFTS FESTIVAL

Gaithersburg - Montgomery County Fairgrounds, exit 11 off I-270. This exciting show features 450 artists and crafters, delicious food, craft demos and children's entertainment. Admission. www.sugarloafcrafts.com. (first full weekend in April & second long weekend in October, third long weekend in November)

BUTLER'S ORCHARD

Germantown - *20874. Phone: (301) 972-3299. www.butlersorchard.com. Hours: Tuesday-Sunday 9:30am-5:30pm. Admission: varies depends on activity or event.*

- STRAWBERRY BLOSSOM TOURS – Late April through Mid-May, An educational group outing for children preschool through 3rd grade. Children experience a working farm; see how food is grown and harvested; enjoy a hands-on planting activity. Tours offered Tuesday - Friday mornings.

- EVENING HAYRIDES – May to December. Bring a group of friends and take a tractor-driven hayride around the farm. Afterward, gather around a crackling bonfire where you can enjoy the refreshments and entertainment you have brought.

- <u>PUMPKIN HARVEST DAYS TOURS</u> - Provide an enjoyable, educational fall trip for preschool through 3rd grade. Take a tractor driven hayride, visit Barnyard Buddies, pick a pumpkin in the pumpkin patch. Tuesdays - Fridays in October.

HAYRIDE IN BUNNYLAND

Germantown - *Butler's Orchard. www.butlersorchard.com. Bring your basket, hunt for eggs, take a hayride in Bunnyland, visit Butler's Country Bunny and barnyard bunnies. (week of Easter)*

PUMPKIN FESTIVAL

Germantown - *Butler's Orchard. Enjoy a hayride, jump in the hayloft, swoosh down the giant slides, visit barnyard buddies, play the rubber duckie derby, and explore the straw maze! Enjoy beautiful fall foliage, live music, hand dipped caramel apples, crafts, and lots more! (Every Saturday & Sunday in October and Columbus Day)*

HOLIDAY OPEN HOUSE

Germantown - *Butler's Orchard. Enjoy a Hayride through the Christmas Trees, Roast Marshmallows Over an Open Fire, Listen to Live Music, Enjoy Hot Apple Cider and Hot Chocolate. Browse their Farm Market Holiday Shop and Custom Wreath Department. Free Admission, no reservations required. (weekend before Thanksgiving)*

CLARA BARTON NATIONAL HISTORIC SITE

Glen Echo - *3801 Oxford Road 20812. Phone: (301) 492-6245. www.nps.gov/clba. Tours: Daily tours on the hour, 10:00am-4:00pm. FREE. Note: In Glen Echo Park, you can enjoy a carousel ride aboard a 1921 restored Dentzel Carousel or enjoy children's productions at Adventure Theatre.*

Clara Barton was a Civil War nurse who went on to establish the American Red Cross. Clara lived here 1897 to 1912. Her late 19th-century home served as the first headquarters of the American Red Cross. Clara never put anything to waste. When construction began on a Red Cross supplies warehouse near our nation's capital, she thought of using the surplus lumber from relief work at Johnstown, Pennsylvania (see *Kids Love Pennsylvania*, Johnstown Flood). Having once served as a hotel for homeless victims of the epic flood, the large warehouse then served as the first permanent headquarters for the organization she started. Hear about her efforts at Antietam Battlefield, too. After the war, the President commissioned her to try to locate tens of thousands of soldiers still missing. It took an organized, systematic effort to locate many with her diligence.

MARCHING THROUGH TIME

Glenn Dale - *Marietta House Museum. 5626 Bell Station Road, 20769. (301) 464-5291. www.pgparks.com. Annual multi-period military and domestic living history encampment. 400+ reenactors representing Romans to Desert storm period merchants and food. Hands-on activities for kids. Admission. (late April weekend)*

MEDIEVAL FAIRE

Glenn Dale - *Marietta House Museum. 5626 Bell Station Road, 20769. (301) 464-5291. www.pgparks.com. Living history camps (11th-15th century); battle reenactments, music, crafts, period merchants, entertainment, food. Admission. (October)*

HOLIDAY CANDLELIGHT TOURS

Glenn Dale - *Marietta House Museum. 5626 Bell Station Road, 20769. (301) 464-5291. www.pgparks.com. Enjoy Federal, Civil War and Victorian era decorations. Program includes reenactor escorts, live music, storyteller, light refreshments. Admission. (December)*

NASA GODDARD SPACE FLIGHT CENTER

Greenbelt - *Visitor Center, Soil Conservation Road, 8800 Greenbelt Road (I-95/495 Capital Beltway - exit 23 to Greenbelt Rd., Rte. 193 east) 20771. Phone: (301) 286-8981. www.gsfc.nasa.gov. Hours: Tuesday-Friday 10:00am-3:00pm and Saturday, Sunday Noon-4:00pm. Open weekdays until 5:00pm (July, August). Admission: FREE. Check the website for the schedule of model rocket launchings.*

The hub of all NASA tracking activities, Goddard is also responsible for the development of unmanned sounding rockets, and research in space and earth sciences including the Mission to Planet Earth. Through interactive exhibits, families explore the Flight Center with a focus on 1958 to the present. Collections include space flight artifacts and photographs. Science on a Sphere (SOS) is a large, mesmerizing 'earth ball' that uses computers and video projectors to display animated data on the outside of a suspended, 6-foot diameter, white sphere. Four strategically placed projectors work in unison to coat the sphere with data such as "3-D surface of the earth and Nighttime Lights," "Moon and Mars" and "X-Ray Sun." To further enhance the experience, catch the movie, "Footprints." The movie consists of a visually rich presentation where the earth appears in a variety of guises, from depictions of the biosphere to planetary views of city lights at night to dramatic examinations about the science of hurricane formation.

In the Science Center, students use the Hubble Telescope computer to "hit" Jupiter with a comet; attempt to put star clusters in order of age; use the Hubble Deep Field image to estimate the number of galaxies in the universe; match before and after images of colliding galaxies; and also learn about the different wavelengths of light by taking pictures of their hands in visible and infrared light. Numerous videos are shown including, Shoemaker-Levy (a comet collision with Jupiter), Star Life Cycle Animations, Age of the Universe and the Hubble Deep Field. Outside, the Center features a full-size rocket garden with many types of rockets, mock-ups, and old flight hardware. This collection is 100% real NASA artifacts. Ask to see the tree that went to the moon.

WASHINGTON REDSKINS FOOTBALL

Landover - *(FedEx Field, I-495/I-95 South to I-95 Exit 17A (Landover Rd. East), turn right on Lottsford Rd. Follow to Arena Drive) 20785. Phone: (301) 276-6800. www.redskins.com.*

Home of the Washington Redskins NFL team playing August thru December (then playoffs). From the days of Slingin' Sammy Baugh through the Joe Gibbs era, Redskins fans have always been some of the most loyal and dedicated in all of sports. It takes teamwork to win a championship and Redskins fans are truly the twelfth man on the field.

DOUBLETREE HOTEL LARGO

Largo - 9100 Basil Court (I-495 exit 17A, set back in corporate park) 20774. The Largo Hotel features 184 perfectly designed guest rooms featuring all of the amenities to make your stay enjoyable. Guest rooms feature the exclusive Sleep Number® Bed, well lit work desk and Complimentary Wireless High-Speed Internet Access. Just 4 miles from Six Flags and 12 miles from DC. When it's time to relax, guests at the Largo Hotel can enjoy the indoor swimming pool and fully equipped, 24-hour fitness center. The Hotel Largo features a full service restaurant and lounge (breakfast buffet, Kids Menu - $5.00). For your convenience, they also offer a lobby shop with light snacks, beverages and microwavable meals available. Micro and Frig in each room. Value rates start around $149.00.

SIX FLAGS AMERICA

Largo - *13710 Central Avenue (I-95 to Largo exit #15A Central Avenue. Head east 5 miles) 20775. Phone: (301) 249-1500. www.sixflags.com/america. Hours: Summer Break, daily 10:30am opening, closing near dark. Weekends only in May* *and September. Admission: Begins around $25.00 for little ones up to $50.00 for most riders. Discount tickets online. Parking additional $15.00.*

Thrilling theme and water-park featuring more than 100 rides, shows and attractions, headlined by the constantly spinning Penguin's Blizzard River raft ride and eight exciting coasters. Younger families enjoy the Pirate themes at Bucanneer Beach and the classic amusement park rides at Whistlestop and Tinseltown (kiddie rides are plentiful and cute). Young families will also like that the music and noise is not loud here. There are plenty of shade trees - especially the entire area of rides near the entrance (right off Main Street). We also liked the fact that many rides were mild enough for many family members to enjoy. Gothan City and the Southwest Territory contained more "thrill" roller coasters although the Batman Thrill Show wasn't too scary for kids to watch as they cheered Batman on. For a classic wooden roller coaster, try the Wild One. And don't forget the price includes Hurricane Harbor water park with the same combo of mild to max rides for all ages.

NATIONAL WILDLIFE VISITOR CENTER

Laurel - *10901 Scarlet Tanager Loop (off of Powder Mill Rd. between the Baltimore-Washington Parkway and Rt. 197 south of Laurel) 20708. Phone: (301) 497-5760. www.pwrc.usgs.gov/. Hours: Daily 10:00am-4:30 or 5:30pm, except Federal Holidays. Trails open at sunrise. Admission: Events are held at the National Wildlife Visitor Center unless otherwise noted and are FREE. Tram Tours are $1.00-$3.00 per person. Tours: Wildlife Conservation Tram Tours are mid-March through mid-November, Saturday & Sunday, 11:30am-3:30pm. Weather permitting. The tram tour offers a ride through woodland and wetland areas guided by an interpreter. A variety of wildlife and evidence of ongoing research here can be seen along the way. Tickets can be purchased in the bookstore.*

The National Wildlife Visitor Center is the largest science and environmental education center in the Department of the Interior. It highlights the work of professional scientists who strive to improve the condition of wildlife and their habitats. Be a field researcher and travel through five life-scale habitat areas. Learn through hands-on interactive exhibits how wildlife research has led to important discoveries. "Play" with scientific tools, press buttons along the way and watch with surprise as creatures appear and hide among the trees. See dramatic dioramas of gray wolves, whooping cranes, canvasback ducks and sea otters displaying true-to-life behavior - up close and in their own environment. If the weather is unkind, stay indoors and peer out their giant Pond Window.

The Visitor Center also offers hiking trails. The Loop Trail - (0.5 km/0.3 mi.) is a paved and fully accessible trail. It leaves the visitor center gallery door and offers views of both Lake Redington and Cash Lake. Goose Pond Trail - (0.3 km/0.2 mi.) parallels the wood's edge as it wanders first through a forested wetland area as it leads to Goose Pond. Laurel Trail - This woodland trail (0.6 km/0.4 mi.) was named for the many Mountain Laurels found along the trail. Visitors have the opportunity to see woodland songbirds and mammals (esp. deer). Cash Lake Trail - (2.3 km/1.4 mi.) travels along the edge of Cash Lake. This trail offers many opportunities to view the lake and its waterfowl, as well as a beaver lodge and evidence of their activity. There is also a seasonal fishing program at Cash Lake, with fishing by permit from the accessible pier and along parts of the shoreline.

PATUXENT WILDLIFE FESTIVAL

Laurel - National Wildlife Visitor Center. Discover wildlife through behind-the-scenes tours, tram tours, live animals, research exhibits and kids crafts. FREE. (second Saturday in October)

MONTPELIER MANSION HOLIDAY TOURS

Laurel - Montpelier Mansion. www.pgparks.com. Refreshments, live holiday music by area performers, tours of the mansion decorated with green and lit by candlelight. (second long weekend in December)

OXON HILL FARM AT OXON COVE PARK

Oxon Hill - *6411 Oxon Hill Road (I-95/495 Capital Beltway exit 3A) 20745. Phone: (301) 839-1176. www.nps.gov/oxhi/. Hours: Daily 8:00am-4:30pm. Admission: FREE. Note: Venture beyond the hilltop and explore part of Oxon Cove Park's 512 acres by strolling along the lower fields or riding the bike path along Oxon Cove. The Woodlot Trail is a steep 1/2-mile trail, marked with yellow blazes on trees, from just below the farm house to the parking lot. Find out how this wooded ravine benefited early farmers. Educators: Lesson Plans - www.nps.gov/ oxhi/learn/education/classrooms/ curriculummaterials.htm*

WOW! - An average dairy cow weighs about 1,400 pounds and can drink an average of 35 gallons of water a day - the equivalent of a bathtub full of water! There are six cattle that live on Oxon Hill Farm.

Oxon Hill Farm operates as an actual working farm, representative of the early 20th century. You can see a farm house, barns, a stable, feed building, livestock buildings and a visitor activity barn. It exhibits basic farming principles and techniques as well as historical agricultural programs for urban people to develop an understanding of cropping and animal husbandry. The most unique story about this place is that of the early farmers of the wheat crops. From the 1890s until the 1950s, Oxon Hill Farm was operated by patients from St. Elizabeth Hospital. It provided therapy as well as food for the patients at the institution.

Each month offers a variety of programs, such as crafts, walks to observe plants and wildlife, wagon rides, and talks about farm life and the animals. Call ahead for reservations. Farming is a year-round business directed by the seasons. In spring, catch some planting corn or sheering sheep. June is dairy month with cows-a-milking. Fall brings the harvest season and cider pressing or sorghum syrup. Winter is a quiet time for walks, hayrides and tracking.

C & O CANAL NATIONAL HISTORICAL PARK

Potomac - *11710 MacArthur Blvd. 20834. www.nps.gov/choh. Phone: (301) 299-3613. Hours: Open All Year 9:00am-4:30pm. (extended summer hours). Admission: $5.00 per vehicle. Tours: one hour Rides offered weekends April-October. $8.00 adult, $6.00 senior (62+), $5.00 child (4-15).*

Take a mule-drawn barge ride on the historic canal. Footbridges are available to see Great Falls. Enjoy the Riley's Lockhouse, the only original C&O Canal lockhouse still open to the public. Displays and a short film interpret the site. Hiking and biking trails are along the historic towpath, a project which took 22 years to build and stimulated economic growth in little towns along the canal. This canal was considered an engineering marvel in its day. The marshy Dierssen Wildlife Management Area is also on site, with trails teeming with wildlife.

WAR OF 1812 ENCAMPMENT

Riverdale Park - Riversdale House Museum, 4811 Riverdale. http://history.pgparks. com/sites_and_museums/Riversdale_House_Museum.htm American and British military and civilian re-enactors prepare for the Battle of Bladensburg. Admission. (second Saturday in August)

RIVERDALE HOUSE WINTER EVENINGS

Riverdale Park - Riverdale House Museum. 4811 Riverdale. http://history.pgparks.com/ sites_and_museums/Riversdale_House_Museum.htm Step back in time to see the candlelit house, with re-enactors, games and refreshments. Admission. (last Thursday and Friday in December)

ROCKVILLE SCIENCE DAY

Rockville - *Montgomery College. http://rockvillesciencecenter.org/rockville-science-day/ The event, which has free admission and parking, annually attracts thousands for an afternoon of fun with math, science, experiments and a look at the future. Entertainment, learning, rockets, astronomy, mammals, reptiles, chemistry, rocks, fossils, minerals and hands-on science. FREE. (Sunday afternoon in late April)*

NATIONAL MUSEUM OF HEALTH & MEDICINE

Silver Springs - *2500 Linden Lane, 20910. www.medicalmuseum.mil/ Phone: (202) 782-2200. Hours: Daily 10:00am-5:30pm (except December 25). Admission and parking are FREE, but donations are accepted.*

Compare a smoker's lung to a coal miner's lung, see the bullet that took Abraham Lincoln's life as well as fragments of his skull and a lock of his hair, touch a real brain or the inside of a stomach if you dare. Try on a pregnancy garment that makes you feel what it's like to be with child, view skeletons and skulls and a stomach-shaped hairball surgically removed from inside a 12-year-old girl. There are live leeches, the world's most comprehensive collection of microscopes dating to the 1600's, a display of kidney stones, a brain still attached to a spinal cord suspended in formaldehyde, and medical artifacts and instruments important in the development of medicine during the Civil War and today's modern hospital.

AIRMEN MEMORIAL MUSEUM

Suitland - *5211 Auth Road, one mile from Andrews Air Force Base (I-495 exit 7B, right onto Auth Road) 20746. http://amm.hqafaf.org/. Phone: (301) 899-8386. Hours: Weekdays 8:00am-5:00pm and during special events.*

The Airmen Memorial Museum stands as a tribute to enlisted airmen who have served in the United States Air Force, the U.S. Army Air Forces, the Army Air Corps and their predecessor organizations. The focus of the Museum's exhibits, programs, publications, oral history interviews and video documentary histories is the "enlisted experience" - the enlisted people. Stories of pioneers in air/space service are sprinkled with Aeronautical Division signal flags, a 1912 leather flying helmet, and a 1st Aero Squadron banner. World War I artifacts include; recruiting posters, an enlisted pilot's uniform, an American bomb and a Distinguished Flying Cross. Items from Sgt. Ray Gallagher and MSgt. John Kuharek, enlisted participants on both atomic missions, are displayed in this comprehensive exhibit detailing the enlisted sacrifices made to ensure the success of the atomic missions. Other World War II artifacts on exhibit include the Norden Bombsight, an A-2 flight jacket, Adolf Hitler's personal stationery (retrieved by an enlisted airmen in war-torn Berlin), and the China-Burma-India Theater sketches of enlisted artist Nathan H. Glick. Bring an enlisted or veteran Airman with you to honor him.

COTOCTIN WILDLIFE PRESERVE AND ZOO

Thurmont - *(US 15 north of town) 21788. www.cwpzoo.com. Phone: (301) 271-3180. Hours: Open daily, 9:00am - 6:00pm (Memorial Day-Labor Day). Daily 10am-5pm (March, April, May). Daily until 5:00pm (September/October). Daily 11:00am-4:00pm (November). Last admission taken one hour prior to closing. Admission: Zoo $16.95 adult, $11.50 child (3-12). Summer fees are slightly higher. Global Safari Ride is $12.00 extra. Note: Camel rides offered May-September.*

From bears to boas, lions to lemurs, macaws to monkeys, panthers to pythons, you'll meet over 450 exotic animals on your Zoo adventure. Newest to the zoo (besides new babies born) is the Amazing Africa exhibit with lions, zebra, antelope and the deadliest snakes of Africa. Look for recent editions including cougars, dingos, tortoises, parrots and lizards. You'll be surprised how close you can get to these creatures at the Conservation Theater Contact Shows. Safely meet and touch a chinchilla, prickly hedgehog, smooth snake or bumpy lizard. Hand-feed animals in the petting area and maybe get to toss a Grizzly bear a special snack. If you take the safari tour, it's conducted in an army surplus troop carrier and not for the faint of heart. You feed giant animals from your open-air seats.

CUNNINGHAM FALLS STATE PARK / CATOCTIN FURNACE / GAMBRILL STATE PARK

Thurmont - *14039 Catoctin Hollow Road (The Manor Area, on U.S. Route 15 and the Houck Area, three miles west of Thurmont, off RT 77, on Catoctin Hollow Road) 21788. www.dnr.state.md.us/publiclands/Pages/western/cunningham. aspx. Phone: (301) 271-7574. Hours: Daily 8:00am-sunset. Admission: Day use service charge is $3.00/vehicle year-round. Out-of-state residents add $1.00. Camping fees.*

Cunningham Falls State Park, located in the Catoctin Mountains, is known for its history and scenic beauty, as well as its 78-foot cascading waterfall. The Falls are located one half mile from the lake in the Houck Area via the Falls Trail. Hiking, swimming, fishing, boating, playgrounds, nine camper cabins, and 171 campsites in two areas are available seasonally. The Houck area has a 43 acre lake and trail to the Falls.

Manor area includes:

- **CATOCTIN FURNACE** - In operation from 1776 to 1903, the iron furnace was an entire community. Founders, miners, clerks, charcoal makers, storekeepers, teamsters, and others were supervised by the iron master. A furnace stack, the iron master's Manor House ruins and a self-guided trail are available.

- **GAMBRILL STATE PARK** (off Rte 40) - All trails, except the Catoctin Trail, are loop trails, and return to the Trailhead Lot. All trails, except the White Oak Trail, are open for hiking, mountain biking, and horseback riding. Stunning overlooks of the surrounding areas. Camping.

MAPLE SYRUP FESTIVAL

Thurmont - Cunningham Falls State Park, Houck Area. See maple syrup made from sap to syrup. Enjoy a pancake breakfast and other family activities. Donation requested. (second and third weekends in March)

LAWYERS MOONLIGHT MAZE

Thurmont - 13003 Creagerstown Road. Pumpkin cannon shoot, largest corn mazes in the state with seven miles of trails. www.lawyersmoonlightmaze.com. Admission. (Friday-Sunday from late September thru October)

MERKLE WILDLIFE SANCTUARY & VISITORS CENTER

Upper Marlboro - *11704 Fenno Road (Route 301 South to Croom Road / Route 382) 20772.   www.dnr.state.md.us/publiclands/Pages/southern/merkle.aspx.   Phone: (301) 888-1410.   Hours: Merkle Wildlife Sanctuary is open daily from 7:00am to sunset. The Visitor Center is open 10:00am-4:00pm Saturday and Sunday only except daily each summer. Admission: $2.00-$3.00 per vehicle.*

- SANCTUARY: The geese arrive in mid-October and stay until late February or early March. About 100 geese stay year-round. During the peak of the season, more than 5,000 geese may be present. Corn, millet and other crops favored by geese are grown for them, adding to the marsh and aquatic plants that flourish in the ponds along the Patuxent River.

- VISITORS CENTER: The exhibits focus primarily on the life history and management of the Canada goose. Other exhibits focus on the habitat of the area. A Discovery Room for children has live snakes, frogs, turtles and other wildlife species. The lower level includes a children's coloring table and a book nook. There is also a gift shop featuring nature items.

- CRITICAL AREA DRIVING TOUR: The four-mile Chesapeake Bay Critical Area Driving Tour (CADT) is open for self-guided driving tours on Sundays from 10:00am-3:00pm throughout the year. The tour begins at Patuxent River Park. Take Croom Airport Road, off Croom Road (north of Merkle). The CADT travels across the Mattaponi Creek onto the Merkle Wildlife Sanctuary. The CADT is open for biking, hiking and horseback riding daily, January through September.

WATKINS REGIONAL PARK

Upper Marlboro - *301 Watkins Park Drive (just one mile south of Six Flags, left on Watkins Park Drive) 20774. Phone: (301) 218-6700. http://outdoors.pgparks. com/Sites/Watkins_Regional_Park.htm Hours: Daytime park hours vary each season.*

The park is 3 minutes from Six Flags and is a must see. It includes the Old Maryland Farm with farm animals petting zoo, Watkins Nature Center, miniature train that runs through the park, miniature golf, an antique carrousel, walking and biking trails and the like. Most activities only require $1.00-3.50 per person. It's a good complement for Six Flags and a wonderful cost-friendly option for families.

KINDERFEST

Upper Marlboro - *Watkins Regional Park. Fall festival that celebrates Prince George's county children and families. Enjoy entertainment, workshops and exhibits, moon bounces, carnival games, pumpkin patch, farm and nature activities. (first Sunday in October)*

WINTER FESTIVAL OF LIGHTS

Upper Marlboro - *Watkins Regional Park. Light up the holidays with this scenic show. Enjoy a festive, animated drive along a 2 1/2 mile course of more than one million twinkling lights, animated displays and arrangements. Admission. (nightly late November thru New Years Day)*

CAPITAL CHALLENGE HORSE SHOW / WASHINGTON INTERNATIONAL

Upper Marlboro - *Show Place Arena / Prince George's Equestrian Center. See Olympians and Olympic hopefuls in one of the largest hunter/jumper equestrian competitions in the U.S. FREE. www.showplacearena.com. (weekends in October)*

GINGERBREAD HOUSE CONTEST AND SHOW

Upper Marlboro - *Darnall's Chance Museum. http://history.pgparks.com/sites_and_museums/Darnall_s_Chance_House_Museum.htm Children of all ages marvel at the creativity and talent of local bakers. Visitors can choose the best houses on display - presented to both favorite adult and child entries. Small Fee. (Thanksgiving thru mid-December)*

HANSEL & GRETEL TEA PARTY

Upper Marlboro - *Darnall's Chance Museum. http://history.pgparks.com/sites_and_museums/Darnall_s_Chance_House_Museum.htm Visit Darnall's Chance when it is decorated like a gingerbread house, listen to the story of Hansel and Gretel and enjoy tea and dessert. Reservations and Fee apply. (third Saturday in December)*

WALKERSVILLE SOUTHERN RAILROAD

Walkersville - *34 W. Pennsylvania Avenue (Rte. 15 north toward Gettsysburg. Follow 15 for 6 miles north then turn right onto Biggs Ford Road) 21793. Phone: (301) 898-0899 or (877) 363-9777. www.wsrr.org. Admission: $8.00-$12.00 per person. Tours: The railroad operates on weekends in October, departing the station at 11:00am, 1:00pm and 3:00pm each day. The railroad also operates on Sundays in May, June, September and October, departing the station at 11:00am and 2:00pm each day. Note: Visitors to the museum will be treated to many educational displays and an operating model railroad (HO scale) known as the "Monocacy Valley Railroad."*

Take a trip back in time . . . on the Walkersville Southern, established in 1991 on the Frederick branch of the old Pennsylvania Railroad. Ride in vintage 1920s passenger cars or on an open flatcar as your rail excursion runs past a 100-year-old lime kiln, and then out into the picturesque Maryland farm country. On a clear day, you can view the Catoctin Mountains west of Frederick. Before returning to the Walkerville Station you will cross the beautiful Monocacy River on the recently reconstructed railroad bridge. The Railroad offers a wide variety of excursion rides on rustic trains, including mystery dinner trains, Jesse James Day, Circus Trains and Teddy Bear Picnics.

BUNNY TRAINS

Walkersville - *Walkersville Southern Railroad. Ride the train with the Bunny. Cookies and juice in the museum while you enjoy model trains and receive an Easter treat. Admission. (weekend before and Saturday of Easter weekend)*

STAR-SPANGLED FIREWORKS TRAIN

Walkersville - *Walkersville Southern Railroad. Visit the carnival in town, have dinner at the fire hall, then take an evening train ride for a view of the fireworks you will never forget. Bring a flashlight and a blanket. Admission. (Friday after July 4th)*

SANTA TRAINS

Walkersville - *Walkersville Southern Railroad. Ride the train with Santa. Admission. (Thanksgiving weekend and first two weekends of December)*

Washington, DC

Chapter 2

A Quick Tour of our Hand-Picked Favorites Around...

Capital - DC Area
Washington, D.C.

Maryland is a generous state; so generous, in fact, that in 1791 they donated the land that became Washington, D.C. To try to name favorites in D.C. is pretty nearly impossible as the entire area is one small place packed with dozens of historical attractions one must see in their lifetime to truly feel American.

Before you fill your day with museum visits, here are some tips to make the visit easier:

Overnight in nearby Virginia suburbs close to a Metro Station so once you get up in the morning - you can easily navigate the Metro into town. If you like to picnic, the National Mall and West or East Potomac Park has dozens of lawn sites to spread out a picnic blanket. You'll be dining, al fresco, by a view of **famous monuments**. As the sun started setting, we especially enjoyed walking the perimeter of the Tidal Basin in Potomac Park with a view of the FDR Memorial and The Jefferson Memorial, as they are backlit towards nightfall. Also, surrounding the White House are oodles of vendors offering the best prices in town on souvenirs and sandwiches.

How To Do Attractions - every family is different but honestly you can "do" as many as your family desires if you work the 10:00am-7:00pm full day. Maybe devote an entire day to the FREE **Smithsonian Museums** & **National Mall** buildings. DC by Foot, a walking tour company, gives FREE, kid-friendly tours infused with games, fun facts and trivia. Or, just wander from one building to the next. Be sure to go online first and print off any "Hunts" (scavenger hunts) that Interest you (ways to engage, not overwhelm young guests). Play pilot in a mock cockpit at America by Air, an exhibition on permanent display at the Smithsonian **National Air and Space Museum**. Teach kids about history at the newly renovated **National Museum of American History** and get a rare look at the original "Star-Spangled Banner," the flag that inspired Francis Scott Key to write the national anthem. The museum's Spark!Lab uses fun activities to help kids and families learn about the history and process of invention through games and conducting experiments plus there's an Under 5 Zone just for pre-schoolers.

Walk among the butterflies or witness a view of the blinding Hope Diamond at the **National Museum of Natural History**.

Maybe following a thread of your favorite President is the best way to tour. **Fords Theatre Museum & Tour** is a newly renovated museum using 21st century technology to transport visitors to 19th-century Washington, DC. The museum's collection of historic artifacts (including the Derringer pistol that John Wilkes Booth used to shoot Lincoln and a replica of the coat Lincoln wore the night he was shot) is supplemented with a variety of narrative devices. As you sit in the theatre for the park ranger presentation, chills run up your spine!

After lunch, go to our favorite wax museum, **Madame Tussauds**. DC's wax museum has a distinctly "Washington" feel, and gives parents the perfect opportunity to give kids a taste of politics without the crowds on the Mall. We interacted with the figures for some amazingly realistic photo ops like: Sitting with Lincoln in Ford's Theatre, Dad discussing decisions of the day in the Oval Office or taking photos with famous presidents. They look so real (in digital pics) that folks on the Metro thought we had actually met the President that day!

Sites and attractions are listed in order by City, Zip Code, and Name. Symbols indicated represent: 🍽 Restaurants   🛏 Lodging

NEWSEUM

Washington - *555 Pennsylvania Ave., N.W. (take Penn Ave all the way to 6th Street and Pennsylvania Avenue, N.W.) 20001. www.newseum.org. Phone: (888) NEWSEUM. Hours: Daily 9:00am-5:00pm. Closed winter holidays. Admission: $24.95 adult, $19.95 senior (65+), $14.95 youth (7-18), FREE child (6 and under). Admission tickets for the Newseum are date and time specific and subject to availability. Tours: 2-Hour Tour Guide Print out and take this guide with you on your next visit and, if you walk fast, you can discover some of the most compelling, revealing and fun exhibits and activities the Newseum has to offer in (about) two hours. Download PDF on Plan your Visit page of their website. Educators: Many students in 8th grade study US Government and the Constitution. The First Amendment Gallery is the place to spend some time getting inspiration for a report. Note: Food Court, two-level Newseum Store.*

The world's only interactive museum of news. The exhibits take you behind the scenes to see and experience how and why news is made. Visitors here can act as editors and put together newspaper front pages. They can also step into a reality ride to the scene of a breaking news story and test their skills as investigative reporters or photographers. Learn about some history from a journalist's point of view - how the media have covered major historical events such as the fall of the Berlin Wall and the Sept. 11, 2001, terrorist attacks. Other great works on display include the Magna Carta, Thomas Paine's "Common Sense," and a 1787 first pamphlet printing of the U.S. Constitution. A major storyline of the World News gallery is the danger reporters face around the globe while reporting the news. Dramatic icons — including a bullet-riddled, armor-reinforced pickup truck used by reporters and photographers in the Balkans — illustrate the dangerous conditions in which journalists often work. In the broadcast studio, visitors can watch "in person" a live TV newscast (most folks never get this chance). Try your hand at being a TV news reporter or photographer in the "Hot Seat" exhibit. A long news bar displays news from around the world. Below the wall are the front pages of daily newspapers from every state and many countries - all diversely covering the same stories. The theater presents great moments in news history and another theater offers a glimpse of vintage newsreels.

OLD TOWN TROLLEY TOURS

Washington - *1000 E St NW (Intersection of 10th & E Streets, NW, across from Fords Theatre) 20004. www.trolleytours.com/washington-dc Tours: $35.00 adult, $26.00 child. Online discounts. "Hop on - Hop off" privileges at 16 conveniently located stops. Trolleys will come by each stop at least every 30 minutes. Free shuttle from area hotels. Tour Includes Free Day Planner Guide - A $10 Value. No Reservations Required.*

A one-of-a-kind fully narrated tour of Washington DC covering over 100 points of interest. The popular Old Town Trolley tour covers Washington's major attractions such as the Lincoln Memorial, Georgetown, Washington National Cathedral, the White House, the museums of the Smithsonian Institution, and Vietnam Veteran's Memorial. The licensed and professional tour guides share colorful anecdotes, humorous stories and well researched historical information. As you tour the nation's capital you will have the opportunity to get off the trolley and visit memorials, museums, and historical points of interest; as well as opportunities for shopping and dining throughout the city. When you're ready, just re-board and it's on with the tour. Your Boarding Pass is your ticket to rejoin the tour at any designated stop.

CLYDE'S AT THE GALLERY

Washington - *707 7th St. NW (take US 50 into town. Follow Metro: Gallery Place / Chinatown) 20004. (202) 349-3700. www.clydes.com. Sit down lunch option in Washington, D.C. Clyde's at the Gallery offers a great Kids Menu for $8.50. Ten entrees to choose from with basics plus something new: Finger Food Platter – hummus & pita, apple wedges, "ants on celery log", carrot sticks. Every Kids Meal is served with a toy, activity sheet & crayons, milk or soft drink, and ice cream or seasonal fruit dessert. Teens will love the Margarita Pizza...adults, be sure to try their seafood – oysters or their meaty crab cakes maybe? Reasonable for D.C. pricing!* **Lunch and dinner served.**

FORD'S THEATRE

Washington - *511 10th Street, NW (take US 50 into town. between E and F Streets-near Metro Center stop) 20004. Box Office: (202) 347-4833. NPS Phone: (202) 426-6924.. www.nps.gov/foth/index.htm. Hours: For museum & tours - the site is open Daily from 9:00am-5:00pm. Final entry into the theatre is at 4:30pm. Admission: Visits to the Ford's Theatre National Historic Site are FREE but do require a ticket. Tickets can be reserved online for a small fee. Tours: Really enjoyed the theatre and museums tour? Extend that feeling with History on Foot tours, each led by an actor in costume. $12.00 per person. Educators: Click on "History & Culture" for background material for reports. Lesson plans are on the NPS Teachers Resources site.*

ACT I

Ford's Theatre Museum preserves and displays over 8,000 artifacts relevant to the assassination of Abraham Lincoln.

The museum uses 21st century technology to transport visitors to 19th-century Washington, DC. The museum's collection of historic artifacts (including the Derringer pistol that John Wilkes Booth used to shoot Lincoln and a replica of the coat Lincoln wore the night he was shot) is supplemented with a variety of narrative devices. Interactive, self-guided exhibits set the stage for guests by painting a social and political picture of Washington, DC, and the United States during the 1860s.

ACT II

Visitors move into the theatre itself for a presentation - either of a one act play or a National Park Service ranger talk - that illuminates the dramatic events of April, 1865. See the Presidential Box (notice how close it is to the stage), the inner door (notice how mangled it is) to the box, and learn many historical tidbits such as the evenings program was publicized as a long awaited appearance of the Commander and Chief so there was an air of anticipation in the theatre that night. Who was supposed to be guests in the box with the President and Mrs. Lincoln that night? Why didn't they come? As you sit in the theatre for the presentation, chills run up your spine!

Standing under the VIP box where President & Mrs. Lincoln sat...

ACT III

The journey continues across the street at the Petersen House, where visitors will learn more about President Lincoln's final hours, the vigil at his deathbed and the subsequent hunt for his assassin.

INTERNATIONAL SPY MUSEUM

Washington - *800 F Street, NW (take US 50 into town. Follow Metro: Gallery Place/ Chinatown) 20004. Phone: (202) 393-7798.. www.spymuseum.org.. Hours: Daily 9:00am-7:00pm (April - early September); Hours vary (October-March). Last Admission: 2 hours before closing. Closed major winter holidays. Admission: $21.95 adult, $15.95 senior (65+), Active duty military, $14.95 child (ages 7-11). Children age 4 and under FREE. All admission tickets for the International Spy Museum are date and time specific and are subject to availability. Advance Tickets are highly recommended. Note: The exhibit spaces are tight (maybe for effect-spies hide in small, hidden passages). The Permanent Exhibition is most appropriate for ages 12+. Be sure to watch the "Briefing Room" video intro before you begin the tour (to orient and "get your cover"). Before your visit (and after), Go to the Family Mission page for games www.spymuseum.org/KidSpy/ family_guide_040714_optimized.pdf. Operation Spy performance and Spy in the City extra fees.*

One of Washington, DC's newer attractions is a big hit with children and adults alike. Packed with high-tech, interactive displays and activities, visitors can take on a spy's cover, test their skills of observation and surveillance, while learning about the history and the future of espionage. Examine over 200 spy gadgets, weapons, bugs, cameras, vehicles, and technologies. Look for the Bond car and a Buttonhole Camera. On mission, climb through duct work, hang from a construction site beam or diffuse an atomic bomb. Learn about the earliest codes - who created them and who broke them. A spy must live a life of lies. Adopt a cover identity and learn why an operative needs one. See the credentials an agent must have to get in - or out. The first half of the museum is interactive but kids may get bored with the second, historical half.

MADAME TUSSAUDS WAX MUSEUM, D.C

Washington - *1001 F Street NW (take US 50 for 9 miles to the corner of 10th and F Street) 20004. Phone: (888) WAX-IN-DC. www.madametussaudsdc.com. Hours: Monday-Thursday 10:00am-4:00pm (last ticket sold at 4:00pm). Friday-Sunday 10:00am-6:00pm (last ticket sold at 6:00pm). During peak season the attraction will stay open later or open earlier as needed. Admission: $22.00 adult, $17.00 child (3-12). Discounts for online purchases and Membership Cards savings. Immortalize your hand in wax! It is a one-of-a-kind memento of visit (extra fee).*

DC's wax museum has a distinctly "Washington" feel, and gives parents the perfect opportunity to give kids a taste of politics without the crowds on the Mall. If you still have time and money left, you have to go to our new favorite wax museum, Madame Tussauds. We've never been to one like this. DC's wax museum has a distinctly "Washington" feel, and gives parents the perfect opportunity to give kids a taste of politics without the crowds on the Mall. We

interacted with the figures for some amazingly realistic photo ops like: Sitting with Lincoln in Ford's Theatre, Dad discussing decisions of the day in the Oval Office, getting arrested sitting next to Rosa Parks on the bus, or taking photos with famous presidents. They look so real (in the digital pics) that folks on the Metro (who took a quick glance at our camera) thought

Hanging out with President Lincoln...

we had actually met the current President that day!

NATIONAL ZOO

Washington - *3001 Connecticut Avenue, NW (I-495 west to exit 33, south on Constitution to entrance. Metro: Zoo) 20008. http://nationalzoo.si.edu. Phone: (202) 633-4800. Hours: Daily 9:00am-4:00pm. Open until 6:00pm (April-October). Closed Christmas Day. Admission: FREE. Parking fee of $22.00. Educators: Curriculum guides, Wildlife Explorer Kits and Activity Sheets are all online on the "Education" icon.*

Most of you are thinking Giant Pandas at the National Zoo. Like babies? Popular areas are: Dandula, the Zoo's young Asian elephant, Cheetah cubs, Tiger cubs or animals in the Kids' Farm. It wouldn't be the National Zoo without a Bald Eagle Refuge. While many animals are always or usually in indoor exhibits, many others, including giant pandas, other bears, seals, and sea lions, and great cats, are usually outdoors. To make your walk around the Zoo more enjoyable, comfortable shoes are recommended. The Zoo is set on hilly terrain and some paths are steep. You can expect to see more animals early in the morning. Print off a scavenger hunt sheet before you visit (on the Info for Visitors web page). Look for ZooLights in December.

ROCK CREEK PARK AND NATURE CENTER

Washington - *5200 Glover Road, NW (take I-495 exit heading northwest to exit 33. Head south on Connecticut, left onto Military Rd. for one mile) 20015. Phone: (202) 426-6829. www.nps.gov/rocr/. Hours: Wednesday-Sunday 9:00am-5:00pm. Closed most national holidays. Admission: FREE. Educators: click on: For Teachers and then Curriculum for grade appropriate lesson plans and scavenger hunts.*

This 2,000-acre park provides a perfect setting for an urban escape or a family outing. Explore a woodland trail. Discover other planets. Touch live animals. Visit a historic flour mill. Visit a 17th century colonial home (Old Stone House). The park has a golf course, tennis courts, picnic tables, bike trails, jogging trails, and horseback riding. The Rock Creek Nature Center is home to the only planetarium in the National Park system and a Discovery Room with a live beehive viewing area. Visitors can watch the bees at work in the hive, visible through glass panes. The hive is connected to the outdoors by a plastic tube. Guided nature walks and curriculum based environmental education programs take place daily.

DC DUCK TOURS

Washington - *(Tours depart Union Station. Take US 50 into town. Look for signs for Union Station as you approach) 20018. www.dcducks.com. Phone: (202) 966-DUCK. Tours: 90 minutes. Daily every hour on the hour starting at 10:00am-4:00pm, (mid-March thru October). $32-$42.00. Off-peak, children are half price. Discounts online.*

DUCKS come from DUKW, a military acronym that designated the vehicle as amphibious military personnel carriers. D stands for the year built, 1942; U for its amphibious nature; K for its all-wheel drive; and W for its dual rear axles. This is the most unusual tour of our nation's capital you'll ever take. . . Land and water in the same vehicle. From Union Station you'll "waddle" down to the mall where you'll see the inspiring monuments and pass the Smithsonian Museums. Then, just after you reach the Potomac River, you'll splash down for a duck's view on the river. The Ducks return to land at Ronald Reagan Washington National Airport under the approach pattern. Hold your ears as incoming aircraft pass over just feet from where you're sitting . . . giving new meaning to "sitting duck"! The wise-quacking captains will entertain you with anecdotes, sneak in some interesting historical facts and tell corny jokes.

FREDERICK DOUGLASS NHS

Washington - *1411 W Street SE (exit 3 north onto Indian Head Hwy, MD 210. Bear right onto MLK Jr. Ave. right on W Street) 20020. www.nps.gov/frdo/. Phone: (202) 426-5961. Admission: FREE. Tours: Ranger-led tours of the home are available daily at 9:00am, 12:15pm, 1:45pm, 3:00pm, and 3:30pm. Tour tickets are available by reservation or on a first-come first-served basis. Tours of the home last approximately 30 minutes. Note: The historic home is set high atop a hill. There are approximately 85 steps between the Visitor Center and the house. Educators: Lesson plans here: www.nps.gov/frdo/forteachers/index.htm.*

The Frederick Douglass National Historic Site is dedicated to preserving the legacy of the most famous 19th century African American. His life was a testament to the courage and persistence that serves as an inspiration to those who struggle in the cause of liberty and justice. This newly restored home to a former slave is where you can begin to learn about his efforts to abolish slavery and his struggle for rights for all oppressed people. Begin with the 17-minute film "Frederick Douglass: Fighter for Freedom." Look for his original piano and documents he published.

FRANKLIN D. ROOSEVELT MEMORIAL

Washington - *900 Ohio Drive, SW (I-295N to I-395N exit signs for Memorials, West Potomac Park at West Basin and Ohio Drive) 20024. Phone: (202) 426-6841. www.nps.gov/fdrm/. Hours: Park ranger in attendance 8:00am-midnight. Wheelchair accessible. The Bookstore opens from 9:00am-6:00pm. All restroom facilities close at 11:30pm. Closed Christmas. Admission: FREE. Metered and free parking (2 to 3 hours) surrounds this memorial. You may have to drive around several times to land a free space. Limited during ball games on the Park fields.*

"The only thing we have to fear...is fear itself". These are the words of our 32nd President, a man who truly knew the meaning of the word courage. Despite, at age 39, being stricken with polio and paralyzed from the waist down, he emerged as a true leader, guiding our country through some of its darkest times: the Great Depression and World War II. The rambling FDR Memorial (it spans 7.5 acres) consists of four "rooms" arranged chronologically to represent

the 32nd President's unprecedented four terms in office. A fountain in the first room flows peacefully, representing the healing effect water had on the president during his term in the Navy and while at Warm Springs, GA. The second room addresses the Great Depression and the hope FDR cultivated with his extensive social programs. The third room represents the war years, 1940-1944 with choppy, unsettling stonework and water. In a stark contrast, the final room projects peace and optimism. A bas-relief resting above a pool of still water depicts FDR's funeral procession. Acknowledging FDR's own physical difficulties, his memorial was the first creation of its kind designed with easy access for people with disabilities. Of all the presidential memorials, this is the most "open" to wander and take many pictures "with" the statues.

HOLOCAUST MEMORIAL MUSEUM, U.S.

Washington - *100 Raoul Wallenberg Place, SW (I-295N to I-395N exit Smithsonian, near the National Mall, just south of Independence Ave., SW, between 14th Street and Raoul Wallenberg) 20024. www.ushmm.org. Phone: (202) 488-0400 Hours: Daily 10:00am-5:20pm, except Yom Kippur and Christmas. Extended hours in the summer. Admission: FREE. Timed tickets required for permanent exhibition; available same day or in advance on their website. Usually sold out by Noon.*

The museum is FREE but they stress that kids under 12 may not enjoy this attraction. There are two "exhibit tracks" to follow: the General Exhibit and Daniel's Story (a softer version for tender hearts and kids). We'd recommend walking through Daniel's Story to everyone BEFOREHAND to prepare you for the intensity to follow in the main exhibit. The permanent collection of the U.S. Holocaust Memorial Museum tells the

We recommend the "kid's version" of the museum FIRST to prepare for learning more...

moving story of the persecution of the Jewish people. It presents a narrative history using more than 900 artifacts, 70 video monitors, and four theaters that include historic film footage and eyewitness testimonies. The exhibition is divided into three parts: "Nazi Assault," "Final Solution," and "Last Chapter." The narrative begins with images of death and destruction as witnessed by American soldiers during the liberation of Nazi concentration camps in 1945. Most first-time visitors spend an average of two to three hours in this self-guided exhibition. Parents and pre-teens or teenagers - be prepared to be changed.

JEFFERSON MEMORIAL

Washington - *East Potomac Park, South end of 15th St., SW on the Tidal Basin (I-295N to I-395N exit signs for Memorials, East Potomac Park at Tidal Basin)*

20024. www.nps.gov/thje/. Phone: (202) 426-6822. Hours: The public may visit the Thomas Jefferson Memorial 24 hours a day. However Rangers are on duty to answer questions from 9:30am to 11:30pm daily. Admission: FREE.

Easily recognizable to Jeffersonian architects, the colonnade and dome memorial reflect Jefferson's love of this architectural style. The graceful, beautiful marble design pays tribute to the third president and primary author of the Declaration of Independence. Inside, there is a large bronze statue and excerpts from his writings on the walls. Jefferson stands at the center of the temple, his gaze firmly fixed on the White House, as if to keep an eye on the institution he helped to create. Museum located in the lower lobby of the memorial.

LINCOLN MEMORIAL

Washington - *900 Ohio Drive, S.W. (I-295N to I-395N exit west Potomac Park, 23rd St. and Constitution Ave., NW) 20024. www.nps.gov/linc/. Phone: (202) 426-6841. Hours: Visitors Center 8:00am-midnight. Park ranger in attendance 24 hours, However Rangers are on duty to answer questions from 9:30am-11:30pm daily. Admission: FREE.*

The most famous of the monuments, this site was used for several of history's greatest moments (including MLK speech). The artist opted to portray Lincoln seated, much larger than life, a symbol of mental and physical strength. As the father of a deaf child, did the artist position Lincoln's hands in the shape of the sign language letters "A" and "L"? Lincoln faces the US Capitol. Murals sculpted by Jules Guerin adorn the temple's inner walls. Emancipation is on the south wall and hangs above the inscription of the Gettysburg Address. Unification is on the north wall, above Lincoln's Second Inaugural Address. The view of the National Mall from this vantage point is spectacular. It gives you chills every time you visit...

NATIONAL MALL

Washington - *(I-295N to I-395N. Follow signs for National Mall exit - stretches between Independence and Constitution Aves.) 20024. Visitor Information: (202) 426-6841. www.nps.gov/nama/.*

Officially, the National Mall is green space that begins at 3rd Street and stretches to 14th Street. Visitors and locals, however, widely use the term to refer to the entire expanse of monuments and museums, from the grounds of the Capitol to the Lincoln Memorial. Pierre L'Enfant's original plans for the city called for this open space and parklands, which he envisioned as a grand boulevard to be used for remembrance, observance, and protest. Today, it serves this purpose, hosting concerts, rallies, festivals, as well as Frisbee matches, family outings, picnics and memorials:

All the presidential Memorials; Vietnam Veterans Memorial (the Wall); U.S. Navy Memorial and Naval Heritage Center (701 Pennsylvania Ave., NW); Korean War Veterans Memorial (West Potomac Park, Independence Ave., beside the Lincoln Memorial); and the National World War II Memorial (East end of the Reflecting Pool, between the Lincoln Memorial and the Washington Monument).

If you like to picnic, the National Mall and West or East Potomac Park have cheap parking spaces (if you can find one) and dozens of lawn sites to spread out a picnic blanket. You'll be dining, al fresco, by a view of famous monuments. Also, near the White House & Washington Monument are oodles of vendors offering the best prices in town on souvenirs

Call a veteran from a Memorial to thank him/her for their service

and sandwiches. It's a block or two walk to lawn space between the Lincoln & Washington Monuments. As the sun started setting, we especially enjoyed walking the perimeter of the Tidal Basin in Potomac Park with a view of the FDR Memorial & The Jefferson Memorial, as they are backlit towards nightfall.

BUREAU OF ENGRAVING & PRINTING TOUR

Washington - *Department of the Treasury, 14th and C Streets, S.W. (I-295N to I-395N exit Smithsonian, near the National Mall, just south of Independence Ave., SW, next to Holocaust Museum) 20228. Phone: (202) 874-2330 (local) or (866) 874-2330. www.moneyfactory.com. Hours: Public Tour: 9:00am-10:45am 11:00am-12:15pm & 12:30pm-2:00pm (every 15 minutes). Extended Summer Hours (May-August): 5:00-7:00pm (every 15 minutes). Visitors Center: Weekdays 8:30am-3:00pm and summer early evenings. The Bureau is CLOSED on weekends, federal holidays and the week between Christmas and New Years. Tours: FREE Tickets are required for all tours from the first Monday in March through the last Friday in August, on a first-come, first-served basis. The ticket booth is located on Raoul Wallenberg Place (formerly 15th Street). They offer same day tickets only. The Ticket Booth opens at 8:00am - Monday through Friday, and closes when all tickets have been distributed. Lines form early and tickets go quickly, most days tickets are gone by 9:00am. Many are in line by 7:00am. No tickets required (September-February). Please plan accordingly. Note: Please be patient with them during this time of heightened security, and be advised that all tour policies are subject to change without public notification. If the Department of Homeland Security level is elevated, the Bureau of Engraving and Printing is CLOSED to the public unless otherwise noted. Strollers not allowed on the tour.*

You'll see millions of dollars being printed during a tour of the BEP. The tour features the various steps of currency production, beginning with large, blank sheets of paper, and ending with the paper money we use every day! The BEP designs, engraves and prints all U.S. paper currency. Established in 1862, the Bureau, at that time, used just six people to separate and seal notes by hand in the basement of the Treasury building. The Bureau moved to its present site in 1914. Though new printing, production and examining technologies have brought us into the 21st century, the Bureau's engravers continue to use the same traditional tools that have been used for over 125 years - the graver, the burnisher, and the hand-held glass. At any given time, you may see millions of dollars roll off the presses in a flash!

WASHINGTON MONUMENT

Washington - 2 15th St. NW & Jefferson Drive (I-295N to I-395N exit National Mall area, Tourmobile stop, Metro Smithsonian stop) 20224. Phone: (202) 426-6841 or (800) 967-2283 reservations. www.nps.gov/wamo/. Hours: Washington Monument are from 9:00am-4:45pm, closed December 25 and July 4th. Open into the evening during summer hours. Admission: Free tickets are distributed for that day's visit from the kiosk on the Washington Monument grounds on a first-come first-served basis. All visitors 2 years of age or older must have a ticket to enter the Monument. Hours for the ticket kiosk are 8:00am-4:30pm, but tickets run out early. Advanced tickets are available through the National Park Service Reservation System. Reservations may be made between the hours of 10:00am-10:00pm. While tickets to the Washington Monument are free of charge, callers to this number will incur a $1.50 service charge and a $.50 shipping and handling fee. Note: Bookstore, restrooms and concessions on site.

Take the fast elevator ride to the top of the Monument for a panoramic view of the city. Most rides make stops to allow viewing of the commemorative stones set along the inside walls of the elevator shaft. Many folks like to start here as Washington was our first President and the view gives you a good feel for the lay of the land in D.C. The 555-foot tall obelisk is marble and is the tallest freestanding obelisk in the world. Why are there two different colors of marble used? The immense structure represents Washington's enormous contribution to the founding of our republic.

NATIONAL MUSEUM OF THE U.S. NAVY

Washington - 805 Kidder Breese Street, SE (I-295N exit 11 St. Bridge/Washington Navy Yard) 20306. Phone: (202) 433-6897. www.navyhistory.org/navy-museum/ national-museum-of-the-united-states-navy/ Hours: 9:30am-4:00pm Monday-Friday, Weekends 11:00am-4:30pm. Note: The NAVAL HERITAGE CENTER is on Pennsylvania Ave. (open daily except Sundays and winter Mondays). www. lonesailor.org. You'll be introduced to an attractive display of ships, aircraft and naval history. Center offers exhibits, Library, and a theater with the wide-screen movie, <u>At Sea</u>, about life on board an aircraft carrier while on a deployment. Also available for viewing is the Navy Log, over 260,000 records of sea service personnel.

Opened in 1963, the Navy Museum is housed in the former 600-foot long Breech Mechanism Shop of the old Naval Gun Factory. Exhibits offer a look at the traditions and contributions of the Navy throughout American history. Popular attractions include the fully rigged fighting top from the frigate Constitution, a submarine room with operating periscopes and a variety of large guns which can be elevated and aimed by the visitor. There is no admission charge.

NATIONAL ARCHIVES

Washington - 700 Pennsylvania Avenue, NW (Take Pennsylvania Ave. all the way into town. Metro Archives station-The Rotunda entrance is on Constitution Ave) 20408. Phone: (202) 357-5000. www.archives.gov/museum/visit/ Hours: Daily 10:00am-5:30pm. Open later each spring and summer. Admission: FREE. Educators: Lesson Plans and biographies can be used for kids' reports.

The Rotunda of the National Archives Building in downtown Washington, DC, contains the permanent exhibit of the Constitution, Bill of Rights, and the Declaration of Independence. An exhibit called the Public Vaults displays over 1,000 fascinating records (originals or reproductions) from the National Archives holdings. Often, the wait may be long, but most say worth it, to enter the Charters of Freedom. See the original Declaration of Independence, U.S. Constitution and Bill of Rights at the National Archives, then stick around to research your own family's immigration records.

PRESIDENT LINCOLN'S COTTAGE

Washington - Armed Forces Retirement Home campus (exit 31 Georgia Ave. south 5 miles. Metro-Georgia Ave - Petworth. Head northeast) 20408. Phone: (202) 829-0436. www.lincolncottage.org. Hours: Visitors Center: Daily 9:30am-4:30pm except Sundays from 10:30am-5:30pm. The site is closed Thanksgiving,

Christmas, and New Year's Day. Admission: $15.00 adult, $5.00 child (6-12). Tours:
One hour, guided tours are offered of President Lincoln's Cottage and a portion
of the Soldiers' Home grounds. Reservations online are highly suggested. This
tour is suitable for children 8 years or older. Monday-Saturday 10:00am, last tour
4:00pm; Sunday Noon, last tour 4:00pm (summer). Last tour at 3:00pm (winter).

Located on a picturesque hilltop in Washington, DC, President Lincoln's
Cottage is the most significant historic site directly associated with Lincoln's
presidency aside from the White House. During the Civil War, President Lincoln
and his family resided here from June to November of 1862, 1863 and 1864.
In part, the Lincolns were seeking privacy to grieve after the death of 12-year
old son Willie. Until recently, little was known about the home. Much has been
pieced together from diaries, letters and newspaper stories. While you may be
thinking you'll get to see the chair or bed Lincoln's family sat on - this museum
instead focuses on the person. "Historical" voices and images illuminate the
compelling stories of Lincoln as father, husband, and Commander in Chief.
Audio and video of actors portray the president and people close to him. A
strong theme is the emancipation of slaves. In "Lincoln's Cabinet Room"

(Visitors Center) visitors can participate in an innovative interactive experience
exploring Lincoln's Toughest Decisions. Students can play the roles of rival
cabinet secretaries and debate the emancipation. The space also has multiple
computer screens showing artifacts and arguments that led to this debate.
We especially like that, before touring the Cottage, visitors first gather in the
theater with their guide for an introduction to the site. An interactive audiovisual
presentation sets the context for the Lincolns' move here. From the theater
room, guests proceed directly to the Cottage.

WHITE HOUSE

Washington - *1600 Pennsylvania Avenue, NW (I-295N to I-395N. Follow signs*
for Monuments or White House exit. Metro: Metro Center, McPherson Square)
20500. Phone: (202) 456-7041. www.whitehouse.gov (White House) or www.nps.
gov/whho/planyourvisit/white-house-visitor-center.htm Hours: Visitors Center
(1450 Pennsylvania Ave, NW): Daily 7:30am-4:00pm. Admission: FREE. Tours:
The White House is currently open only to groups (of 10 or more) who have made
arrangements through a congressional representative. These self-guided tours
are available from 7:30am-11:30pm, Tuesday through Thursday and 7:30am-
1:30pm Fridays and Saturdays (excluding federal holidays), and are scheduled
on a first come, first served basis. You are given a specific entry time.

Park Rangers lead Walks Around the (Presidents) Park at 9:30am, 11:30am
(themed) and 1:30pm each day.

- WHITE HOUSE VISITOR CENTER: All visits are significantly enhanced if visitors stop by the White House Visitor Center located at the southeast corner of 15th and E Streets, before or after their walking or White House group tour. The Center features many aspects of the White House, including its architecture, furnishings, first families, social events, and relations with the press and world leaders, as well as a 14-minute video titled: White House, Reflections from Within. Allow between 20 minutes to one hour to explore the exhibits.

- WHITE HOUSE TOUR: You are given a specific entry time. There are many items you can't bring onto the property. The tour is self-guided with guards and Secret Service people in every room. You

1600 Pennsylvania Avenue...
America's most famous address

aren't rushed through and they willingly answer questions. The entry has lots of interesting displays and artifacts. Some of the rooms you can peak into are the East Room, Green Room, Blue Room, Red Room, State Dining Room and then out through the North Portico. It is definitely an impressive place to visit.

The guided OUTSIDE tour combined with the Visitor Center and online video presentations give you the best "feel" for the White House without actually going inside. I think they realize citizens still want to know about the President's house but can't always go through the "hoops" necessary to secure an inside visit these days. The White House Historical Association also sponsors a sales area. Please note that restrooms are available, but food service is not.

CAPITOL BUILDING, UNITED STATES

Washington - *(take Pennsylvania Ave. all the way in to east end of the National Mall) 20540. Phone: (202) 737-2300 or (800) 723-3557. www.visitthecapitol.gov. Hours: Monday-Saturday 8:30am-4:30pm except for Thanksgiving Day, Christmas Day, New Year's Day and Inauguration Day. Admission: FREE. Visitors must obtain free tickets for tours on a first-come, first-served basis, at the Capitol Guide Service kiosk located along the curving sidewalk southwest of the Capitol (near the intersection of First Street, S.W., and Independence Avenue). Ticket distribution begins at 9:00am daily. Or, online. Tours: Guided tours of the building leave every 15 minutes from the Rotunda. Note: A limited number of free passes to the House*

and Senate galleries are available by contacting your representative's office, by phone or stopping by their offices across the street from the Capitol building.

The Capitol is one of the most widely recognized buildings in the world. It is a symbol of the American people and their government, the meeting place of the nation's legislature, an art and history museum, and a tourist attraction visited by millions every year. The bright, white-domed building was designed to be the focal point for DC, dividing the city into four sectors and organizing the street numbers. Begun in 1793, the Capitol has been built, burnt, rebuilt, extended, and restored. An 180-foot dome is adorned by the fresco Brumidi painting (took him 20 years to complete). The Rotunda, a circular ceremonial space, also serves as a gallery of paintings and sculpture depicting significant people and events in the nation's history. The Old Senate Chamber northeast of the Rotunda, which was used by the Senate until 1859, has been returned to its mid-19th century appearance. The third floor allows access to the galleries from which visitors to the Capitol may watch the proceedings of the House and the Senate when Congress is in session...learning firsthand how a bill becomes a law. The Visitors Center, an underground facility, includes an exhibition gallery, orientation theatres, a large cafeteria, gift shops and restrooms, allowing greater access to public tours of the Capitol and shorter waits for tours. Another feature is a walking tunnel connected to the Library of Congress.

LIBRARY OF CONGRESS

Washington - *101 Independence Ave, SE (I-295N to I-395 exit D Street. Follow signs. Metro: Capitol South) 20540. Phone: (202) 707-8000.. www.loc.gov. Hours: Monday-Saturday 8:30am-4:30pm. Admission: FREE public tours. Tours: Docents lead scheduled public tours that are offered Mondays through Saturdays in the Great Hall of the Thomas Jefferson Building of the Library of Congress. Tours are limited to 50 people. For more information on guided tours, ask at either of the information desks in the Visitors' Center of the Jefferson Building (west front entrance). You may enter this building on the ground level under the staircase at the front of the building, located directly across from the U.S. Capitol.*

FREEBIES: Kids and Families - Log on, play around, learn something. Teachers - More than 10 million primary sources online. (www.loc.gov/visit/activities-for-kids-and-families/)

The world's largest library is home to much more than just books. At the Library of Congress, kids can see a perfect copy of the Gutenberg Bible, personal papers of 23 presidents, a collection of Houdini's magic tricks, the Wright Brothers' flight log books and more. Equipped with new information desks, a visitors' theater features a 12 minute award winning film about the Library and interactive information kiosks. The Visitors' Center enhances the experience of approximately one million visitors each year.

SMITHSONIAN INSTITUTION

Washington - *(I-295N to I-395N located on the National Mall exit and may be entered from many directions. Follow signs.) 20560. Phone: (202) 357-2700 or (202) 633-1000 (voice). www.smithsonian.org. Hours: All museums are open from 10:00am-5:30pm, daily. Admission: FREE. Educators: Click on "Educators"*

button and you'll find a wealth of exciting approaches to curriculum and related crafts or projects! Have your kids go to the Smithsonian Kids pages to explore before they go - their pages are whimsical and short - meant to pique interest, not destroy it. Note: Docents are available in many popular galleries daily to answer visitor questions between 10:30am and 2:30pm, Mondays through Saturdays and Sundays from noon to 4:00pm.

A visit to Washington, DC is not complete without experiencing at least one of the 14 Smithsonian museums. The Castle is the original building, completed in 1855, which provides an overview of the entire offering to help your family determine which museums interest you the most (you probably can't do them all). Be sure you have on your walking shoes. DC by Foot, a

The original Smithsonian Museum is a great place to start your visit

walking tour company, gives FREE, kid-friendly tours (gratuity recommended) infused with games, fun facts and trivia. Or, just wander from one building to the next. Be sure to go online first and print off any "Hunts" (scavenger hunts) that interest you (ways to engage, not overwhelm young guests). The following are highlights of the myriad of exhibits and activities offered especially for children. Maybe only choose two to explore each visit.

- **ON THE MALL**: Outside the National Air and Space Museum, a scale model of the solar system entitled Voyage: A Journey through our Solar System helps children grasp the magnitude of the world around them. During the summer months, a ride on the world's oldest carousel, near the Arts and Industries Building, is a sure treat.

- **AMERICAN ART MUSEUM**: (Gallery Place Metro station at 8th and F Streets N.W. Open 11:30am-7:00pm). The Smithsonian American Art Museum is dedicated exclusively to the art and artists of the United States. All regions, cultures, and traditions are represented in the museum's collections, research resources, exhibitions, and public programs. The collection features colonial portraits, nineteenth-century landscapes, American impressionism, twentieth-century realism and abstraction, New Deal projects, sculpture, photography, prints and drawings, contemporary crafts and decorative arts, African American art, Latino art, and folk art. There's a neat display of license plates from every state that write out the Preamble to the Constitution (clever). They also have a good collection of portraits of Presidents. You may especially like the Washington and Lincoln studies (ever study Lincoln's eyes?). The Civil War space is good, too.

- **HIRSHHORN GALLERY**: The Smithsonian's modern art museum's "Young at Art" program introduces young visitors to different artistic disciplines through hands-on activities. Participants can act in a play, create portraits in chocolate, make clay sculptures, and more. A great place to start your visit Saturdays, drop in for an "Improv Art" program - including a tour of the gallery with a special activity sheet and an art project to take home. The museum also offers regularly-scheduled guided family tours.

- **NATIONAL AIR & SPACE MUSEUM**: Play pilot in a mock cockpit at America by Air, an exhibition on permanent display at the Smithsonian National Air and Space Museum. The large space provides a world-renowned collection of flying

See the _ACTUAL_ Wright Brother's famous airplane...WOW...

machines from the Wright Brothers' Kitty Hawk Flyer to the Apollo 11 Command Module. Kids can see a moon rock, Lindbergh's Spirit of St. Louis and a variety of special films. The museum's IMAX theatre provides large format and 3-D glimpses of space and beyond. (fee for IMAX shows AND Planetarium shows). Enclosed within the Museum is the Albert Einstein Planetarium. Not only does the planetarium have a spectacular star field instrument, but it has been upgraded to include a first-of-its-kind, Sky Vision™ dual digital projection system and six-channel digital surround sound. For the first time, you'll feel the sensation of zooming through the cosmos with a blanket of color and sound. Infinity Express: A 20-Minute Tour of the Universe; Cosmic Collisions, or Stars Tonight (free) program.

- **NATIONAL MUSEUM OF AMERICAN HISTORY**: Also known as "America's Attic," this popular museum houses such treasures as the

First Ladies' inaugural gowns, Dorothy's Ruby Red Slippers, Mr. Roger's sweater, Abraham Lincoln's top hat, Lewis and Clark's compass, Custer's buckskin coat, Thomas Jefferson's bible, Edison's light bulb and the flag that inspired "The Star-Spangled Banner." (see separate listings about the creation of this flag and poem in the Baltimore listings). Your mouth will drop when you first turn the corner and see it! The museum's Spark!Lab uses fun activities to help kids and families learn about the history and process of invention through

Early Americans hauled 25 pails of water (at 21 lbs each!) just to do a load of laundry...

The "priceless" Hope Diamond...

games and conducting experiments plus there's an Under 5 Zone just for pre-schoolers. A new transportation exhibition (and the largest exhibition to open in the museum), America on the Move, explores the world of transportation, including real artifacts from historic Route 66.

- **NATIONAL MUSEUM OF NATURAL HISTORY**: Walk among the butterflies or witness a view of the blinding Hope Diamond at the National Museum of Natural History. After seeing a digitally-restored Triceratops or dining in the special dinosaur café, check out the famous Insect Zoo. Kids can learn all about these creatures and non-squeamish types are allowed to handle them for an up-close look. The newly renovated Mammal Hall shows some of the museum's specimens in lifelike, realistic settings. The Ocean Hall is the newest permanent exhibition—and the largest exhibit—that explores the ancient, diverse, and constantly changing nature of the ocean, the long historical connections humans have had with it, and ways in which we are impacting the ocean today.

- **NATIONAL MUSEUM OF AFRICAN AMERICAN HISTORY and CULTURE**: (15th and Constitution Ave., NW) It has close to 37,000 objects in its collection related to such subjects as community, family, the visual and performing arts, religion, civil rights, slavery, and segregation. Personal items such as Harriet Tubman's silk shawl, Rosa Parks dress she was sewing the day of refusal, Louis Armstrong's trumpet, James Brown's cape, Jim Crow era "Colored" signage and a segregated drinking fountain, feet and wrist shackles, Muhammad Ali's boxing headgear, and modern artifacts such as President Barack Obama's campaign office.

- **NATIONAL MUSEUM OF THE AMERICAN INDIAN**: (4th Street & Independence) Experience culture at the National Museum of the American Indian, where FREE programming from storytelling and dance festivals to music performances by Native composers is available based on changing monthly performance schedules. The four story brilliantly lighted atrium captures your senses to explore the simple chronicle of people's courageous survival to present day accomplishments. The site offers live performances by American Indians full of color and sound.

- **NATIONAL POSTAL MUSEUM**: Located next to Union Station, the National Postal Museum offers its young visitors insights into the interesting world of mail service. Children can create a souvenir postcard, learn about the history of the Pony Express and the legend of Owney the Postal Dog, and participate in a direct mail marketing campaign. Climb up into the cab of an Interstate Mail Truck and blow the bell and whistle. 2 Massachusetts Ave., NE. Metro: Union Station.

- **SACKLER GALLERY** @ The National Museums of Asian Art: Through the Sackler Gallery's ImaginAsia, kids visit a featured exhibition with a special guide written for children and create an art project to take home. Other special family programs include Asian dance and music lessons, storytelling, and more.

NATIONAL GALLERY OF ART

Washington - *4th Street & Constitution Avenue, NW (I-295N to I-395N to National Mall exit between Third and Seventh Streets) 20565. www.nga.gov. Phone: (202) 737-4215. Hours: Monday-Saturday 10:00am-5:00pm, Sunday 11:00am-6:00pm. Closed Christmas and New Years. Admission: FREE. NOTE: Ask for the "Great Picture Hunt" at the info desk which lists paintings of special interest to kids.*

This fine art museum contains a collection of European and American works in chronological order with recognizable names including da Vinci, Renoir, Monet and Whistler. The new NGAkids Still Life interactive encourages young artists to explore the world around them by arranging artistic elements and everyday objects into works that mirror those of the old masters. But there are surprises in store, as some of the objects unexpectedly spring to life! Experiment with spatial arrangements, size variables, and perspective angles, then switch modes and add layers of textured "brushstrokes" to create a more abstract image. This Art Zone activity is suitable for all ages. Visitors with children can also participate in drop-in workshops, take several postcard tours of the collection using a packet of cards with pictures of objects and questions for discussion or rent a family-oriented audio tour. Outside, browse through the National Gallery of Art's Sculpture Garden and enjoy the fresh air at the same time (they have benches to "sit a spell", if needed).

CHERRY BLOSSOM FESTIVAL

Washington - *Washington, DC's annual National Cherry Blossom Festival is a celebration of the coming of spring and commemorates the gift of 3,000 cherry trees given to the U.S. by Tokyo mayor, Yukio Ozaki in 1912. The two-week festival includes many cultural, sporting and culinary events culminating with the Festival Parade and DC's Sakura Matsuri Japanese Street Festival, presenting over 80 organizations highlighting Japanese performances, arts, crafts and food. The Parade showcases entries from across the country and around the world, including Ringling Bros. And Barnum & Bailey circus, lavish floats, gigantic helium balloons, exciting international performance groups, marching bands and celebrity guests. Also, The Smithsonian Kite Festival on the grounds of the Washington Monument. www.nationalcherryblossomfestival.org. Most events are FREE. (first two weeks of April, beginning end of March)*

WHITEHOUSE EASTER

Washington - *White House Lawn. www.whitehouse.gov/easter/. This annual tradition dates back to 1878 and President Rutherford B. Hayes. Children ages 3 to 6 can frolic on the South Lawn searching for over 24,000 wooden eggs that have been hidden throughout the grounds. There is also an Easter celebration at the Ellipse including entertainment, music, storytelling and food giveaways for the whole family to enjoy.*

Reservations in advance a must. FREE.

AMERICA'S INDEPENDENCE DAY PARADE

Washington - *Constitution Avenue. www.july4thparade.com Celebrate the nation's birthday in the nation's capital. Don't miss the parade, with more then 100 marching units stepping out at noon along Constitution Avenue. When that's over, popular music groups entertain from mid-afternoon until the fireworks at Washington Monument. FREE.*

SMITHSONIAN FOLKLIFE FESTIVAL

Washington - *National Mall. National, even international, celebration of contemporary living traditions. The Festival typically includes daily and evening programs of music, song, dance, celebratory performance, crafts and cooking demonstrations, storytelling, illustrations of workers' culture. The Festival encourages visitors to participate - to learn, sing, dance, eat traditional foods, and converse with people presented in the Festival program. www.festival.si.edu/. FREE. (first two weekends, Thursday-Sunday, in July)*

HOLIDAY HOMECOMING

Washington - *www.washington.org/holidayhomecoming/. Warm up your holiday season with spectacular art exhibitions and lively performances in the nation's capital. Lighting of the National Christmas Tree (White House Ellipse), Discovery Theatre children's performances (Discovery of Light), house tours, Creche Nativity display and Christmas Pageant at National Cathedral. Some events require fee. (December)*

Chapter 3
Central
Area

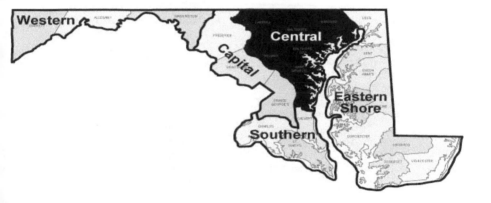

Aberdeen

- Ripken Stadium / Ironbirds
- U.S Army Ordnance Museum
- Annapolis Ice Cream Company
- Annapolis Symphony Orchestra
- Buddy's Crabs & Ribs
- Chick & Ruth's Delly
- Historic Annapolis Museum
- Maryland State House
- Sandy Point State Park
- Schooner Woodwind
- U.S. Naval Academy
- Annapolis Maritime Museum
- Chesapeake Children's Museum
- Discover Annapolis Trolley Tour
- Pirate Adventures On The Chesapeake
- Watermark Cruises/Walking Tours
- Family Fishing Adventures
- All American Fourth Of July Celebration
- Kunta Kinte Celebration
- Maryland Renaissance Festival
- Maritime Republic Of Eastport's Annual Tug Of War
- Pumpkin Walk
- Greens Show
- William Paca Holiday Open House

Annapolis (Eastport)

- Carrol's Creek Café

Annapolis (Shady Side)

- Oyster Fest

Baltimore

- Baltimore Area Sports
- Baltimore Symphony Orchestra
- Charm City Circulator
- Geppi's Entertainment Museum
- Maryland Historical Society Museums
- National Museum Of Dentistry
- Oriole Park At Camden Yards
- Walters Art Museum
- Flag House & Star Spangled Banner Museum
- Frederick Douglass - Isaac Myers Maritime Park

Baltimore (cont.)

- Hyatt Regency Baltimore
- Port Discovery Museum
- Reginald F. Lewis Museum Of Maryland African American History & Culture
- LaCrosse Museum And National Hall Of Fame
- Baltimore Streetcar Museum
- National Great Blacks In Wax Museum
- Maryland Zoo In Baltimore
- Baltimore Museum Of Art
- Maryland Aviation Museum, Glenn L Martin
- B & O Railroad Museum
- Urban Pirates, Baltimore City
- American Visionary Art Museum
- Babe Ruth Birthplace
- Baltimore Museum Of Industry
- Fort McHenry National Monument & Historic Shrine
- Preakness Celebration
- Charles Village Summer Festival
- Honfest
- Latinofest
- Artscape
- Baltimore Book Festival
- Ukrainian Festival
- Czech And Slovak Festival
- Russian Festival
- Monumental Occasion

Baltimore & Columbia

- Toby's Dinner Theatre

Baltimore (Columbia)

- Hilton Columbia

Baltimore (Hanover)

- Medieval Times Dinner Show

Baltimore, Inner Harbor

- Harborplace
- Baltimore Spirit Cruises
- National Aquarium In Baltimore
- USS Constellation
- World Trade "Top Of The World"
- Maryland Science Center
- Baltimore Maritime Museum

Brookeville
- Sharp's At Waterford Farm

Churchville
- Brad's Produce Corn Maze

Columbia
- Boat Float
- Symphony Of Lights

Darlington
- Darlington Apple Festival

Edgewater
- Historic Londontown
- Smithsonian Environmental Research Center

Ellicott City
- Enchanted Forest & Clarkland Farm
- Ellicott City B&O Railroad Station Museum
- Patapsco Valley State Park

Fort George G. Meade
- National Cryptologic Museum

FrienDship
- Herrington Harbour Inn

Galesville
- Pirate's Cove Restaurant

Greenspring Valley
- North Run Farm Maze

Havre De Grace
- Concord Point Lighthouse
- Havre De Grace Decoy Museum
- Havre De Grace Maritime Museum
- Laurrapin Grille
- MacGregors Restaurant
- Skipjack Martha Lewis
- Susquehanna Museum Of Havre De Grace Lock House
- VanDiver Inn
- Susquehanna State Park
- Independence Celebration

Kingsville
- Gunpowder Falls State Park

Linthicum
- National Electronics Museum

Lutherville
- Fire Museum Of Maryland

Monkton
- Ladew Topiary Gardens

Owings Mills
- Soldier's Delight Natural Environmental Area

Parkville
- Johnny Appleseed Festival

Savage
- Terrapin Adventures

Timonium
- Sugarloaf Crafts Festival
- Baltimore Area Pow-Wow
- Maryland State Fair
- Festival Of Trees

Towson
- Hampton National Historic Site

Union Mills
- Civil War Encampment Living History
- Old-Fashioned Corn Roast Festival

West Friendship
- Farm Heritage Days
- Carroll County Farm Museum

Whiteford
- Applewood Farm

Woodbine
- Days End Farm Horse Rescue

A Quick Tour of our Hand-Picked
Favorites Around...   **Central Maryland**

The Central portion of the state enters from northern Maryland, crossing over the Tydings Memorial Bridge over the Susquehanna River in Havre de Grace along the way. Major interstates I-83, I-70 and I-95 meander a little and then travel diagonally through the middle of the state, through Baltimore and then fork due south to Annapolis.

The first family-friendly town you hit on your way south through the state is **Havre de Grace** (pronounced haver da grace). Maybe try an overnight at a B&B, and then walk to any waterfront museum, a skipjack tour or a quaint restaurant – each with their specialties clearly presented on the menu. Because this is a walkable town, we consider all of Havre de Grace one big attraction.

Maryland is a very kid-friendly state and the perfect place for some serious sidetripping. A logical choice is a trip to **Baltimore**, where you can explore the acclaimed Inner Harbor museums and shops...especially the big ship, the **USS Constellation** in port. Audio players allow you to listen as a young girl's grandpa shares stories about the Constellation's magnificent power on the waters of combat. Surrounding **Inner Harbor** are some pretty historic sites. Baseball great **Babe Ruth's Birthplace** is just down the street from Camden Yards. Or, visit the actual spot where the "**Star Spangled Banner**" originated at Ft. McHenry or the Flag House where a small group of women created the famous flag.

What kids don't love trains at some point in their childhood? Remember the Monopoly game you played at home and one property marked the **B&O Railroad**? What about visiting the original huge trains, miniature trains, trains you can ride – all here and all presented in short presentations inside and outside. Haven't had enough? Travel a little ways off the connecting outerbelt and you'll find another quaint railroad station: the **Ellicott City B&O Railroad**. The surrounding little town has dozens of whimsical shops, too.

When it comes to offbeat, Maryland is home to some bizarre, yet amusing attractions like the **Museum of Dentistry** in Baltimore, which includes George Washington's dentures and crazy people who use their teeth to lift things! We found another extremely unique and a little creepy museum at Fort Meade Military base. The **National Cryptologic Museum** is all about secret codes and deciphering them. Talk about stories that make you wonder who's watching (or listening to) you!

The farthest southern point of this chapter is the capital city of **Annapolis**. While it is extremely steeped in history, it's a walking town full of hidden gems like **Chick n Ruths**, **Buddys**, **Annapolis Ice Cream**, little shops, the city dock boats and oh, the sailing adventures! Entering historic Annapolis is like opening a treasure chest but to be sure you don't overdue it - try a schooner, sailboat, pirate or water taxi **Boat Cruise**. You won't be disappointed. If you want to be sure you get a great overview of Maryland history by land, try the **Historic Annapolis Museum** using an audio stick self-guided tour. Our description of the museum and city offerings will give you just what you need to explore "kid-friendly" sites. Don't leave Annapolis without touring the **U.S. Naval Academy**. Try to get there by Noon formation, when the entire brigade forms up to march to lunch.

Maryland gets a lot of attention for their succulent blue crabs, plucked from the Chesapeake Bay and transformed into pink crustaceans that you can dissect for dinner. It seems silly to don a bib and "tools" for a meal but the reward is the yummy meat in the middle. We found the best crab at Crab/BBQ joints downtown and just off interstates. Just follow the signs…

Sites and attractions are listed in order by City, Zip Code, and Name. Symbols indicated represent: 🍴 Restaurants   🛏 Lodging

RIPKEN STADIUM / IRONBIRDS

Aberdeen - *873 Long Drive (I-95 NORTH take the MD-22 exit - number 85 - towards Aberdeen/Churchville) 21001. www.ironbirdsbaseball.com. Phone: (410) 297-9292.*

Home of baseball's best known family. Tours of the stadium, which includes the Ripken Museum exhibit, are offered during the Aberdeen Ironbirds off-season (October-May).

The New York-Penn League affiliate for the Orioles plays seasonal home games, has a Kids Club, and hosts the Cal Ripken World Series and All-Star Games for the league. The name "IronBird" is a product of two distinct tie-ins that Cal wanted to incorporate into the team's image. "Iron" is a reference to Cal's streak of 2,632 consecutive games played, surpassing the record previously held by Lou Gehrig. Ripken is now known as baseball's all-time "Iron Man." The "Bird" part of the name refers to Cal playing his entire 21-year career in an Orioles uniform.

CAL RIPKEN WORLD SERIES

Aberdeen - Cal, Sr.'s Yard, a youth-sized version of Oriole Park at Camden Yards, located adjacent to Ripken Stadium. www.ripkenbaseball.com. Baseball games between 10 U.S. and 5 International teams competing for the Cal Ripken World Series championship title. Admission. (2nd full week in August)

U.S ARMY ORDNANCE MUSEUM

Aberdeen - (I-95 exit onto Rte. 22 going towards Aberdeen. Exit Rte. 40 west to Rte. 715 south) 21005. Phone: (410) 278-3602. www.ordmusfound.org. Hours: Daily 9:00am-4:45pm. Closed National Holidays except for Armed Forces, Memorial, Independence and Veterans Days. Admission: Free Day Pass will be issued only at the "Maryland Ave. Gate". This gate is on Rt. 715. The Rt. 22 gate will not issue any passes.

You can now visit the Ordnance Museum at Aberdeen Proving Ground as a civilian. Inside the museum, you'll find a collection of small arms, artillery, combat vehicles and ammunition. Outside is more impressive at the Proving Ground. Drive the "Mile of Tanks" at the 25 acre Tank & Artillery Park. A park full of real tank trucks is pretty eye-popping for little (and big) guys.

ANNAPOLIS ICE CREAM COMPANY

Annapolis - 196 Main Street 21401. (443) 482-3895 or www.annapolisicecream.com. For the freshest, in-store-made ice cream look for their Penguins on Main Street. 100% natural and gourmet ice cream plus seasonal favorites like homemade hot cocoa. They make ice cream fresh nearly every day. During the summer, you can pretty much be sure that the ice cream you are eating today was made within the last 24-36 hours! With more than 35 homemade ice cream selections (like coffee, Oreo, apple pie, and peanut butter vanilla!), Annapolis Ice Cream Company caters to every unique ice cream palate - and every flavor is so "on" because they use real ingredients mixed in (ex. Real coffee, real apple pie, peanut butter) - it makes the difference. And, a grand banana split is only around $8.00! So-o-o very good. _____ 🍽

ANNAPOLIS SYMPHONY ORCHESTRA

Annapolis - *Maryland Hall for the Creative Arts, 801 Chase Street 21401. Phone: (410) 263-0907. www.annapolissymphony.org.*

The music you treasure, the orchestra that loves to play it. They present classics, Holiday Pops and kid-friendly Family Series concerts. Free Labor Day weekend concerts in the Parks.

BUDDY'S CRABS & RIBS

Annapolis - 100 Main Street 21401. (410) 626-1100 or www.buddysonline.com. Family-owned and operated with 22 windows overlooking Main Street and the City Dock. Specializing in steamed crabs, baby back ribs, seafood, steaks, chicken, salads, daily buffets (seafood lunch $15.00, dinner $25.00). All kids twelve and under eat free (from the kids menu) with each full priced adult entree ordered. Free Balloons, Free Coloring pads. They find themselves different from most other restaurants because they cater to families with kids. Their slogan says it all... "WE LOVE KIDS!!" This was the site of my FIRST blue crab training with mallet and knife! I would recommend the fresh and flavorful buffet with a side of blue crab to "dissect" if you dare. Not for the seafood squeamish, those crabs. A hoot for me for sure!

CHICK & RUTH'S DELLY

Annapolis - 165 Main Street 21401. Daily for breakfast, lunch and dinner. Old fashioned milk shakes, ice cream, too. (410) 269-6737 or www.chickandruths.com. Their menu takes a while to look over as there are tons of things to order. Ask for Delly homefries with breakfast - yum. Now, Ted, the 2nd generation owner is the ambitious one flitting about performing impromptu magic tricks tableside. The best part of breakfast here is their nickname: "Flag'n Eggs" cause each morning as the crowded restaurant is on their second cup of coffee - everyone in the place, customers and employees alike, gets up in unison and recites <u>The Pledge of Allegiance</u>. An act of spontaneous patriotism? No, it's an Annapolis tradition that dates back more than three decades. The Pledge is recited every day at 8:30am (Monday through Friday) and 9:30am Saturday and Sunday. What a great way to start your journey around the historic state capital!

HISTORIC ANNAPOLIS MUSEUM

Annapolis - *99 Main Street (historic Foundation site/Museum Store, corner of Main & Greene Sts.) 21401. Phone: (410) 267-6656. www.annapolis.org. Hours: Monday-Saturday 10:00am-5:00pm, Sunday 11:00am-5:00pm. Open later on weekdays in the summer.*

Tours: Audio Guide self-guided walking tour is $5.00 per stick. When you stop *in front of one of the numbered locations on the corresponding audio tour map, simply enter that number into the digital player and hear about the building and its history. Purchase one and share or pick different themes for each person. History buffs really enjoy these tours, thoroughly, while the rest of the family may want to listen in here and there so it makes it nice for everyone. Some can shop while others are touring. Note: Drive across the Spa Creek Bridge into Eastport on a mid-week evening and you'll see people lining the shore, on the bridge and anchored in the water to watch the Annapolis yacht Club's Wednesday Night Races. Locals and visitors time their tips to waterfront restaurants and the Naval Academy's sea wall (great spot for kids viewing) to watch more than 150 sailboats race, 20 at a time.*

Discover the Museum without Walls that is Annapolis – through the doorway that is HistoryQuest – where your Annapolis adventure begins! The complete orientation center (in a 1790s building) features movies, exhibits and artifacts on display...in a very simple, interesting format (free to look around museum). Kids need to do the scavenger hunt worksheet for a sweet prize once they complete it. Especially look for the Death's Head Printers Block reminiscent of the Annapolis Tea Party. We liked their Window Rails. Look up at the present, look down at the past. Now that you're oriented, get your tour materials and then begin your walk past churches, a courthouse, the Old Treasury, The US Naval Academy (see separate listing), St. John's College campus, homes and taverns. Stop in for a visit to the **BANNEKER-DOUGLASS MUSEUM** (84 Franklin Street) in the

first African American Episcopal Church of Annapolis which focuses on African-American life and history. The facility features an Annapolis Underground exhibit which explores the archaeology of African American life in town and another exhibit, Deep Roots, Rising Waters, explores the history of African Americans

Such a fun town to walk and explore!

in the state from the 1630s to the Civil Rights Movement. Wander some more and look for the house whose resident wrote "Anchors A Weigh" (Zimmerman House), or the birthplace of the only Roman Catholic signer of the Declaration of Independence (**CHARLES CARROLL HOUSE**). Othersigners have homes here: **WILLIAM PACA HOUSE** (186 Prince George St) and **CHASE LLOYD HOUSE** (22 Maryland Avenue). Most are open to tour. Another home is named after the ship burned after a discovery of a hidden shipment of tea was found making Annapolis its Revolutionary War "tea party". (**PEGGY STEWART HOUSE**). The Stewart House was also owned by the fourth (and youngest) signer of the Declaration, Thomas Stone. Pass by, and maybe explore inside, the State House - the oldest state capital in continuous legislative use. Many linger at the heart of the city, the City Dock. City Dock has been the center of the town's maritime life for over 300 years. Today, work and pleasure boats share the use of "Ego Alley." There's a waterside park and a memorial commemorating the 1767 arrival in Annapolis of KUNTA KINTE, immortalized by his descendant, Alex Haley, in Roots. You'll love the endearing sculpture of Alex Haley reading to children. Story boards on Compromise street and a display at the Market House complete the memorial.

MARYLAND DAY

Annapolis - Historic sites downtown. Learn about Diamondback Terrapins, Chesapeake Retrievers and other Maryland state symbols during this kid-friendly event. (March 25 or thereabouts)

MARYLAND STATE HOUSE

Annapolis - 91 State Circle 21401. www.mdarchives.state.md.us/msa/homepage/ html/statehse.html. Phone: (410) 974-3400. Hours: Monday-Friday 9:00am-5:00pm, Saturday-Sunday 10:00am-4:00pm. Closed major statewide holidays. Tours: Available daily at 11:00am and 3:00pm. This is an indoor stop for many walking tours of town, also. Educators: For teaching guides to many important events and issues in Maryland and US history, please visit the Web site: www. teachingamericanhistorymd.net.

The Maryland State House is the oldest state capital in continuous legislative use, and the only state capital to have been a US capitol. Construction began in 1772; the legislature first met here in 1779. Features include the largest wooden dome in country built without nails. To the right of the front door is the Old Senate Chamber where the Continental Congress met. This room has been restored to its original appearance and features a mannequin of George Washington dressed as he was when he resigned his commission. There are

a number of portraits of early governors of Maryland by Charles Willson Peale, as well as Peale's celebrated portrait of Washington, Lafayette and Tilghman at Yorktown. The President's desk as well as some of the other desks and chairs in the room are original pieces made for the State House in 1796-1797 by Annapolis cabinetmaker John Shaw. The US Congress met here from November 1783 to August 1784 and ratified the Treaty of Paris in this building, formally ending the Revolutionary War.

STATE HOUSE BY CANDLELIGHT

Annapolis - *Maryland State House. Decorated for the holiday season; a variety of musical entertainment. State House guided tours. (first weekend in December)*

SANDY POINT STATE PARK

Annapolis - *1100 E. College Pkwy 21401. (western terminus of the Bay Bridge, off US Rtes 50/301 at exit 32) Phone: (410) 974-2149. www.dnr.state.md.us/ publiclands/Pages/southern/sandypoint.aspx Admission: Off peak $3.00 per vehicle. Peak $4.00-$7.00 per person.*

Offering sandy beaches with swimming, playgrounds, hiking, crabbing, fishing and an excellent view of the Bay Bridge, the park also features boat ramps, a marina and boat rentals.

MARYLAND SEAFOOD FESTIVAL

Annapolis - *Sandy Point State Park. www.mdseafoodfestival.com. Traditional Maryland seafood fare, crab soup cookoff, arts and crafts, music, family-oriented entertainment. Admission. (second weekend in September)*

LIGHTS ON THE BAY

Annapolis - *Sandy Point State Park. Annual drive through holiday lights show sponsored by the Anne Arundel Medical Center (benefits hospital). Admission. (month-long in December)*

SCHOONER WOODWIND

Annapolis - *80 Compromise Street (Marriott Waterfront) 21401. Phone: (410) 263-7837. www.schoonerwoodwind.com. Admission: $43.00-$46.00 adult, $41-$44 senior (60+), $29.00 child (mid-April to Labor Day). Includes a snack and soft drink.*

"Woodwind" sails up to four times daily throughout the summer season from the Annapolis Marriott Waterfront Hotel. Raise the sails, steer the boat or sit back and relax on a two-hour sail. All cruises sail by the United States Naval Academy and then into the Chesapeake Bay. Sailing under the Chesapeake Bay Bridge is a fabulous experience as are the breathtaking sunsets over the historic Annapolis skyline. Learn many little-known historical facts along the way. "Woodwind" is a replica of the classic, fast wooden schooners that were built as "yachts" in the early part of this century. Her handsome mahogany brightwork, gleaming chrome and roomy cockpit distinguish her from cargo carrying work vessels.

U.S. NAVAL ACADEMY

Annapolis - *Armel-Leftwich Visitors Center, 52 King George St., Gate 1 (at the foot of King George Street) 21402. Phone: (410) 293-TOUR. www.navyonline.com. Hours: Daily 9:00am-4:00 or 5:00pm except holidays. Adults (over 16 years of age) please bring photo ID to show at Gate 1 for entrance. Tours: Public walking tours are given until 3:00pm. Cost is $9.00-$11.00 per person (1st graders and up). Led by Academy guides - the best way to get an insiders view of the Yard. We'd recommend this tour for older kids and adults as it covers many detailed facts. Note: Dry Dock Restaurant open for lunch. If taking the self-guided tour, be sure to get a campus map. It's not that hard to navigate the campus.*

John Paul Jones, "the Father of the American Navy" is buried here... Armel-Leftwich Visitors center.

The graduation hat toss is a recognizable Commissioning Week tradition and when you explore this 338-acre campus, known as "the Yard," you'll discover that the Naval Academy is defined by many traditions. Whether on self or guided tours, begin at the information center in the

The massive gift shop and the Freedom 7, America's first manned spacecraft flown by Naval Academy graduate Alan Shepard, are here, too. Begin by viewing the film: "*Leaders of Character Serving the Nation*," which chronicles the intensely structured and rigorous days and nights of the midshipmen. Stops on the tour include Bancroft Hall, known as "Mother B," the largest dormitory in the United States, and home to the entire brigade of midshipmen. If you are visiting during the school year, you may be able to see Noon Formation, when the entire brigade forms up to march to their midday meal. Another stop is the US Naval Academy Chapel, "The Cathedral of the Navy," located on the highest ground of the Yard, towering with its copper dome. The crypt

and sarcophagus of Revolutionary War hero John Paul Jones lie beneath the chapel. His legend is forever linked to the immortal words, "I have not yet begun to fight!" The Naval Academy Museum (Preble Hall on Maryland Ave.) is packed with Academy memorabilia, beautiful model ships and exhibits on American naval history. What's that peculiar statue on the Yard? It's probably "Tecumseh." Midshipmen toss pennies in his quiver for good luck and refer to him as "the god of 2.0," the minimum passing grade. Before you leave, be sure to see the Herndon Monument, site of perhaps the most famous and enduring rite of passage in the USNA. To signal the end of their "plebe" status, first-year midshipmen work together to reach the top of the 21-foot monument, greased for the occasion by members of the upper classes. Legend has it that the student who successfully places his Dixie Cup hat on the pinnacle of the monument will be first admiral of his class.

JOHN PAUL JONES DAY

Annapolis - *U.S. Naval Academy. Wreath laying, flag raising, historical presentations, children's activities, fifes and drums, John Paul Jones warrant signings. (second weekend in July)*

ANNAPOLIS MARITIME MUSEUM

Annapolis - 723 Second Street (Foot of Second Street & Back Creek on Bayshore Drive) 21403. Phone: (410) 295-0104. www.amaritime.org. Hours: Thursday-Sunday 11:00am-3:00pm. Note: Summertime maritime concerts are regularly scheduled. Thomas Point Lighthouse tours available mid-summer.

Come to the Barge House to see the exhibit, the Thomas Point Lighthouse Experience, and the short documentary, Legacy of the Light, a virtual tour of the lighthouse. Visitors also learn about the natural history of the oyster and the vital role it plays in the health of the Chesapeake Bay. The exhibits tell the story of the hard-working people who harvested, shucked, packed, and shipped oysters from this old oyster processing building. Kids can stand in an authentic shucking stall, in the very footprints the shucker wore into the wooden slats and hear stories of workers who once walked these same floors.

- **THOMAS POINT SHOAL LIGHTHOUSE** - Come aboard the icon of the Chesapeake Bay and the last screwpile lighthouse left on its original location. Learn about how lighthouse keepers lived, why many other lighthouses on the Bay met their demise, and how one preserves an old lighthouse. The tour includes a safety check-in and orientation at the Thomas Point Shoal Lighthouse Interpretive Center at the Annapolis Maritime Museum's Barge House, a 30-minute boat ride to the lighthouse, an on-board docent-led tour, and a 30-minute return boat ride. Allow three hours for the excursion. Tours are $70.00 per person. The tour involves some physical exertion so it's almost like you're on a sea voyage adventure like Huck Finn through potentially heavy seas, climbing up a steep ladder and through a small hatch-a trap door on the lighthouse deck!

CHESAPEAKE CHILDREN'S MUSEUM

Annapolis - *25 Silopanna Road (pass the Naval Academy Stadium, right on Taylor, right onto Spa Road. Left on Silopanna) 21403. Phone: (410) 990-1993. www.theccm.org. Hours: Daily 10:00am-4:00pm. Admission: $5.00 per person (age 1+).*

Live animals are the highlight of an exhibit on Aquatic and land-living creatures representing regional wildlife. Kids can then climb aboard a ten-foot boat and dock to act out their own watermen scenes (Props-life jackets, nets, plush crabs and fish - add to the realism of the exhibit). Toddlers adore the wooden train table, just at their height. Preschoolers make buildings and towns with the block set, often with help from their grown ups. In Body Works, kids can explore inside Stuffee, or climb up into a real dental chair (or, let mom do it and YOU be the dentist). There's an art workspace with creative, recycled materials or Center Stage full of costumes and a dramatic curtain. At Around the World, little visitors can visit a home in Colombia; Shop in the market place; Bring rainforest puppets to life; Say hello to Rosita the red-tailed boa constrictor or the new Owl on display.

DISCOVER ANNAPOLIS TROLLEY TOUR

Annapolis - *(depart from Visitors Center or Historic Annapolis) 21403. Phone: (410) 626-6000. www.discover-annapolis.com. Admission: $18.00 adult, $9.00 youth (11-15), $3.00 (10 and under). Tours: Daily (April - November) departing 3-4 times per day beginning at 10:30am. Note: dogs are welcome on the tour.*

You will "Discover Annapolis" from a trolley – which is a little bus with big windows. The tour takes one hour. You'll travel down charming streets laid out over three centuries ago. Friendly guides point out all the major points of interest including the City Dock, the State House, handsome colonial mansions, beautiful Victorian homes, sailboats along the waterfront, and much more. You'll enjoy spectacular water views from three bridges. Drive along all sides of the Naval Academy as the guide describes the academic and athletic programs of Navy. There are about 1300 buildings in Annapolis at least a century old, representing 15 different architectural styles. This tour focuses on the largest and oldest of those 1300 buildings, with special attention on the Georgian style (harmonious and balanced) named after the Kings George who ruled Britain much of the 18th century. Annapolis has the highest concentration of Georgian buildings in America. The one-hour, air conditioned (or heated) trolley tour also promises some surprises.

PIRATE ADVENTURES ON THE CHESAPEAKE

Annapolis - *311 3rd Street 21403. www.chesapeakepirates.com. Phone: (410) 263-0002. Tours: The Sea Gypsy sails seven days a week (April-Labor Day) at 9:30am, 11:00am, 12:30pm, 2:00pm, 3:30pm, and 5:00pm, and then Weekends only thru October. Tickets are $22.00 per person age 3 and over, $12.00 for children under the age of 3. Tours return to dock 75 minutes after departure. Arrive 30 minutes prior for check-in, facepainting and dress-up!*

Come aboard for a Pirate Cruise as your children enjoy life as a pirate while you relax and enjoy the ride. We encourage you to arrive 30 minutes prior to sailing time to allow time to register and to transform your child into a pirate. Children will have the opportunity to have their faces painted with mustaches, mermaids, anchors, sharks, and more. Young buccaneers can also choose a pirate vest and sash from their treasure chest to wear for the voyage. The crew will gather the group for a rousing "AARGH" and then board Sea Gypsy for departure at sailing time. High energy staff fill the entire trip with activities. Watch out for their signature fire water cannons.

WATERMARK CRUISES & WALKING TOURS

Annapolis - *Slip 20, Annapolis City Dock   21403. www.watermarkcruises.com.*
Phone: (410) 268-7600. Fireworks Cruises and Christmastime candlelight walks.

THOMAS POINT LIGHTHOUSE CRUISE: (90 minutes). Cruise out to the Chesapeake Bay to view the National Historic Landmark, Thomas Point Lighthouse. Built in 1875, it was the last to be manned on the Bay. You will learn more about the history of such points of interest as Providence, The Bay Bridge and Tolly Point as well as the historic lighthouses on the Chesapeake. Cruise departs at 4:30pm on weekends and holidays. ($23/$10 per person)

RIVER & BRIDGES CRUISES: (40 minutes): Just the right amount of time to take a leisurely, historical or natural cruise for younger sailors. Maybe the Spa Creek or Severn River, Chesapeake Bay bridges. The kids get to take turns being captain and receive a sticker! ($16/$6 daily April-early October)

WATER TAXI: Take a taxi to waterfront restaurants on Spa & Back Creeks. $3.00-$8.00 per person.

COLONIAL STROLL (90 minute walking tour): Tour the heart of Annapolis and the U.S. Naval Academy as a colonial attired tour guide leads the way. Kids become history detectives, looking for unusual architecture, "speed bumps" and ghost marks. Your guide brings a basket of curiosities to visually connect the history told. Tour includes exteriors of the Maryland State House and famous historic mansions as well as the interior of the U.S. Naval Academy Chapel and Crypt. Tour leaves from the Visitors Center on 26 West Street (City Dock) at 10:30am. $16.00/Adults, $10.00/Children 3-11, Daily spring thru October. Children ages 2 & under are free. PHOTO ID REQUIRED for adult admittance into Academy grounds. If you like to take walking tours of streets full of historic buildings - here's your match. Good tour for state history students and older.

FAMILY FISHING ADVENTURES

Annapolis - *410 Severn Avenue, Annapolis City Dock   21403. http:// familyfishingadventures.com. Phone: (410) 279-8325. Sails: 4 times daily (May-October). Admission: $20.00 per person, $16.00 child under 5.*

Welcome aboard the Sea Dragon for interactive fishing adventures where the kids are immersed in the world of fishing and crabbing, learning how to fish and preserve the Chesapeake Bay. Families board a 30 foot vessel for an hour and 45 minute trip. Once on deck, the crew takes over for hassle free instruction.

ALL AMERICAN FOURTH OF JULY CELEBRATION

Annapolis William Paca House and Garden. www.Annapolis.org. Period music and entertainment, Revolutionary War re-enactors, historical figures, readings of the Declaration of Independence and patriotic crafts. (July 4th)

KUNTA KINTE CELEBRATION

Annapolis - City Dock. www.kuntakinte.org. African-American ethnic festival featuring exciting performances. Unusual displays of arts, crafts. Children's tent and delicious ethnic cuisine. Admission. (weekend in September)

MARYLAND RENAISSANCE FESTIVAL

Annapolis - Crownsville Road. www.rennfest.com. 16th century English festival with 10 stages, 5,000 seat jousting arena, zoo performers, 140 food and craft shops. Admission. (weekends in September and October)

MARITIME REPUBLIC OF EASTPORT'S ANNUAL TUG OF WAR

Annapolis - Second Street, next to Chart House. www.themre.org. The longest tug of war over a body of water in the world. The tug of war between the maritime Republic of Eastport and Downtown Annapolis features 1700 foot rope, more than 450 tuggers, and more than 1,000 spectators. Proceeds benefit charity. (last Saturday in October or first Saturday in November)

PUMPKIN WALK

Annapolis - Hammond Harwood House. www.hammondharwoodhouse.org. Old-fashioned fall fun especially for children. Festivities include story telling, apple bobbing, a parade and more. Admission. (third Friday in October)

GREENS SHOW

Annapolis - Hammond Harwood House. www.hammondharwoodhouse.org. This event features the sale of fresh holiday decorations from the 18th century. Tour the house dressed in holiday splendor. Admission. (second weekend in December)

WILLIAM PACA HOLIDAY OPEN HOUSE

Annapolis - William Paca House. www.Annapolis.org. Period home enhances candlelight and daylight tours of the William Paca House in all of its holiday grandeur. Admission. (almost daily in December)

CARROL'S CREEK CAFÉ

Annapolis (Eastport) - 410 Severn Avenue 21403. www.carrolscreek.com. (410) 263-8102. Located on the famous Restaurant Row in the Eastport section of Annapolis, Carrol's Creek is tucked in the Annapolis City Marina. A short stroll over the Spa Creek Bridge, the restaurant has a great view of the Wednesday night sailboat races. With a stunning view of the historic skyline and harbor, they feature regional American dishes with an emphasis on seafood and outside dining is available. Lunch serves gourmet style sandwiches and plates ($9.00-$15.00 average). Their Maryland Cream of Crab Soup rich with jumbo lump crabmeat and a touch of sherry, was judged Maryland's Best.

OYSTER FEST

Annapolis (Shady Side) - 1814 East West Shady Side Rd. Great food including raw oysters, oyster fritters, fried oysters, oyster stew, crab cakes, fresh fish, cream of crab soup, picnic food, desserts and refreshments. Musical entertainment and children's activities. Following the house tour, kids head to the pier where they can hoist up an oyster cage and learn about the live shrimp, shellfish, worms, fish, and crabs they find inside. http://captainaverymuseum.org/ Thanks to a new 75-foot pier, boaters have direct access to the Captain Salem Avery House. Admission (age 13+). (third Sunday in October)

BALTIMORE AREA SPORTS

Baltimore -

- **BALTIMORE RAVENS** - Football. MT & T Bank Stadium. (410) 261-WAVE or www.baltimoreravens.com. The NFL Baltimore Ravens play home games here (not far from Inner Harbor) and the stadium gives tours on non-game days by appointment.

- **BALTIMORE ORIOLES** - Baseball. Oriole Park At Camden Yards. (410) 685-9800 or www.theorioles.com. The famous park is home to the American League Orioles. Take A Stroll Through Oriole Park at Camden Yards On A Ballpark Tour! (by appointment, $5.00-$7.00) Come see Camden Yards from a whole new perspective! Enjoy the charm of the ballpark from club level suites, the press levels, and even the Orioles dugout!

BALTIMORE SYMPHONY ORCHESTRA

Baltimore - *Joseph Myerhoff Symphony Hall, 1212 Cathedral Street   21201. Phone: (410) 783-8000. www.bsomusic.org.*

The Baltimore Symphony Orchestra has been playing strong since 1916. The Grammy Award-winning orchestra performs more than 150 concerts annually including outdoor summer concerts (which often conclude with fireworks) and Family Fun Zones before concerts.

CHARM CITY CIRCULATOR

Baltimore - *Federal Hill & Inner Harbor/Mt. Vernon & Penn Station / B&O Railroad to Harbor East 21201. www.charmcitycirculator.com.*

Fast, frequent and free...that's the trademark of downtown Baltimore's new shuttle bus system. Visitors have an easy and convenient way to navigate the city. The FREE shuttles run every 10 minutes from early morning to late night, daily, so it is easy for your family to hop on and off to shop, visit a museum or attraction, browse or dine.

GEPPI'S ENTERTAINMENT MUSEUM

Baltimore - *Camden Station   21201. www.geppismuseum.com. Phone: (410) 427-9438. Hours: Tuesday-Sunday 10:00am-6:00pm. Admission: $10.00 adult, $9.00 senior (55+), $7.00 student (5-18). Special game day reduced admission.*

On TV and radio, in the papers and comic books - even toy stores - pop culture has performed magic for years. This new museum features colorful, chronologically arranged displays that explore 230 years of American life. From rare toys and antique advertising to comic books, movie posters and animation, the journey through history takes visitors from the late 1700s right up to today. Look for famous characters like Superman, Spiderman and Batman. Each chronological period highlighted in the museum is anchored by a centerpiece exhibit representing a historically significant character in pop culture. These artifacts have come from the world-famous private collection of museum founder and Diamond Comic President, Stephen Geppi.

MARYLAND HISTORICAL SOCIETY MUSEUMS

Baltimore - *201 W Monument 21201. Phone: (410) 683-3750. www.mdhs.org. Hours: Vary by location. Society Museum: Wednesday-Saturday 10am-5pm. Sunday Noon-5pm. Admission: Varies by museum, generally $6.00-$9.00 / person (age 13+). On the first Thursday every month, the MdHS offers free museum admission. Educators: http://www.mdhs.org/education/teachers/lesson-plans*

MARYLAND HISTORICAL SOCIETY MUSEUMS (cont.)

Discover the people and events that shaped the state of Maryland. The bombardment of Fort McHenry, Francis Scott Key's original manuscript of the "Star Spangled Banner", hear the stories of civil rights activists, and the difficulties and successes of colonists. Don't miss Tench Tilghman's Revolutionary War uniform and Eubie Blake's eyeglasses.

• MARITIME EXHIBIT: The museum tells the story of the notorious Privateer Clipper ships of the War of 1812 and the rich history of the town's ports. Privateers, shipbuilders, immigrants, merchants, and sailors sought their fortunes in this waterfront community, home to the world-famous Baltimore clipper schooners. These vessels, known then as pilot-boat schooners, were the fastest in the world and carried cargos both legal and illegal. On a single voyage in 1814, one of the most famous captains, Thomas Boyle, captured 14 British vessels and 48 prisoners, and returned with cargo worth over $100,000.

• BALTIMORE CIVIL WAR MUSEUM: 601 S President St. (443) 220-0290. Thursday-Monday 10:00am-4:00pm. $2-$3.00. The Baltimore Civil War Museum, housed in the 1849 train station - one of the oldest in the nation - examines the events of that day and highlights Maryland's divided loyalties and critical role as a border state during the war. Learn the story of the first deaths of the Civil War at the Pratt Street Riot. In addition, visitors will hear the story of the stations important role in the escape of enslaved African Americans via the Underground Railroad. www.baltimorecivilwarmuseum.com

NATIONAL MUSEUM OF DENTISTRY

Baltimore - *31 S Greene Street (MD 395 to downtown, exit MLKing Blvd. Right on Baltimore, right on Greene) 21201. www.dentalmuseum.org. Phone: (410) 706-0600. Hours: Monday-Friday 9:00am-4:00pm. Admission: $7.00 for Admission and Audio Tour. $5.00-$6.00 each for Seniors (60+), college students, and children (ages 3-12). Educators: Quizzes and worksheets are downloadable under the Educators/Resources page.*

Discover the power of a healthy smile at this Smithsonian affiliate. The infamous Doc Holliday was a student at the Baltimore College of Dental Surgery, founded in 1840 as the first dental school in the world. An appropriate place, then, for the Dr. Samuel D. Harris National Museum of Dentistry, a fabulous interactive facility that showcases the evolution of dentistry.

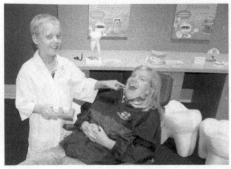

Interactives include: Guess the Smile, Amazing Feats - using teeth to write, to waterski, to pull, to paint; Mouth Power - meet Mouthy and take up a tooth chair to pretend dentistry. Want to know the history of the tooth fairy? What about a whole room devoted to Spit? Modern-day forensics feature the section explaining how DNA in teeth can be used to identify missing persons and solve criminal cases. Among the pieces in its collection are George Washington's dentures (no, they weren't wooden; they were ivory) and a set of dental instruments used by Queen Victoria. We loved this museum!

ORIOLE PARK AT CAMDEN YARDS

Baltimore - *333 W Camden Street (follow Russell Street to Camden Yards signs) 21201. http://baltimore.orioles.mlb.com/bal/ballpark/tours.jsp. Phone: (410) 685-9800.*

The famous park is home to the American League Orioles. Take A Stroll Through Oriole Park at Camden Yards On A Ballpark Tour! (by appointment, $6.00-$9.00, 1 hour and 30 minutes) Daily times during regular season - schedule varies for game days. Come see Camden Yards from a whole new perspective! Enjoy the charm of the ballpark from club level suites, the press levels, and even the Orioles dugout!

WALTERS ART MUSEUM

Baltimore - *600 N Charles Street, entrance on Centre St. 21201. Phone: (410) 547-9000. www.thewalters.org. Hours: Wednesday-Sunday 10:00am-5:00pm and until 9:00pm on Thursdays. Admission: FREE for permanent collection. FREEBIES: Waltee's Quest game online. Waltee Club Card kids club. Look for ArtCarts games and books on weekends and during school breaks.*

The Walters Art Museum offers a variety of extraordinary programs where you can make cool art, see live performances, play dress up, or tour the museum with a kid-friendly passport designed to foster discovery and engagement (scavenger hunt or audio tours). Listen to lively storytelling in the galleries during festivals, watch a family-friendly video in the cozy Family Art Center, create a piece of original artwork during drop-in hours, celebrate your birthday, and earn a scout patch. Every third Saturday of the month is Walk, Wonder and

Create Family Tours. Their permanent collection includes Egyptian Mummies and medieval armor. The newly installed Renaissance and Baroque Galleries includes works by masters Raphael and Bernini. The Palace of Wonders features paintings, artifacts and furniture all arranged as they might have been in the home of a wealthy European collector during old time periods.

FLAG HOUSE & STAR SPANGLED BANNER MUSEUM

Baltimore - 844 E Pratt Street (Little Italy, 2 blocks east of Inner Harbor) 21202. Phone: (410) 837-1793. www.flaghouse.org. Hours: Tuesday-Saturday10:00am-4:00pm. Admission: $6.00-$8.00   per person. Tours: Guided tours last approximately 45 minutes but they are happy to adapt to your schedule. Just let them know when you arrive.

A museum dedicated to the story of Mary Young Pickersgill who made the enormous 30 x 42-foot Star-

A giant life-size flag awaits you at the entrance...

Spangled Banner that flew over Fort McHenry during the War of 1812 and inspired Francis Scott Key to write the poem that became our National Anthem. The new Star-Spangled Banner Museum, adjacent to the Flag House, houses an orientation theatre film and exhibits on the American Flag, Mary and the War of 1812. The unique feature of the museum is the Great Flag Window, a glass wall the same size, color and design of the original Star-Spangled Banner!

Visitors to the Flag House are given a personalized tour of the 18th-century home of Mary Young Pickersgill. You'll learn how Mary, a widowed flag maker and mother, made the flag. How do you hand sow a flag so large? The 90 pound flag made of wool bunting was recreated by local ladies and laid on display in the parlor to help you imagine the task these 1800 era women undertook. As you tour, you'll

Mary Pickersgill's actual flag still survives and now hangs at the Smithsonian Institution's National Museum of American History.

realize how contemporary Mary and her family were for their time. Who would guess their large commissioned project would inspire patriotism even now!

Discovery Gallery is a hands-on room where the kids dress up and then color their own Star Spangled flag to take home. Cook for your family at a replica of the Flag House kitchen, design your own flag and fly it on the gallery's flagpole, tell a story at the puppet stage or try games and toys from long ago.

FREDERICK DOUGLASS - ISAAC MYERS MARITIME PARK

Baltimore - 1417 Thames Street, Fells Point (near the intersection of Caroline St) 21202. Phone: (410) 685-0295. www.douglassmyers.org. Hours: Daily 10:00am-4:00pm. Admission: Self-guided tours $2.00-$5.00 (age 6+).

This park features a re-creation of the first marine shipyard and marine railway operated by African Americans, as well as the Sugar House, the oldest remaining industrial building on the waterfront. Frederick Douglass lived in Baltimore for a time and worked in the maritime trades (before he became a famous abolitionist) and Isaac Myers founded the shipyard and the first black maritime unions. Baltimore was home to one of the largest populations of free blacks before the Civil War, many of whom worked here. After the Civil War, other ethnic workers asked not to work with Blacks and so many were fired - they needed work and new, black owned shipyards were established for a time. Wander through a once busy shipyard railway and a deep-water pier; monuments to Douglass and Myers; exhibits concerning African American maritime history; and the Sugar House view.

HYATT REGENCY BALTIMORE

Baltimore - 300 Light Street 21202. Perfectly located, this Four-Diamond Inner Harbor hotel offers a luxurious haven in the midst of the city's premier attractions with many rooms providing an excellent Harbor View. Stroll to Camden Yards, the National Aquarium or a skywalk to HarborPlace, and then return to the downtown Baltimore harbor hotel to enjoy features like pillow top Grand beds, flat screen TVs, summer sundeck and outdoor pool, tennis, a giant fire pit, or shoot some hoops on a rooftop deck. Several styles of restaurants are on the premises. This property is often part of Baltimore Inner Harbor family packages. (410) 528-1234 or www.hyattregencybaltimore.com.

PORT DISCOVERY, THE CHILDREN'S MUSEUM

Baltimore - *33 Market Place (corner of Lombard Street and Market Place) 21202. Phone: (410) 727-8120. www.portdiscovery.org. Hours: Tuesday - Friday: 9:30am - 4:30pm, Saturday: 10:00am - 5:00pm, Sunday: Noon - 5:00pm. Summertime open Mondays, too. The Museum is closed Thanksgiving Day, Christmas Day, and on Mondays during the months of October through May, except during select Maryland Public School holidays. Admission: $14.95 (age 2+). 3rd Friday of every month (4-8pm) is $2.00 admission!*

Note: Unlike most kids museums, this one is stroller accessible throughout. Concerned about safety? The treehouse structure is clear and steps surround it so you can follow your kids with your eyes or feet. Exits have family check-out station bracelets, too.

Port Discovery, the Children's Museum in Baltimore, offers three floors of interactive, educational exhibits and programs for children ages 2-10 years old. Use your problem solving and critical thinking skills to climb, slide and glide your way through this three-story urban treehouse. Visit the farm area and look under interactive hanging signs to learn all about life on the farm, including how milk is made, or what a fowl is. Barter, sell or trade your new crops at the roadside market. Shop for farm-fresh fruits and vegetables and then use the giant crane to move hay bales from the market to the train for transport. Every kid enjoys the Wonders of Water as they pump, squirt or float objects through a maze of streams, dams and waterfalls (rain coats and crocs are provided). Creative? Act, puppet or design skits or artwork. Step right up to a realistic gas station or uncover secret hieroglyphics that provide clues to solving the mystery inside the tomb. Play hostess, waitress, cook or cashier in a realistic diner. Pick up clues using your detective-sharp research, literacy and problem solving skills to find out what happened to the missing members of the Baffled family. P.S. Don't forget to crawl through the sink, it could lead you to clues on the other side!

REGINALD F. LEWIS MUSEUM OF MARYLAND AFRICAN AMERICAN HISTORY & CULTURE

Baltimore - *830 East Pratt Street, just east of Inner Harbor 21202. Phone: (410) 263-1800. http://lewismuseum.org. Hours: Wednesday-Saturday 10:00am-5:00pm, Sunday Noon-5:00pm. Admission: $6.00-$8.00 (age 7+).*

See 400 years of progress in one day. The African American experience, from tobacco and ironworking to education and law, shows there is not an industry or profession that has not been touched by the accomplishments of African Americans. Discover how ancient-African skills influenced laborers here. Try your hand at some of the most difficult occupations, including caulking and the art of oystering. Meet several families and follow their lives from slavery to freedom and equality. Listen to historical music. Get to know famous African Americans including Frederick Douglass and Harriet Tubman. Follow Benjamin Banneker, Eubie Blake, Joyce Scott and others as they guide you through understanding African American traditions of music, art, and storytelling. And, new, take the self-guided tour, "The Generations Tour: 400 Years, 12 Objects, 1 Hour." Follow the lives of two fictitious characters - Chima and Gladys - as they take you on a journey through the museum's collection. Their stories lead you to 12 exhibits in the gallery that cover 400 years of African American history. Great way for youth to explore the highlights of this museum.

LACROSSE MUSEUM AND NATIONAL HALL OF FAME

Baltimore (Sparks) - *2 Loveton Circle. 21152. www.us-lacrosse.org. Phone: (410) 235-6882. Hours: Weekdays 9:00am-5:00pm. Admission: FREE.*

This modern museum spans the history of lacrosse from Native American origins to modern times. Relive the origins of America's oldest sport. View the all-time greats of lacrosse in the beautiful Hall of Fame Gallery and study their outstanding accomplishments through state-of-the-art computer interactives, striking sculptures, vintage equipment and uniforms, and ancient artifacts. Capture the thrill of playing lacrosse during the multimedia show "Lacrosse: The Spirit Lives" and their historical documentary "More than a Game: A History of Lacrosse."

BALTIMORE STREETCAR MUSEUM

Baltimore - *1901 Falls Road 21211. www.baltimorestreetcar.org. Phone: (410) 547-0264. Hours: Sunday Noon-5:00pm (April-December). Open Saturdays (June-October). Admission: $8.00-$10.00 per person (age 4+). Family max + $24.00.*

Admission includes: Unlimited rides on original Baltimore streetcars and a guided carhouse tour. Visit Trolley Theatre and view the new 10 minute orientation video, Baltimore and Streetcars, about trolleys and how they built the cities, including, of course, Baltimore. The Trolley Theatre, is a 3/4 scale trolley model that you can sit in.

NATIONAL GREAT BLACKS IN WAX MUSEUM

Baltimore - *1601-03 E North Avenue (395 north onto South M L K Blvd. East onto E. Baltimore St and quickly north onto SR-2. East onto US1) 21213. Phone: (410) 563-7809. www.greatblacksinwax.org. Hours: Tuesday-Saturday 9:00am-5:00pm, Sunday Noon-5:00pm. Summers open Monday also. Admission: $12.00-$15.00 (age 3+).*

The museum houses more than 100 life-size and lifelike wax figures presented in dramatic and historical scenes, and takes you through the pages of time with wax figures featuring special lighting, sound effects and animation. Harriet Tubman, Benjamin Banneker and Billie Holiday, as well as many other national figures, chronicle the history of African people from around the globe. The experience is highlighted by a dramatic walk through a replica slave ship complete with Middle Passage history. Visitors enter the cramped hold of a slave ship replica to witness a story of struggle, survival, and triumph. Another kid-focused area is the: And a Little Child Shall Lead Them: Black Youth in the Struggle delivers the message that children have been called upon to take up the mantle of freedom and justice throughout history and around the world. Some of the exhibits are marked PG as the history portrayed can be gruesome, however a great way to study black history in America.

MARYLAND ZOO IN BALTIMORE

Baltimore - *Druid Hill Park 21217. Phone: (410) 366-LION. www.marylandzoo.org. Hours: Daily 10:00am-4:00pm. Open Friday-Monday only in January & February. Extended summer weekend hours. Closed only Thanksgiving and Christmas. Admission: $14.00-$18.00. Reduced winter pricing. Parking is free.*

Journey from Africa to the Arctic on this wooded, 180-acre setting in Druid Hill Park. Otters, polar bears, bats and even skunk are here. Plus the regular lions, tigers and bears. A new tram system transports visitors from the main gate to the zoo's central plaza. Another highlight is the Polar Bear Watch, a state-of-the-art exhibit about life on the edge of the Arctic, featuring an area where guests can watch Alaska and Magnet, the zoo's polar bears cavorting in and out of the water. Children will create lifelong memories as they hop across lily pads, perch in an oriole's nest, play on a giant barn silo slide, a tree slide or groom friendly goats at the hands-on Children's Zoo. Look for baby chimps or maybe a new elephant.

BALTIMORE MUSEUM OF ART

Baltimore - *Art Museum Drive at N Charles and 31st Sts. 21218. Phone: (410) 396-7100. www.artbma.org. Hours: Wednesday-Sunday 10:00am-5:00pm. Admission: FREE. Note: Gertrudes open for lunch and dinner.*

Home to a wonderful collection of Matisse, Picasso and 19th century and contemporary art, plus a scenic sculpture garden. Three different self-guided kits invite kids to dress up, sketch, or sing their way through the galleries; available Thursdays, Saturdays, and Sundays 11:00am-3:00pm. A Grand Legacy Family Guide will help you explore five centuries of European art. Matisse for Kids Guide is a fun way to discover the Museum's renowned Cone Collection. During extended evening hours, enjoy family-friendly activities including music, performances, guided tours, hands-on workshops, and more. Outdoor sculpture gardens.

MARYLAND AVIATION MUSEUM, GLENN L MARTIN

Baltimore (Middle River) - *701 Wilson Point Road, Hanger 5 at Martin Airport 21220. Phone: (410) 682-6122. www.mdairmuseum.org. Hours: Wednesday-Saturday 11:00am-3:00pm. Admission: $1.00-$3.00 (age 6+).*

The site is dedicated to the promotion, preservation, and documentation of aviation and space history in the state of Maryland. Outside planes with names like Thunderchief, Thunderflash, Phantom, Sabor and Voodoo entice the kids to look around some.

B & O RAILROAD MUSEUM

Baltimore - *901 West Pratt Street (I-395 exit to MLKing St. to Pratt St, west a couple of blocks) 21223. Phone: (410) 752-2490. www.borail.org. Hours: Monday-Saturday 10:00am-4:00pm, Sunday 11:00am-4:00pm. Admission: $18.00 adult, $16.00 senior (60+), $12.00 child (2-12). Train rides are offered Wednesday through Sunday, April through December and weekends in January. Note: A café is on the premises as well as a delightful, large gift shop.*

Baltimore & Ohio Railroad Pioneers

The world's first telegraph line was erected between Baltimore and Washington, D.C., in 1844. Baltimore's Mount Clare Station, which was built in 1830 as the first railroad station in the country, was the receiving point of Samuel

Morse's famed "What hath God wrought" message. Today the station is the B&O Railroad Museum, a great place to learn about the history of the railroad that brought fame and fortune to Baltimore and which earned immortality on the Monopoly board! Ride the FIRST MILE of track in America, see them restoring old trains, learn the simple science of locomotion, get caught up in railroad flicks, and get a great view of the newly restored giant Roundhouse (the slumber house). The 20-minute train ride (just the right length for antsy kids) has an interesting narrative accompanied by travel folk music. Younger kids marvel at the operating 60 foot HO gauge model railroad outside. The model railroad is a cute way for little engineers to push buttons to hear train whistles and horns or hear the conductor shout "all aboard." There are several trains you can board. Some are unusual - how was the spiked Clearance Car used? What a wonderful and incredibly historical train attraction!

STEAM DAYS AT THE B & O

Baltimore - B & O Railroad Museum. Celebration of American railroading including special programs, entertainment and train rides. Admission. (Labor Day weekend)

HOLIDAY FESTIVAL OF TRAINS AT THE B&O RAILROAD

Baltimore - Baltimore and Ohio Railroad Museum. The kick-off of the B&O's winter holiday celebration featuring model train gardens. Admission. (Thanksgiving through December)

URBAN PIRATES, BALTIMORE CITY

Baltimore - Ann Street Pier, Thames Street, Fells Point 21224. Phone: (410) 327-8378. www.urbanpirates.com. Admission: $22.00 general, $12.00 child (2 and under). Tours: take place several times during the weekends in April, May, September and October and everyday from Memorial Day thru Labor Day. Reservations are required.

Dress, talk and tie ropes like a pirate; fight enemies with water cannons; navigate treacherous waters; and discover hidden treasures during an interactive excursion around the Inner Harbor on Fearless. The 48' long ship with a 17-foot beam and 3-foot draft can accommodate up to 49 passengers. Arrive 30 minutes before your cruise to check in and allow the crew to transform you into pirates with costumes, tattoos and face painting. Remember, pirates are not afraid to get a little wet. If you prove yourself worthy being a member of the crew, you get a share of the booty and take home a few trinkets from the treasure chest. Dance a jig and sing sea shanties all the way home.

AMERICAN VISIONARY ART MUSEUM

Baltimore - *800 Key Hwy, Inner Harbor (Key Hwy for 1.5 miles to corner of Covington & Key) 21230. Phone: (410) 244-1900. www.avam.org. Hours: Tuesday-Sunday 10:00am-6:00pm. Admission: $15.95 adult, $13.95 senior (60+), $9.95 student/child (age 7+). Metered parking nearby.*

This museum only exhibits art produced by folks who have no formal training (farmers, housewives, doctors, auto mechanics…you get the picture). Between the six week themed temporary installations, you can always tour the permanent collection. The Giant Whirligig & Sculpture Plaza is Baltimore's newest and already most beloved outdoor sculptural landmark. Fifty-five feet tall, this brilliant, multicolored wind-powered sculpture was created in the central plaza as a salute to Federal Hill and "Life, Liberty & The Pursuit of Happiness" by 76 year-old mechanic, farmer and visionary artist, Vollis Simpson. Free to visit anytime. The Sculpture Plaza functions as the ground level connector to Federal Hill and Baltimore's Inner Harbor.

BABE RUTH BIRTHPLACE

Baltimore - *216 Emory Street 21230. Phone: (410) 727-1539. www. baberuthmuseum.org. Hours: Daily, except Mondays 10:00am-5:00pm. Open Mondays in the summer. Admission: $10.00 adult, $8.00 senior, $5.00 child (5-16).*

The Babe Ruth Birthplace is located just three blocks west of Camden Station (follow the 60 painted baseballs along the sidewalk). George Herman "Babe" Ruth was born February 6, 1895 on Emory Street, a Baltimore row house that is now just a long fly ball from Oriole Park at Camden Yards. The Baltimore Orioles signed Ruth to his first pro contract. Some of the priceless artifacts the Babe Ruth Museum holds in its collections are: a near-complete team set of 1914 International League Baltimore Orioles baseball cards (including the rookie card of a 19-year-old pitcher named George Ruth, Jr.) or a baseball bat given to Ruth by Shoeless Joe Jackson sometime between 1915 and 1916. This thick-handled, 38 3/4 ounces of baseball history is the only one known to exist - a game-used bat shared by Shoeless Joe and the Babe. A wonderful place to "get to know" a baseball hero!

BALTIMORE MUSEUM OF INDUSTRY

Baltimore - *1415 Key Hwy, Inner Harbor 21230. www.thebmi.org. Phone: (410) 727-4808. Hours: Tuesday-Sunday 10:00am-4:00pm. Admission: $12.00 adult, $9.00 senior, $7.00 student/child.*

Step back in time to the Industrial Revolution at the Baltimore Museum of Industry, with its vividly recreated workshops on machining, printing, garment-making and metalworking. Walk through an 1886 bank building or step into the 1910 Bunting Pharmacy where Noxzema was invented. Experience the local innovations that touched the world - from the world's first disposable bottle cap to America's first umbrella company. Students become garment workers and hand sewers and learn about life in a turn-of-the-century garment shop. As they work, they hear about labor activist "Mother Jones" and her crusade to rid the world of abominable working conditions for children. Learn Baltimore's role as one of the busiest and most important ports in America. See a replica of an early dock and dockmaster's shed. Walk through the original 1865 Platt Oyster Cannery structure, the only surviving cannery building. Look outside and see the coal-fired S.S. Baltimore, the only operating steam tugboat on the East Coast. To get the best value, it is better to visit on weekends or part of a group tour so the kids can actually dress up and participate in the re-enacting areas like the cannery and clothing factory.

FORT MCHENRY NATIONAL MONUMENT & HISTORIC SHRINE

Baltimore - *End of 2400 E. Fort Avenue (I-95 exit 55) 21230. Phone: (410) 962-4290. www.nps.gov/fomc. Hours: Daily 9:00am-5:00pm. Admission: Entrance fee to the historic fort is $10.00 for adults 16 and over. Children 15 and under are admitted free of charge. Educators: A new, and wonderfully organized, Lesson Plan is available at this link: www.nps.gov/fomc/forteachers/lessonplansandteacherguides.htm.*

FORT MCHENRY NATIONAL MONUMENT (cont.)

Fort McHenry National Monument and Historic Shrine is a star-shaped fort best known for its role in the War of 1812, when its successful defense against the British bombardment inspired Francis Scott Key to write the words that became our national anthem. "O say can you see, by the dawn's early light, ...Whose broad stripes and bright stars ...were so gallantly streaming!" This historical event happened over Fort McHenry during the Battle of Baltimore, September 13-14, 1814. Watch the orientation film and look at the day's calendar of interpretive programs (in season). The movie is wonderfully done with a grand interactive patriotic finish! See the long stick rockets that glared red in the sky or the huge cannonball bombs designed to explode in air. Regardless of the "rockets red glare, the bombs bursting in air," the defenders of Fort McHenry stopped the British advance on Baltimore and helped to preserve the United

States of America – "the land of the free and the home of the brave." Within the actual fort you may enter some rooms that have visuals and audio plays or an electric map. The special kid-friendly Defenders' Room has unique hands-on activities. Because soldiers here were so close to the harbor and town, they could purchase seafood, chocolate and spices. Touch and smell everything they ate and then try on some very authentic looking apparel and be a soldier for a moment. Following the Battle of Baltimore during the War of 1812, the fort never again came under attack. However, it remained an active military post off and on for the next 100 years. Highly recommended National site!

FLAG DAY, NATIONAL PAUSE FOR THE PLEDGE OF ALLEGIANCE

Baltimore - Fort McHenry National Monument. Annual National Pause ceremony and program, band concert, parade of state flags, entertainment, fly-over and fireworks. (Flag Day, June 14th)

GLORIOUS FOURTH

Baltimore - Fort McHenry National Monument. Join the garrison of the Fort and patriotic citizens of Baltimore for fife and drum music, cannon firing, a musket salute for 18 states, period dancing and games. Twilight ceremony. (July 4th weekend)

DEFENDERS' DAY- A STAR-SPANGLED BANNER WEEKEND

Baltimore - Fort McHenry National Monument. Large War of 1812 re-enactment, musket firing, artillery demos, noted authors, children's programs, fireworks, ship-to-shore bombardment and military band concert. Admission. (second weekend in September)

LIVING AMERICAN FLAG PROGRAM

Baltimore - Fort McHenry National Monument. 3,500 plus 3rd, 4th and 5th graders from public, private and home schools in Maryland recreate the first "Human Flag" (Living American Flag). (morning of October 6)

PREAKNESS CELEBRATION

Baltimore - East on Pratt St to Market Place. www.preaknesscelebration.com. Hot air balloon festival & Parade with Marching bands, clowns, equestrian units, and floats in a salute to the Preakness Stakes the following weekend. (second Saturday in May)

CHARLES VILLAGE SUMMER FESTIVAL & PARADE

Baltimore - St Paul & 23rd St. www.charlesvillage.net. A vibrant colorful procession, featuring creative floats, art cars, marching bands, and more, captures the heart and soul of this diverse urban village. Voted Baltimore's best parade, this funky event includes bands, antique cars, dogs on skateboards, food and craft. Various prizes will be awarded in several categories. (first weekend in June)

HONFEST

Baltimore - Hampden. www.honfest.net. HonFest is a unique celebration that pays homage to the neighborhoods, the language and the people of Baltimore. Over 20,000 people flock here each year at HonFest to join in the festivities. The highlight of the day is the crowning of Baltimore's Best Hon. What is a Hon? The term Hon is actually a friendly Baltimore greeting and comes from the word "honey". However, the women who become Baltimore's Best Hon are a vision of the sixties-era women with beehive hairdos, blue-eye-shadow, spandex pants and something, anything leopard print! During HonFest you too can get your own beehive in their Glamour Lounge, listen to talented local musicians, and peruse the work of local artists, while you stroll "downy Avenue". (second Saturday in June)

LATINOFEST

Baltimore - Patterson Park. www.latinofest.org A lively weekend of Hispanic art and culture, Latin music, Hispanic cuisine, costumed dancers and family activities. Admission. (last weekend in June)

ARTSCAPE

Baltimore - Mt Royal Avenue Corridor. The region's premier celebration of the arts; continuous music, children's activities, food, artists' market. www.artscape.org. (full weekend in July)

BALTIMORE BOOK FESTIVAL

Baltimore - Mount Vernon Place. www.baltimorebookfestival.com Celebration of the literary arts; local bookstores, publishers, storytellers, author signings, crafts, refreshments and entertainment. . FREE. (fourth long weekend in September)

UKRAINIAN FESTIVAL

Baltimore - St Michael Ukrainian Catholic Church, 2401 Eastern Avenue. Enjoy Ukrainian dance groups, ethnic food, pierogy eating contest, 40 vendors, eggs and children's area. www.baltimoreukrainianfestival.com. (second weekend in September)

CZECH AND SLOVAK FESTIVAL

Baltimore - The Cathedral of Mary Our Queen, 5300 North Charles St. Ethnic costumes, food, bands, and dancing. Sokol gymnastics, vendors, exhibits, instrumental and vocal music. www.czslha.org. Admission. (third Sunday in October)

RUSSIAN FESTIVAL

Baltimore - Holy Trinity Russian Orthodox Church. www.russianfestival.latest-info.com. Celebration of Russian culture and food, homemade breads, samovar, live Balalaika Orchestra, chorus, dancers, imports. Admission. (third full weekend in October)

MONUMENTAL OCCASION

Baltimore - Mount Vernon Place. Annual lighting of the Washington Monument by the Mayor and First Family of Baltimore. www.promotionandarts.com. Live entertainment, refreshments, colorful fireworks finale. (first Thursday in December)

TOBY'S DINNER THEATRE

Baltimore & Columbia - *5625 O'Donnell Street / 5900 Symphony Woods Rd. 21224. Phone: (866) 998-6297 or (800) 888-6297. www.tobysdinnertheatre.com.*

Toby's offers Broadway musicals, live orchestras and service while you choose from 7 main entrée buffets, 7 salad bars and make-your-own sundae bar. Kids like the variety of food (and desserts) and are usually good about then sitting through a lively musical production like: _Footloose_, _Annie_ or _It's A Wonderful Life_. $43.50-$62.00.

DOUBLETREE HOTEL COLUMBIA

Baltimore (Columbia) - 5485 Twin Knolls Road, off Rte. 175, just west of I-95 21045. http://doubletree3.hilton.com/en/hotels/maryland/doubletree-by-hilton-hotel-columbia-BWICHDT/index.html. (443) 539-1119. Situated in a park-like setting, this place offers standard guest rooms that are welcoming with warm, yet vibrant color scheme and modern decor. All rooms include complimentary high-speed wireless internet services, complimentary use of the indoor pool, jacuzzi, exercise facilities and sauna. Morgan's restaurant serves great chicken (Frangelico) and steak (Cajun) dishes as well as Maryland crab. The children's menu runs around $5.00 and offers so many well-portioned kids foods. _____

MEDIEVAL TIMES DINNER & TOURNAMENT

Baltimore (Hanover) - _Arundel Mills, 7000 Arundel Mills Circle 21076. Phone: (443) 755-0011 or (888) WE-JOUST. www.medievaltimes.com. Shows: Wednesday - Sunday at 5:00pm or 7:00 / 7:30pm. Admission: $36.95-$59.95 per person. Tax & gratuity not included. Includes dinner, beverages and live show. Childrens and vegetarian menus available. Note: Due to some choreographed fighting scenes in the tournament, small children may become frightened by the bashing sounds of sword against sword (it appears very real)._

Set inside an 11th century-style castle, this show allows guests to become lords and ladies of the court. As you are assigned seating, you'll also be assigned a knight to cheer for and a "take home" crown to wear to show your support for that knight. You sit with others who join in cheering as serfs and wenches dressed in period costumes serve the feast of fresh vegetable soup, roasted chicken, spare rib, herb basted potato, a pastry and beverages. In order to honor medieval tradition, guests eat their meals without silverware (your kids will love having to eat with their hands!). As the lights dim, the story begins with the battle-weary King and his Knights returning to the Castle. The King calls for a grand tournament to determine the realm's new champion. As everyone is feasting, the Knights spar in games and jousts. As the plot thickens - we all hope truth, honor and love will eventually triumph. The villain is revealed in the final minutes of the show bringing the crowd to their feet - cheering for the brave hero to defend the castle. The beautiful horses and quick displays of sword and jousting ability make this show so engaging!

HARBORPLACE

Baltimore, Inner Harbor - *Inner Harbor (Light Street and Pratt Street) 21201. Phone: (410) 332-4191. www.harborplace.com.*

Indoor and outdoor eateries, shopping (many souvenirs related to Crabs and sports) and live entertainment on the waterfront.

- **PHILLIPS SEAFOOD** - On the edge of the harbor serving extensive seafood menus, plus sandwiches, beef and chicken entrees. A wide variety of offerings and friendly staff make this busy Baltimore institution a great place for firsttime visitors to get acquainted with the city's number one culinary attraction: the Blue Crab. The tasty crustaceans are served in many forms: Crab Imperial, crab dip, crab cakes. Authentic Maryland Style Seafood is tradition at Phillips so come prepared to feast! Festival Buffet. (www.phillipsseafood.com/locations-and-menus/baltimore).

- **BALTIMORE'S WATER TAXI** - (www.thewatertaxi.com) can provide water transport to more than 30 attractions and neighborhoods. Look for the blue and white boats. One price for all-day unlimited on-off service. $8.00-$14.00 per person.

BALTIMORE WATERFRONT FESTIVAL

Baltimore - Inner Harbor and surrounding area. Seafood cooking demos, entertainment, maritime exhibits, sailing races, family fun and Chesapeake Bay exhibits. (last long weekend in April)

BALTIMORE'S FOURTH OF JULY CELEBRATION

Baltimore - Inner Harbor. Entertainment including a fireworks display over the Inner Harbor. Admission for 4 hour Harbor Cruise. (July 4th)

DRAGON BOAT RACES

Baltimore Inner Harbor - www.returnofthedragons.com Corporate sponsored teams compete in chessie (dragon) boat races for Catholic charities. Daylong elimination heats determine winner of the Dragon Cup. (second Saturday in September)

BALTIMORE SPIRIT CRUISES

Baltimore, Inner Harbor - *561 Light Street 21202. Phone: (410) 727-3113 or (800) 695-LADY. www.spiritcruisesbaltimore.com. Tours: 75-minute interactive tour, the only Inner Harbor sightseeing cruise from the Inner Harbor past Ft. McHenry and back. Kick-back and relax as you take in the sites and enjoy an animated narration of Baltimore's rich history. They will give you an insider's view of Baltimore's historic places and the world-famous Inner Harbor. $15.00-*

$20.00 (April-October). Lunches run around $35.00-$42.00 adult, Dinners around $50.00-$60.00. Children under 11 are about half price.

They cruise just about everyday with lively lunch, dinner and special event cruises. Also, a one-hour scenic, narrated tour is offered. An original Baltimore cruise line, they offer the most themed tours in Maryland. Basic lunch menus include: Caesar Salad, Herb Roasted Boneless Breast of Chicken, Roasted Red Potatoes, Green Beans Almondine, Dinner Rolls with Butter. Decadent Chocolate Cake, Coffee, Tea, Decaf, Soft Drinks and Juices. If you love Maryland blue crab, try their weekend Crab Fest cruises. Or, for the kids, Easter Brunch with Bunny or Christmas Brunch with Santa.

NATIONAL AQUARIUM IN BALTIMORE

Baltimore, Inner Harbor - *501 East Pratt Street, Pier 3, Inner Harbor (I-95 to I-395 to Pratt Street, turn right) 21202. Phone: (410) 576-3800. www.aqua.org. Hours: Open daily until 5:00pm and Fridays until 8:00pm with seasonal extended morning and evening hours. Admission: $39.95 adult, 34.95 senior (65+) and $24.95 child (3-11). Dolphin Show and 4D Immersion Theater extra. Note: for safety, strollers must be checked; free front-and backpacks are available to carry babies. Educators: Click https://aqua.org/learn/learning-tools for PDF versions of activity sheets on dozens of grade appropriate topics.*

Take a short walk across the promenade from the World Trade Center to the National Aquarium where stingrays (look for butterfly rays), sharks and sea turtles will greet you on the first level to start your adventure...up close! You might visit during a feeding of sharks. Each exhibit brings new surprises, including a blackwater Amazon River forest with schools of dazzling tropical fish, giant river turtles, dwarf caimans, and pygmy marmosets - the smallest species of monkey in the world. And in the Upland Tropical Rain Forest, keen observers may spot colorful birds, golden lion tamarins (monkeys), two-toed sloths, red-bellied piranhas, iguanas and even poison dart frogs, as they wander on pathways through the dense tropical foliage. The 8-minute intro film in Australia is very helpful for kids to learn differences in extreme geography. Australia Wild Extremes has fish that shoot water from their mouths, encounters with the Outback's deadliest snake and relaxing sounds of a 35-foot cascading indoor waterfall. Visit with multi-colored jelly fish live or on their webcam. And don't forget the shark ring or giggling at the dolphin show at the adjoining Marine Mammal Pavilion. Trek across Maryland's varied terrain in the Waterfront Park outdoors or take in a high definition sensory drama at the 4D Immersion Theater.

USS CONSTELLATION

Nearly 200' long and 300 crew aboard... it was a 19th Century floating city!

Baltimore, Inner Harbor - *301 E. Pratt Street, Pier 1, Inner Harbor (follow signs to HarborPlace, just on other side, waterside) 21202. www.constellation.org. Phone: (410) 539-1797. Hours: Daily 10:00am-4:30pm. Extended to 5:30pm or 6:00pm (May-October). Admission (squadron pass for visits up to 2 ships): $15.00 adult, $13.00 senior (60+) and teens, $7.00 child (6-14). Add just a few dollars on to see all of the maritime ships in the Inner Harbor piers.*

Built in 1854, this is the last all-sail warship built by the U.S. Navy and the only Civil War era naval vessel still afloat. History comes "alive" with hourly hands-on demonstrations and self-guided audio tours. Before you head up the stairs to the ship, be sure to get a complimentary audio tour wand.

This will help guide you and help you to learn more about what life was like on board. Using a "Youth" or "Adult" number system, you follow a modern girl through the ship. Discover how sailors lived on board - officers in their own cubbies and shipmen on hundreds of hammocks hanging from the ceiling - no, not for naps - for good, swaying sleep before the next watch. What's a Powder Monkey? Learn how this mighty sailing machine was powered, propelled and controlled. What technology did they have and what did they eat? Interactives include steering the ship or ringing the loud ship's bell to tell time. Listen for the cannon firings!

WORLD TRADE CENTER "TOP OF THE WORLD"

Baltimore, Inner Harbor - *401 E. Pratt Street (World Trade Center, 27th floor) 21202. Phone: (410) 837-VIEW. www.viewbaltimore.org. Hours: Daily 10:00am-6:00pm (spring, summer). Some longer summertime hours. Wednesday-Sunday hours (mid September thru late May). Admission: $4.00-$6.00 (ages 3+).*

Start your visit to the city at the Top of the World Observation Level, where the

beauty of the resurgent city will unfold before you - from all sides - harbor and downtown. Enjoy a spectacular panoramic view of Baltimore's skyline, as well as photo-map guides featuring local attractions, hotels and neighborhoods. It's a good place to get a sense of the city. The observation level also contains exhibits about Baltimore and its economic renaissance. The World Trade Center is the tallest pentagonal building in the world. You will have a wonderful view of the city from an elevation of 423 feet.

MARYLAND SCIENCE CENTER

Baltimore, Inner Harbor - *601 Light Street (a couple of blocks from Inner Harbor @ Key Hwy & Light) 21230. Phone: (410) 545-5927. www.mdsci.org. Hours: Monday-Friday 10:00am-5:00pm, Saturday 10:00am-6:00pm, Sunday 11:00am-5:00pm. Closed Mondays in the fall and winter. Open until 8:00pm on Fridays. The IMAX theater is open after hours for evening shows; the Observatory is open after hours on Fridays for Stargazing Fridays; and the Kids Room closes one hour prior to museum closing Saturdays through Thursdays and two hours prior to close Fridays. Admission: $18.95-$24.95 (age 3+). Note: Beakers Café & Science Store. Look for online specials such as Fridays After Five discounted admission evenings. IMAX theater and Planetarium shows extra fee.*

Dinosaurs. Planet Earth. The Human body. Outer space. Chesapeake Bay life. The Kids Room (under age 8 play area). Science Sir Isaac Newton never imagined. At the Maryland Science Center you'll find three floors of demonstrations to exercise your imagination and challenge your mind. See exciting combustible reactions, eye-boggling optical illusions and learn about lasers. Hands-on exhibits include a voyage through the human body and learning how microbes work for us. Traveling exhibits abound, so there's always something new see and learn. Real time connections to real time science. So much to see and do - all in a Please Touch environment. Live Maryland crustaceans and their fellow Chesapeake citizens inhabit the Blue Crab water exhibit. A kinetic, energetic, hands-on exhibit powered by you and looking at space by 3-D or satellite image.

BALTIMORE MARITIME MUSEUM

Baltimore, Inner Harbor - *802 S. Caroline Street (Piers 3 & 5) 21231. Phone: (410) 783-1490 or (877) NHCPORT. www.historicships.org. Hours: Daily 10.00am - 5:00pm. Extended Hours in the Summer. Admission: Squadron Pass (up to 2 ships) - $15.00 adult, $13.00 senior (60+) and teen, $7.00 youth (age 6-14). Best to combine with ships in the Inner Harbor...especially the USS Constitution.*

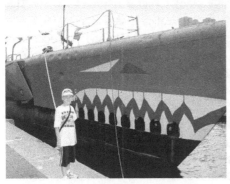

The US Coast Guard Cutter Taney, US Submarine Torsk, Lightship Chesapeake, and the Seven Foot Knoll Lighthouse tell a story of American power and technology. Over sixty years ago, two of the ships of the Baltimore Maritime Museum were involved in events that changed the history of the world. US Coast Guard Cutter Taney was an amphibious command ship for the Battle of Okinawa, one of the bloodiest battles in US Naval history. By virtue of her 50 year career, she is the last surviving warship afloat today from the December 7, 1941 Japanese attack on Hawaii. On August 14, 1945, the USS Torsk fired a torpedo which hit home, sinking a Japanese coastal patrol vessel. This dramatic moment was to become the last naval action of World War II, as the Cease Fire was declared the next day.

The US Lighthouse Service first assigned Lightship 116 to the Fenwick Island Shoal (DE) Station from 1930-33; after that assignment she marked the entrance to Chesapeake Bay. Crew accommodations included two-man staterooms for the enlisted men, a crew's mess, and an electrically powered galley and refrigerator unit (a major advancement for 1930).

The Seven Foot Knoll Lighthouse, the oldest surviving screw-pile lighthouse, was built as an aid to navigation on the Chesapeake Bay. The lighthouse is free of charge to tour.

A Lighthouse Ship?

All of these actual pieces of history are docked together at the Inner Harbor - a convenient way to witness early 1900s sea life on the Chesapeake and American ocean waters.

SHARP'S AT WATERFORD FARM

Brookeville - *4003 Jennings Chapel Rd, off Rte 97 20833. Phone: (410) 489-2572. www.sharpfarm.com.*

Sharp's at Waterford Farm is a 530 acre working farm located in western Howard County. The farm produces field corn, soybeans, and grazes hundreds of goats, sheep, and cattle. There are production greenhouses that are full of organic herbs, vegetables, and flowers. A nature trail meanders through 100 acres of woodland under forestry management. Hayrides, picnics, farm animals, a nature trail, and family entertainment or tours round out the offerings at this farm. While tours require a $7.50 per person admission, the animals are always delighted to see you venture down to the barnyard. Visit them anytime during our open hours. No admission or parking fees.

Open House Days are educational programs available to Home-school groups or children not visiting with a school group.

- SPRING - Spring is the season of planting in the greenhouse, geese hatching on the ponds, gardens and fields being planted, and the farm ponds wake up to a new year. They feature 6 tours in the spring.

- SUMMER - What a great summer mini-vacation for your camp or family group. All spring tour programs will continue into the summer.

- FALL - Each fall they offer pumpkin picking, hayrides, campfires, corn mazes, farm animals, observation beehives, nature trails and much more. They offer 4 programs in the fall season.

BRAD'S PRODUCE CORN MAZE

Churchville - *550 Asbury Road. www.bradsproduce.com. This farm is a full-time farming operation raising fresh produce, flowers and grain. In the fall, they open the Corn Maze Adventure. Each year with a different theme. Each maze is designed to share history, too. Hayrides to the Pumpkin patch on weekends. Admission. (Labor Day thru end of October)*

BOAT FLOAT

Columbia - *Lake Kittamaqundi, across from Columbia Mall. A challenge to design and build a person-powered, corrugated cardboard boat capable of racing a 200-yard course. www.hocoboatfloat.com. Admission to participate. FREE to watch. (second Saturday in June)*

DARLINGTON APPLE FESTIVAL

Darlington - *Shuresville Road. www.darlingtonapplefest.org/. Take a step back in time. Apples, pumpkins, mums, crafts, entertainment, art, country market & refreshments. Apple pie contest. (first Saturday in October)*

HISTORIC LONDONTOWN

Edgewater - *839 Londontown Road 21037. www.historiclondontown.org. Phone: (410) 222-1919. Hours: Wednesday-Sunday 10:00am-4:30pm (mid March-November). Monday-Friday only (winter). Admission: $12.00 adult, $10.00 senior (62+), $7.00 child (7-17), $3.00 preschool (4-6). Educators: Excellent unit studies on topics such as Early Maryland & Colonial Foodways are found here: www. historiclondontown.org/index.php/education/teacher-resources.*

Discover new remnants of colonial merchant town life circa 1693 on the South River. The "lost town" was a major port of call in the 1730s for ships taking tobacco to Britain and bringing African slaves, indentured workers, and convicts to Maryland. By the 19th century, London Town was abandoned. The mansion, tavern/home and gardens are open for tours but we'd recommend starting at the orientation Visitors Center.

Learn about tavern life in a major 18th-century seaport town with a visit to the William Brown House. Discover native and imported medicinal plants in the Richard Hill Garden, and give your legs a workout by strolling London Town's eight-acre woodland garden. Talk to archaeologists at work rediscovering the lost Town of London in the largest ongoing archaeological dig in Maryland. Watch as workmen recreate a town using materials and tools that would have been used in the late 17th-and early 18th-centuries. During special events at London Town, you can hearth cook your own meal over the fire in the circa 1710 Lord Mayor's Tenement using period recipes and ingredients; play colonial games and learn about 18th-century medicine; try your hand at colonial carpentry, and help fire a cannon; live, work, and play as a colonial child; dip your own candles; and throw tomahawks.

SMITHSONIAN ENVIRONMENTAL RESEARCH CENTER

Edgewater - *647 Contrees Wharf Road (Follow Central Ave. (Md. 214) east to stoplight at Md. 468 (Muddy Creek Road). Turn right (south). Proceed about 1 mile) 21037. Phone: (443) 482-2200. www.serc.si.edu. Hours: Monday-Saturday 9:00am-4:30pm, except National holidays. Admission: Walking trails are free. Many programs and canoe tours require a minimum fee (~$10.00).*

Pick up your trail map at the Reed Education Center when you sign in and explore two self-guided nature trails: The Java History Trail Is a 1.3-mile walking path through field, forest and marsh that deals with the history of the land and the people who lived and worked on it. Using the interpretive panels along the path, this is a self-guided walk through local history. Family Programs are offered each month. Families and individuals of all ages enjoy creating animal track castings, designing plankton, night-time owl searches and Saturday canoe tours of Muddy Creek.

ENCHANTED FOREST & CLARKLAND FARM

Ellicott City - *10500 Rte. 108, Clarksville Pike (Rte. 29 to Rte. 108 west 2 miles) 21042. Phone: (410) 730-40409. www.clarklandfarm.com. Hours: Tuesday-Sunday 10:00am-5:00pm (April-early November). Admission: Petting Zoo and Enchanted Forest $6.00 per person. Additional $2.00 for hayrides or pony rides.*

Once upon a time, there was a wonderful storybook park in Ellicott City called The Enchanted Forest. Opened in 1955, it thrilled and delighted

generations of families from far and wide throughout the next 30 years. Sadly, it closed to the public in the late 1980s. The folks on this farm are slowly restoring many of the Storybook characters back to display park quality. Look for Mother Goose and her Gosling, the six Mice that pulled Cinderella's Pumpkin Coach

(and the big pumpkin coach!), Papa Bear, the bell-shaped Flowers, two giant Lollipops, a number of Gingerbread Men, a large Candy Cane, the Little Red Schoolhouse, the Crooked House and the Crooked Man, the Easter Bunny's House, the Beanstalk with the Giant at the top and the beautiful Birthday Cake. You can now also see Snow White, Sleeping Beauty, Robin Hood, the Three Little Pigs' straw, stick and brick houses, the Rainbow Bridge, and Little Boy Blue, the Old Woman's Shoe and the Three Bears House. The scenes are woven throughout the petting farm area and into a forested area.

The Clark family has been farming in Howard County since 1797. Visit the 540-acre farm and see a wide variety of animals: goats, sheep, donkeys, pigs, alpacas, calves, horses, ponies, turkeys, ducks, chickens, bunnies, and turtles. You can feed the animals and visit the Barnyard area where you can touch and pet them. They offer hay rides through the storybook farm fields and a number of play areas for the children. Pony rides are available all day, every day that they are open. Too cute!

<u>PUMPKIN WEEKENDS</u>

Ellicott City *- Clark's Elioak Farm. Each weekend provides a little different theme – Storytime at the Farm, Pumpkin Growing Contest, Pumpkin Patch, Teddy Bear Farm visit, homemade cider, face-painting, hayrides, Scarecrow making, and Pumpkin Chucking. www.clarklandfarm.com. Admission. (month-long in October)*

<u>ELLICOTT CITY B&O RAILROAD STATION MUSEUM</u>

Ellicott City *- 2711 Maryland Avenue (I-695 exit 13 on MD 144 toward Catonsville. Travel 4 miles, cross over the Patapsco River bridge and into town.) 21043. Phone: (410) 461-1944. www.ecborail.org. Hours: Wednesday-Sunday 10:30am-4:30pm. Friday-Sunday only (February-March). Closed most holidays. Admission: $4.00-$6.00 ages 2+.*

This 19th-century museum profiles the oldest terminus for the first 13 miles of track of the first commercial railroad in America! Walk through history from the 1830s thru the Civil War up to the great flood. See the cluttered Agent's Living Quarters as the first items transferred by rail were products, not people. People came later. Notice the ladies and gents had separate waiting rooms upstairs. Folks dressed in period costume inform you about each room. Exhibits include the fascinating 40-foot HO scale teaching railroad and audio-visual presentation. Only ten minutes long, the movie quickly tells you who and why the railroad was built and this is followed by a light show of the path the B&O rails took. The "climb aboard" outside caboose is fun for play and photos. The adorable old downtown of Ellicott City is just footsteps away - with quaint shops and cafes making this stop a perfect day trip for every member of the family. Kids will

love the Museum gift shop and the toy stores downtown.

PATAPSCO VALLEY STATE PARK

Ellicott City - *8020 Baltimore National Pike (I -95 take I-195 to Rt. 1 (Exit 3) toward Elkridge to South St. Turn right) 21043. Phone: (410) 461-5005. Hours: Daily 9:00am-dusk. http://dnr2.maryland.gov/publiclands/Pages/central/patapsco. aspx*

The park extends along 32 miles of the Patapsco River, with 14,000 acres and five developed recreational areas. The Avalon Visitor Center houses exhibits spanning over 300 years of history along the Patapsco River. Housed in a 19th century stone dwelling in the Avalon Area, the center includes a re-creation of a 1930's forest warden's office. View the Thomas Viaduct – world's longest multiple-arched stone railroad bridge or hike the Grist Mill Trail – A 1.5 mile paved and accessible trail for the disabled along the river. (Avalon Area) Walk across the Swinging Bridge – a 300 foot suspension walkway over the river or hike to Bloede's Dam – world's first internally housed hydroelectric dam. (Orange Grove Area) Visit the Daniels Area fish ladder to learn about Maryland's first barrier free river to shad and herring migrations. Recreational opportunities include hiking, fishing, camping (primitive and cabins), canoeing, horseback and mountain bike trails, as well as picnicking for individuals or large groups in the park's many popular pavilions.

NATIONAL CRYPTOLOGIC MUSEUM

Fort George G. Meade - *Colony Seven Road (I-95 to Rte. 32 east/Ft. Meade, exit Canine Rd) 20755. http://www.nsa.gov/about/cryptologic_heritage/museum/ index.shtml. Phone: (301) 688-5849. Hours: Monday-Friday 9:00am-4:00pm. Admission: FREE. Note: Vigilance Park outside is home to actual spy planes used for secret missions. FREEBIES: Ask the attendant for a decoder and Picture Scavenger Hunt to make the visit even more engaging.*

Codemakers and Codebreakers. Located adjacent to NSA Headquarters, the Museum collection contains thousands of artifacts of the cryptologic profession - the most secret organization in the United States. Catch a glimpse of some of the most dramatic moments in history, using cryptology machines and techniques. Learning past secrets, some events in American and world history may take on a new meaning. Peek into a once secret world - the cracking of enemy codes and the protection of American communications. Look at Union code books and Confederate cipher cylinders. Learn about Code Talkers - Native Americans who used their own language and terms in radio transmissions - they NEVER made mistakes and codes were NEVER broken!

Check out the world's only remaining Enigma - the German encrypting machine that Allied intelligence cracked to glean knowledge that assisted in winning the Battle of the Atlantic and facilitated the ending of WWII. And, look at everyday life applications. Government and top security level companies use Biometrics - human fingerprints or eye scans as password IDs - machines and technology developed from military security needs. Even the post office uses cryptology. Metered mail uses a 2D bar code encryption system. There are several areas where parents might want to watch movies while the kids use their free cipher disk and activity book to try to decode messages and win a small prize. This place is so secretive and so interesting!

HERRINGTON HARBOUR INN

Friendship - 7161 Lake Shore Drive, Rte 261, 20758. www.herringtonharbour.com (410) 741-5100. Beautiful beachfront Caribbean style lodging, featuring fantastic Bay views, chickee huts and palm trees. Each of the "cottage-style" rooms offers a coffee maker, microwave, mini-fridge, and some have private patio hot tubs surrounded by colorful tropical murals. The suites offer full kitchens with a living area. Have tropical slushies on the patio overlooking the Olympic-sized resort pool, or jump in and enjoy. Better yet, enjoy the private beach and play in the Bay. Other resort amenities include a game room, Peddle Boats, Kayaking (Both one and two-person boats.), Playground, Volleyball, Croquet & Tennis Court, Shuffleboard Area, Picnic Facilities (grills available) on the water's edge. Rentals available for all sports activities. Homemade continental breakfast included with some awesome muffins and coffee cake plus cereal, fresh fruit, bagels, various fruit juices, etc. Rates begin around $100.00 per night (peak), hovering around $200 for suites and weekend hot tub rooms. Mangos restaurant on premises with Kids Menu (~$5.00). Why go all the way to Florida when these folks have the cozy tropical feel on the popular Bay coast. We used it as a haven to rest and relax after day trips to neighboring sites.

PIRATE'S COVE RESTAURANT

Galesville - *4817 Riverside Drive (on the West River, end of Rte. 255) 20765. (410) 867-1861 or www.piratescovemd.com. Boat Races on Tuesday / Wednesday nights (summer). Pirates Cove Restaurant & Marina is the place to enjoy fine classic seafood dining the year round with the scenic charm of the West River. They highly recommend the Broiled Seafood Platter (~$25) or their Crab Imperial. And it's the home of the "Cannon Ball Crab Cake". The Children's Menu has variety. Fried shrimp, steak, spaghetti, chicken, hamburger and grilled cheese (~6.00-$8.00). Lunch/Dinner/Sunday Brunch.* 🍽 _____

NORTH RUN FARM MAZE

Greenspring Valley - *North Run Farm, 1703 Greenspring Valley Road. . Hayride to pick your own pumpkin patch, GPS designed corn maze, farm animal zoo, barnyard fun. www.northrunfarm.com Admission. (long weekends late September thru early November)*

CONCORD POINT LIGHTHOUSE

Havre de Grace - *(Lafayette & Concord Streets) 21078. Phone: (410) 939-1498. Hours: Weekends 1:00-5:00pm (April-October). http://concordpointlighthouse. org/*

The Concord Point light is one of the oldest lighthouses in continual use on the East Coast. It was part of a navigational improvement effort to enhance the safe flow of goods down the Susquehanna River to the ports of Baltimore and Philadelphia. Kids love the giant iron key used to open the lighthouse door. There are only about 35 steps up to the top where there is a great view of the Chesapeake Bay. Wander around the light keepers house on the property. Learn about the first keeper who was also a quirky hero of a self-prompted "battle" between British ships and one man, John O'Neill, on shore. When he ran out of cannon balls, he began to use potatoes instead - the first potato gun! On the grounds behind the lighthouse is one of the cannons used by John O'Neill in his near solitary-attempt to defend the town.

HAVRE DE GRACE DECOY MUSEUM

Havre de Grace - *215 Giles Street (on the waterfront near Tydings Park) 21078. Phone: (410) 939-3739. www.decoymuseum.com. Hours: Monday - Saturday 10:30am - 4:30pm, Sunday Noon - 4:00pm. Admission: $6.00 adult, $5.00 senior (60+), $2.00 youth (9-18). Note: Each Saturday and Sunday, local carvers provide carving demonstrations to the public in the R. Madison Mitchell Shop, located behind the museum's main facility.*

Located on the banks of the historic Susquehanna Flats, the Havre de Grace Decoy Museum houses one of the finest collections of working and decorative Chesapeake Bay decoys ever assembled. Not only exhibits, but tours and demonstrations are regularly scheduled. The newer areas, by the entrance,

have many hands-on exhibits for kids. The museum's main gallery features "What is a Decoy?" A look at the dozens of decoys in this gallery demonstrates that the appearance of any decoy depends upon the species of animal being imitated, the purpose of the decoy, the region in which the decoy is carved,

Why a two-headed decoy?

and the unique approach of the carver. "What is a Decoy?" also features a popular diorama that freezes in time a gathering of prominent carvers during an afternoon in the early 1940s. Look for the two-headed duck decoys (part of the scavenger hunt sheet kids can ask for). Compare different styles and see a recreated workshop setting. "Gunning the Flats" explores the history of waterfowling on the Susquehanna Flats, an area long noted for its bounty of waterfowl. What is a body Booting? Or a sinkbox? The town's waterfowling traditions truly make Havre de Grace the "Decoy Capital of the World!"

We love "please touch" exhibits...

DUCK FAIR

Havre de Grace - *Decoy Museum grounds. 50 carvers, collectors and artists, live and silent auctions, kids activities, retrievers, carving competition. (second weekend in September)*

DECOY AND WILDLIFE ART FESTIVAL

Havre de Grace - *Decoy Museum & Middle and High Schools. 175 or so carvers, collectors and artists. Live auction, special exhibits, retriever demos and carving competitions. (first full weekend in May)*

HAVRE DE GRACE MARITIME MUSEUM

Havre de Grace - *100 Lafayette Street (on the waterfront, near Tydings Park) 21078. Phone: (410) 939-4800. www.hdgmaritimemuseum.org. Hours: Wednesday-Saturday 10:00am-5:00pm, Sunday 1-5pm (April-mid October); Weekends only (rest of year). Admission: $3.00 per person (ages 8+).*

The museum tells the story of the region's rich maritime heritage. Changing exhibits on boating are the mainstay. They have a boat building school on the premises where you can observe or tour (Tuesday night is live boat building). BEYOND JAMESTOWN: LIFE 400 YEARS AGO portrays the lives

of the Native Americans in the Upper Bay Region and contact with European Settlers. It features a replica of Captain John Smith's exploratory shallop, near life-size dioramas, and so much more. Ring the ships' bell or play with real 19th century boating tools. Try using these 200 year old tools to "caulk" the boat cracks yourself. Try casting nets, too. On the North side of the Yacht Basin are the entries to the city's Promenade, a half-mile boardwalk that follows the shoreline and overlooks the confluence of the Susquehanna River and the Chesapeake Bay. A quaint surprise.

LAURRAPIN GRILLE

Havre de Grace - *209 North Washington Street (take Rte 155 east into downtown) 21078. Phone: (410) 939-3663. www.laurrapin.com. Where Northern California meets the Chesapeake Bay. Items like spring rolls, pizza, muffalattas or crab on the same menu. The newbie kid gourmet will enjoy their meatloaf and steak and potatoes, too. Lunch around $10 and dinner around $20. Daily for dinner. Saturday and Sunday brunch.*

MACGREGORS RESTAURANT

Havre de Grace - *331 Saint John Street   21078. www.macgregorsrestaurant.com. Phone: (410) 939-3003. Originally a bank built in 1924, all tables here have a water view. The two-tiered all glass upscale casual dining room features lunch ($12.00-$15.00), dinner (around $20.00), lite fare and Sunday Brunch. We have to highly recommend the award-winning Rockfish and their garlic chive mashed potatoes! Mild gourmet sauces are served and fit each entrée perfectly. Children's Menu (everything from crab pretzels to sliders to spaghetti - most around $9.00), balloons and coloring books.*

SUSQUEHANNA MUSEUM OF HAVRE DE GRACE LOCK HOUSE

Havre de Grace - *817 Conesto Street (follow signs into town) 21078. Phone: (410) 939-5780. www.thelockhousemuseum.org. Hours: Thursday-Sunday 1:00-5:00pm (April-October). Admission: Donations accepted.*

Why is a lockhouse right next to a river? The canal was built as a water staircase because the river was too shallow for large cargo boats. Why did they use a leather scoop on board? Where was the parking lot for boats ready for shipping? Listen to a 160 year old xylophone and secret birthday music box. In the kitchen, learn how to make an old fashioned snow ball treat. Look for the high chair that turns into a stroller. Why is it better to have rounded

Help move a 4000 lb. pivot bridge..with just a push...

travel trunks vs. a flattop. At the end of the tour, make sure the kids help move the pivot bridge. You just moved 4000 pounds! Fun things to learn in every room - and you get to touch most items.

PIRATE FEST

Havre de Grace - *Susquehanna Museum. Come experience the fun of living history, pirate style. (second weekend in July)*

CANDLELIGHT TOUR

Havre de Grace - *Historic City Streets. Tour of homes, museums, and B&Bs in historic HdG. Admission. (second Sunday in December)*

VANDIVER INN

Havre de Grace - *301 South Union Avenue (corner of Fountain) 21078. Phone: (800) 245-1655. www.vandiverinn.com.*

The Vandiver Inn is an 1886 Victorian mansion located two blocks from the Chesapeake Bay in historic Havre de Grace, Maryland. What a nice treat! The owner greeted us on the front porch where we later sat during a heavy rainstorm. The kids were apprehensive at first - being in such an old mansion - but soon eased and began exploring all the nooks and crannies. One night, our family, some staff and the owner's son, watched a movie in the parlor - "Movies at the Mansion." All the staff are gracious but not pretentious.

Breakfast and the amenities weren't so "foo-foo" that our kids wouldn't enjoy - more like homemade eggs or pancakes with oodles of blueberries. The Vandiver Mansion has nine elegant rooms, many with fireplaces. The adjacent Murphy & Kent Guest Houses provide an additional eight rooms.

This Country Inn really tries to cater to family getaways, family reunions (take over the mansion!) and weddings or corporate meetings. Girls love that every room is decorated differently. All rooms are air conditioned and four of their new suites feature luxury Jacuzzi tubs. All of their rooms offer private in-room baths, full breakfast every morning, cable TV, phones w/data ports, high speed wireless internet, voice mail, hair dryers, irons and many other amenities. (rates around $100-$150 per night).

The Inn is surrounded by historic homes, museums, golf, shopping, antique stores, marinas and water-oriented activities. As you walk towards downtown - you'll notice many other friendly neighbors wave from their adorable restored homes. Since the "downtown" is only one mile long, you can walk to everything. You'll love the charming streets and people.

SUSQUEHANNA STATE PARK / STEPPINGSTONE MUSEUM / ROCKS STATE PARK

Havre de Grace - *4122 Wilkinson Road (I-95 exit 89, off Rte. 155 west to Rte. 161. Turn right on Rte 161 and then right on Rock Run Rd.) 21084. Phone: (410) 557-7994.http://dnr2.maryland.gov/publiclands/Pages/central/susquehanna.aspx*

This park is located on land bordering Deer Creek. A popular feature of the park is the throne-like rock formation called "The King and Queen Seats," where, according to legend, Indian Chieftains once sat in tribal council. Rock climbing, picnicking, hiking, tubing, wading, canoeing, fishing, bow hunting and photo ops are plentiful. Susquehanna State Park also contains a very family friendly campground with traditional campsites and cabins.

The Falling Branch area of **ROCKS STATE PARK** is located about 5 miles north of the main part and features a 17-foot scenic free-falling waterfall - the second highest vertical falls in the state. Historical sites include the **ROCK RUN GRIST MILL**, Archer Mansion and Jersey Toll House. The stone mill is open on weekends all summer operating using a 12-ton water wheel, which runs on a limited basis.

STEPPINGSTONE MUSEUM: Visitors can spend the afternoon touring the sites of a once-working Harford County farm. The farmhouse, furnished as a turn-of-the-century home, charms the visitor as a guide invites you to

share the daily life of the period. With no electricity, what did kids do for fun? Tours include the formal sitting room, sleeping quarters, and kitchen with its wood burning stove and ice box. Can you find the toaster? In the other buildings, maybe watch a woodworker, blacksmith or weaver. Our favorite building is the recreated tomato cannery. Kids did this as a summer job. They begin by scalding the fruit to loosen the skin and peel. Then they pack (on a giant wheel conveyor!), cap, cook, label and store the canned product. They even have equipment to make Catsup. Very interesting and well displayed processes in here! www.steppingstonemuseum.org (888) 419-1762. (weekends 1:00-5:00pm, $3.00 - ages 13+).

SUMMER FUN DAY

Havre de Grace - *Steppingstone Museum. Children's activities, ice cream eating contest, turtle races, frog jumping contest, sack races, face painting, food and the famous lawnmower races. Admission. (second Sunday in July)*

FALL HARVEST FESTIVAL

Havre de Grace - *Steppingstone Museum. Scarecrow making, hayrides, clowns, storytelling, pumpkin painting, apple bobbing, crafts, food, tours, country music, clogging and corn shelling. Admission. (fourth weekend in September)*

HOLIDAY OPEN HOUSE @ STEPPINGSTONE

Havre de Grace - *Steppingstone Museum and Park. Farmhouse decorated for the holidays, cookies, cider & more. FREE. (first weekend in December)*

INDEPENDENCE CELEBRATION

Havre de Grace - *Tydings Memorial Park. Carnival, Parade, Concert & Fireworks. (first few days of July)*

GUNPOWDER FALLS STATE PARK / JERUSALEM MILL

Kingsville - *2813 Jerusalem Road 21087. Phone: (410) 592-2897. http://dnr2. maryland.gov/publiclands/Pages/central/gunpowder.aspx*

Gunpowder Falls State Park features numerous scenic areas on 18,000 acres in the Gunpowder River Valley. The park features over 100 miles of trails, trout streams and the historic Village of Jerusalem, an 18th century grist mill company town. A Visitors Center Museum in the town displays artifacts and there's a blacksmith shop and gun factory on the premises. Seasonal Revolutionary and Civil War era living history demonstrations and encampments are held here (www.jerusalemmill.org or 410-877-3560).

Nearby **NORTH POINT STATE PARK** (in Fort Howard, off Rte. 20, 410-477-0757) features the Defenders' Trail used during the War of 1812. Other park areas include a rail trail, swimming beach, and a marina. Guided trips with local outfitters are available for flatwater and moving water kayaking, canoeing, fishing, catamaran sailing, windsurfing and natural history walks.

NATIONAL ELECTRONICS MUSEUM

Linthicum - *1745 W Nursery Road (Route 295 South (Baltimore Washington Parkway), Take West Nursery Road exit, turn left at light) 21090. Phone: (410) 765-0230. www.nationalelectronicsmuseum.org. Hours: Monday-Friday 9:00am-4:00pm, Saturday 10:00am-2:00pm. Admission: $3.00-$5.00.*

You can learn about TVs, radios, cell phones, and even see a working original Edison cylinder phonograph. The museum houses the first American radar ever built (used in Pearl Harbor to detect incoming Japanese planes), a lunar camera just like the one used to photograph Neil Armstrong's moon landing, and the SCR 584 - a giant radar unit that visitors can enter and explore! The educational gallery features hands-on exhibits. Use their hands on equipment to generate electricity and experiment with magnetism. Learn how electromagnetic waves power our cell phones, cook our food, and help us see into space. Become part of a human battery. Take a look at an operational amateur radio station capable of worldwide communications by voice, Morse code, digital modes, and television. See the type of radar that detected the attack on Pearl Harbor on December 7, 1941. Learn how radar led to the household microwave oven or try a hands on demonstration of phased array beam steering. Go under the sea in an Interactive demonstration of passive and active underwater sounds and then go to a room where you can see yourself in infrared.

FIRE MUSEUM OF MARYLAND

Lutherville - *1301 York Road (I-695 exit 26B, one block north) 21093. Phone: (410) 321-7500. www.firemuseummd.org. Hours: Saturdays 10:00am-4:00pm (May-December). Wednesday-Saturday, Sundays 1-4:00pm (June-August). Closed July 4th and Christmas. Admission: $14.00 adult, $12.00 senior (62+) and firefighters, $6.00 child (2-18).*

This nice, active museum still exhibits operational hand pumps, steam engines and water tower - something from each era. In the Discovery Room, pull an old fire alarm in your 1800s neighborhood, then run to the telegraph station and punch in the message to dispatch units to the fire. Climb aboard a real engine cab and turn on the siren or flash the lights.

LADEW TOPIARY GARDENS

Monkton - *3535 Jarrettsville Pike (I-95 take Exit 74 to MD Route 152. Follow MD Route 152 northwest to the dead end at MD Route 146 (Jarrettsville Pike) and go left) 21111. Phone: (410) 557-9466. www.ladewgardens.com. Hours: Daily 10:00am - 5:00pm (April-October). Admission: $10.00-$13.00 adult, $4.00 child for Garden & Nature Walk. Home tours extra $5.00. Tours: daily 11am-3pm. Note: Ask the Admissions desk for the Kids Scavenger Hunt sheet before you walk the gardens. Garden storytimes each week - nature story and craft. Ladew Café for lunch.*

The most outstanding topiary garden in America features 15 different themed flower and hedge gardens on 22 acres. What is "topiary"? The art of trimming and training shrubs or trees into unnatural ornamental shapes. See bushes

See the hunter (jumping the fence) and the two dogs ahead in hot pursuit...

shaped like swans, trophies or simple rows of boxes and triangles. A topiary of two riders atop horses and a pack of hounds pursue a cunning green fox across the front lawn. A caterpillar crawls through a whimsical garden. Make a game of who can identify the shape first. There's also a yellow garden (everything with a yellow cast) or the White Garden or the Pink Garden (you get the idea). How about the Garden of Eden (look for the apple tree) or a real Secret Garden or the Keyhole Garden - only one small hidden door in and out.

Browse or cool off in the historic manor house, café, or gift shop. The Manor Tour begins with the poodle and dog house topiary near the front porch. Inside, notice all the stirrup cups shaped like many things. Why is the staircase called a glide? Why the coin in the banister? Our favorite room was the oval room built around an oval desk with a secret passageway to outside. The Nature Walk at Ladew is a 1.5 mile trail through the woods and fields of the Ladew property. In addition to educational stations along the trail, there is a short boardwalk through wetland forest and marsh. Look for frogs and fish in the ponds.

CHILDREN'S DAY AT LADEW TOPIARY GARDENS

Monkton - Ladew Topiary Gardens. Live entertainment, interactive performances for children of all ages, treasure hunt, face painting and balloons. Admission. (second Sunday in September)

CHRISTMAS AT AN ENGLISH COUNTRY HOUSE

Monkton - Ladew Topiary Gardens. Festively decorated manor house; fresh greens, unique holiday decorations for sale. Admission. (second weekend in December)

SOLDIER'S DELIGHT NATURAL ENVIRONMENTAL AREA

Owings Mills - *5100 Deer Park Road, near the Liberty Reservoir (I-795N to exit 7B on Franklin Blvd, west. Turn right on Church Road, left on Berrysman Lane, then left on Deer Park Road) 21117. Phone: (410) 922-3044. http://dnr2.maryland. gov/publiclands/Pages/central/soldiersdelight.aspx Hours: Sunrise to sunset.*

The area supports over 39 rare, threatened or endangered plant species, as well as, rare insects, rocks and minerals. Visitors will enjoy hiking on the trails or stopping by the visitor center to enjoy interpretive exhibits (find out what a serpentine barren is?). They offer a Scavenger Hunt inside the Center, too. Trails are only open to hikers. Equestrians and cyclists are not permitted due to the sensitive nature of the area.

* SERPENTINE TRAIL (2.5 miles) - Visitors will traverse a large section of the serpentine barren while hiking this trail. This area consists mainly of grassland, but also passes through wetland areas and an oak forest.

* CHOATE MINE TRAIL (1.1 miles) - Hikers will pass by the historic Choate Mine. This chrome mine was operated from 1818 to 1888. It was briefly reopened during World War I for ore extraction. This loop trail connects to the Red Run Trail and Dolfield Trail.

- RED RUN TRAIL (0.9 mile) - Hikers will travel through sections of serpentine grasslands as well as the oak forest. This trail offers the only "stream side" hiking opportunity at Coldioro Dolight as visitors hike along the banks of Red Run.

JOHNNY APPLESEED FESTIVAL

Parkville - *Webers Cider Mill Farm, Rte 695 exit 30B north. www.webersfarm.com. Hayrides, apple picking, farm animals, fresh pressed apple cider and baked fruit pies. (last full weekend in September)*

TERRAPIN ADVENTURES

Savage - 8600 Foundry Street, Savage Mill 20763. www.TerrapinAdventures.com. Phone: (410) 925-9574. Hours: Daylight runs early March-November. Weekends only in cooler months. Admission: each activity has a fee from $15-$55

For some no sweat adrenaline, scale one of the 12 routes of the 43-foot-high Terrapin Tower. Conquer all 25 elements of a Challenge Course. Experience two G's of force on the Giant Swing, and enjoy the thrill of gliding through the forest canopy on a Zip Line. The new Terrapin Explorer Kids Course offers 22 elements of fun for ages 5-9. Learn new skills while you explore local parks, rivers, and the Chesapeake Bay on guided kayak tours and nature hikes, mountain bike rentals and tours, sailing and windsurfing, fly and reel fishing, geo-caching, horseback trail riding, rock climbing, rappelling, and river tubing.

SUGARLOAF CRAFTS FESTIVAL

Timonium - *Maryland State Fairgrounds. www.sugarloafcrafts.com. This exciting show features 350 artists and crafters, delicious food, craft demos and children's entertainment. Admission. (last weekend in April & first weekend in October)*

BALTIMORE AREA POW-WOW

Timonium - *Maryland State Fairgrounds. www.baic.org. Intertribal gathering of Native American dancers, drummers, artists, crafts persons, and friends; public is cordially invited. Admission. (second weekend in July)*

MARYLAND STATE FAIR

Timonium - *Maryland State Fairgrounds. www.marylandstatefair.com. Livestock, crafts, produce, farm and garden exhibits, food, midway rides, Thoroughbred horse racing, and entertainment. Admission. (last Friday in August thru Labor Day)*

FESTIVAL OF TREES

Timonium - Maryland State Fairgrounds. www.festivaloftrees.kennedykrieger.org. Ring in the holiday season with crafts, ginger bread gardens and much more at this benefit of the children of Kennedy Krieger Institute. Admission. (Thanksgiving weekend in November)

HAMPTON NATIONAL HISTORIC SITE

Towson - *535 Hampton Lane (I 695) eastbound or westbound: Take Exit 27B, Dulaney Valley Road northbound) 21286. www.nps.gov/hamp. Phone: (410) 823-1309. Hours: Grounds open daily 8:30am-5:00pm. VISITOR CENTER OPEN: 9:00am-4:00pm Thursday-Sunday except Thanksgiving, Christmas, and New Year's Day. Admission: FREE. Tours: Explore the farm with a Ranger. A 30-minute presentation including visit to worker's quarters occurs twice daily.*

Once the largest house in America, the site tells the story of enslaved African Americans, indentured servants, industrial and agricultural workers, and owners and interprets the economic and moral changes that made this lifestyle obsolete. The self-guided tour of this farm and grounds includes original slave quarters that tell the story of the family who lived here for more than 150 years, as well as slaves and indentured servants. Scenes from Hampton's past include a colonial merchant shipper amassing thousands of acres of property along Maryland's Chesapeake shore; indentured servants casting molten iron into cannons and ammunition for the Revolutionary army; and enslaved people loading barrels of grain, iron, and timber onto merchant ships bound for Europe that would return with luxury goods.

CIVIL WAR ENCAMPMENT LIVING HISTORY

Union Mills - Union Mills Homestead. www.unionmills.org. Living history, demos, food both days, ice cream social, music, clowns, pony rides, and tours of Homestead and grist mill. Fee per vehicle. (second weekend in July)

OLD-FASHIONED CORN ROAST FESTIVAL

Union Mills - Union Mills Homestead. Chicken platters, applesauce, rolls, sliced tomatoes, roasted corn, and tours of Homestead and grist mill; art, music and vendors, too. www.unionmills.org. Admission. (first Saturday in August)

FARM HERITAGE DAYS

West Friendship - Howard County Living Heritage Farm. www.farmheritage.org. Family fun, antique farm equipment, wagon, train and pony rides, petting zoo, arts and crafts show, live music, food. Admission. (fourth weekend in September)

CARROLL COUNTY FARM MUSEUM

Westminster - *500 South Center Street 21157. Phone: (410) 386-3880. http:// ccgovernment.carr.org/ccg/farmmus/default.asp. Hours: Saturdays & Sundays Noon-5:00pm (May-October). Also Tuesday - Friday 10:00am-4:00pm (July & August). Admission: $5.00 adult, $3.00 senior (60+) or youth (7-18).*

The Farm Museum takes you back to a bygone era filled with country charm and old-fashioned ingenuity. The Museum grounds include original farm structures, such as the Farmhouse and a bank barn, built in 1852-53. Other buildings include a Smokehouse, Broom Shop, Saddlery, Springhouse, Living History Center, Wagon Shed, General Store exhibit, Firehouse, and a One-room Schoolhouse. Take a self-guided tour through the Living History Center where artisans demonstrate old-time skills. At various times, demonstrated skills may include broom making, tinsmithing, blacksmithing, quilting, spinning, weaving, basket making, and hearth cooking.

CIVIL WAR LIVING HISTORY REENACTMENT

Westminster - Carroll County Farm Museum. Witness Living History in the remaking as various regiments occupy the grounds surrounding the family farmhouse. Guests may visit the camps. Artisans demo skills from the 1800s. Admission. (first weekend in May)

BLACKSMITH DAYS

Westminster - Carroll County Farm Museum. Blacksmiths set up forges and demo "smithy" skills; hands-on opps and farmhouse tours. Admission. (third weekend in May)

COMMON GROUND ON THE HILL

Westminster - Carroll County Farm Museum. www.commongroundonthehill.org. Four stages of music, folk, Blues, old-time, bluegrass, world arts and crafts, ethnic foods, and family "world village". Admission. (second weekend in July)

OLD-FASHIONED JULY 4TH CELEBRATION

Westminster - Carroll County Farm Museum. Fireworks, old-fashioned family picnic, games, food, crafts and farmhouse tours. Admission. (July 4th)

STEAM SHOW DAYS

Westminster - Carroll County Farm Museum. Antique farm machinery, antique cars, working demos, flea market, hayrides, farmhouse tours, sawmilling, and food for sale. Admission (second weekend in September)

FALL HARVEST DAYS

Westminster - *Carroll County Farm Museum. Scarecrow making, wagon rides, apple butter making, country food, crafts, entertainment, puppet theater, games, farmhouse tours. Admission. (first weekend in October)*

HOLIDAY TOUR

Westminster - *Carroll County Farm Museum. Museum is decorated in holiday fashion with Santa visits, food sales, holiday music, and mule pulled wagon rides. Holiday teas. Admission. (weekends in December)*

APPLEWOOD FARM

Whiteford - *www.applewoodfarm.org. Petting zoo, hayrides, pony rides, pick-your-own pumpkins, decorated barn, train gardens, children's maze. Admission. (weekends in October)*

DAYS END FARM HORSE RESCUE

Woodbine - *1372 Woodbine Road 21797. www.defhr.org. Spring Carnival - Petting zoo, pony rides, games. All proceeds benefit abused, neglected horses. www.defhr.org. Admission. (third or fourth Saturday in June). Fall Festival - Horses in costume. Petting zoo, pony rides, games and prizes. All proceeds benefit abused, neglected horses. Admission. (last Saturday in September)*

Chapter 4
Eastern Shore
Area

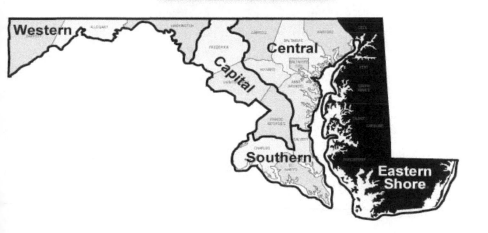

Berlin
- Assateague Island National Seashore & State Park

Cambridge
- Blackwater National Wildlife Refuge
- Hyatt Regency Chesapeake Bay Resort
- Richardson Maritime Museum & Boatworks
- Skipjack Nathan Of Dorchester
- Fly In

Chesapeake City
- C & D Canal Museum

Chestertown
- Chesapeake Farms

Chestertown
- Schooner Sultana
- Chestertown Tea Party

Crisfield
- Crisfield Walking Tours
- Janes Island State Park
- Smith Island Cruises & Smith Island
- Tawes, J. Millard, Historical Museum

Deal Island Harbor
- Skipjack Race & Land Festival

Easton
- Pickering Creek Audubon Center
- Tuckahoe Steam & Gas Show

Elkton
- Milburn Orchards

Federalsburg
- Wheat Threshing, Steam And Gas Engine Show

Grasonville
- Chesapeake Bay Environmental Center

Hurlock
- Choptank Riverboat Co.

North East
- Day Basket Factory
- Elk Neck State Park And Forest

Ocean City
- Assateague Adventure
- Jolly Roger Amusement Parks
- OC Boardwalk
- OC Boat Tours
- OC Life-Saving Station Museum
- Princess Royale Resort Hotel
- Ripley's Believe It Or Not!
- Wheels Of Yesterday
- Easter Kids Fair
- Oktoberfest

Ocean City, West
- Frontier Town Western Park
- OC Jamboree

Pocomoke City
- Delmarva Discovery Center
- Sturgis 1-Room School Museum

Princess Anne
- Olde Princess Anne Days

Queen Anne
- Tuckahoe State Park

Queenstown
- Wye Island Natural Resources Management Area

Ridgely
- Grand Illumination And Candlelight Caroling Walk

Rising Sun
- Plumpton Park Zoo

Rock Hall
- Eastern Neck National Wildlife Refuge
- Rock Hall Museum
- Waterman's Museum

Salisbury
- Comfort Inn Salisbury
- Delmarva Shorebirds Baseball
- Pemberton Hall Plantation
- Salisbury Zoo
- Salisbury Pewter Outlet
- Ward Museum Of Wildfowl Art

Smith Island (Ewell)
- Bayside Inn

Snow Hill
- Furnace Town Heritage Museum
- Mt. Zion One-Room School Museum
- Pocomoke River State Park
- Purnell Museum

St. Michaels
- Chesapeake Bay Maritime Museum

Taylors Island
- Island Grille

Tilghman Island
- Chesapeake Sailing Cruises
- Tilghman Island Summer Seafood Festival

Wye Mills
- Wye Grist Mill And Museum

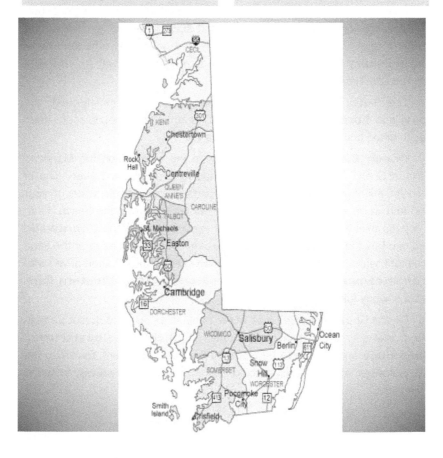

A Quick Tour of our Hand-Picked Favorites

Eastern Shore Maryland

The Maryland Eastern Shore is a fairly wide peninsula between the Chesapeake Bay and the Atlantic Ocean. It has hundreds of miles of shoreline, ocean resorts, farmland, forests, modest cities and small historic towns.

Salisbury is the largest "city" with 24,000 residents. It's the regional hub for transportation, shopping, education and services. Plant yourself at one of many hotels on the main shopping strip and go on day trips from here. The **Salisbury Zoo** is a FREE zoo with an open-air walkway to "visit" with animals. We liked "hanging out" with the lemurs.

The town of Snow Hill is not far and presents a casual, mostly shady, old iron village, **Furnace Town**, to explore. Different crafters set up space each day to demo and display their old-timey wares.

Ocean City is the big tourist draw in the summer on the Maryland Eastern Shore. It offers a clean beach, fun for the kids, and every kind of food you might possibly crave. With anticipation of cool Atlantic water on your skin and warm sand under your feet, this is Americana at the beach. Grab a colorful beach umbrella and chair and settle in or walk the **Boardwalk**. You can buy the flip-flops you forgot, the t-shirt you adore, gaze at the sand sculptors, while juggling your ice cream cone and OC fries. A short drive away is **Assateague Island** (wild ponies) or **Frontier Town Western Park** full of cowboy fun.

On the Chesapeake Bay side of the peninsula you'll find quaint Eastern Shore towns in every nook and cranny. **St Michaels**, **Chestertown**, **Cambridge** and **Crisfield** are some of the most prominent. Exploring the little waterfront towns of the Maryland Eastern Shore is a great way to spend a weekend.

Cambridge is home to eagles and other creatures – especially at the **Blackwater National Wildlife Refuge**. Crisfield is a cute "crabbing" port for watermen working or cruises out to the laid-back **Smith Island**. Take the Crisfield walking tour and be sure to try a giant slice of Smith Island cake before you head back to the mainland. While St. Michaels is predominantly flocked by lazy day adults, kids find their haven at the **Chesapeake Bay Maritime Museum**. The eerie, walk-on oyster boat could tell stories…and it does! As you enter different portals, a waterman shares a tale or two of life on these waters.

Sites and attractions are listed in order by City, Zip Code, and Name. Symbols indicated represent:

 Restaurants   Lodging

ASSATEAGUE ISLAND NATIONAL SEASHORE & STATE PARK

Berlin - *7307 Stephen Decatur Hwy (from OC, take Rte. 50 bridge west, turn left onto Rte 611 south) 21811. www.assateagueisland.com Phone: (888) 432-2267. Hours: Visitor Center 9:00am-5:00pm daily. Admission: Day use $3.00 per person.*

Begin your Maryland visit to Assateague Island National Seashore in the family-oriented Barrier Island Visitor Center, located at the end of Rte. 611, just prior to crossing the bridge to the island. Pick up a park map, enjoy the aquariums, or watch a film about the island. Cross the bridge to Assateague and explore the barrier island. Short, self-guided walks or bike trails run through the park (trail is 3.5 miles long). View magnificent marshlands, beautiful beaches and miles of water. The island is home to the wild ponies made famous in the novel "Misty of Chincoteague." The name Assateague comes from a Native American word thought to mean "the marshy place across." The island is ideal for camping (primitive), fishing, clamming, crabbing, canoeing and kayaking. Bring your own car-top boat or rent a canoe at the Bayside Picnic Area (daily during summer and on spring or fall weekends).

BLACKWATER NATIONAL WILDLIFE REFUGE

Cambridge - *2145 Key Wallace Drive (Rte. 16 south) 21613. Phone: (410) 228-2677. www.friendsofblackwater.org. Hours: Refuge open Dawn to dusk. Visitors Center open Monday-Friday 8:00am-4:00pm, Weekends 9:00am-5:00pm. Admission: $3.00 per vehicle. Note: Orientation video is about 20 minutes long.*

The endangered Fox Squirrel...

Then pick up a Wildlife Drive Map and head on the driving path. Want to make this a game? Ask the ranger for a waterfowl checklist and see how many you can find.

This is a prime resting and feeding area for migrating waterfowl. Huge flocks of ducks, geese and swans migrate through in November and December. As a major stop on the Atlantic Flyway, Blackwater is a vital haven for waterfowl, as well as a sanctuary for the threatened American bald eagle and the endangered Delmarva fox squirrel. These squirrels are much less active - we saw one taking a nap! The largest nesting population of bald eagles on the East Coast hang out here each year. What makes the refuge attractive? Why do they farm corn and soybean? Why do they drain the pond in summer? If you decide not to venture into the refuge, you'll find a rapidly growing Butterfly and Beneficial Insect Garden. And if you look out the

window at the rear of the building, you will see their Osprey Cam platform off in the distance. The second floor contains a bird-watcher's observatory overlooking the marsh. You never have to leave the building to catch some great views of wildlife (especially helpful if the weather isn't cooperating).

EAGLE FESTIVAL

Cambridge - *Blackwater National Wildlife Refuge Visitor Center. Festival celebrating eagles and other birds of prey, featuring live animal programs and children's activities. (second Saturday in March)*

HARRIET TUBMAN UNDERGROUND RAILROAD STATE PARK

Cambridge (Church Creek) - *4068 Golden Hill Road (near Blackwater Refuge, about 12 miles south of town off of Rte 335) 21622. www.dnr.state.md.us/ publiclands/eastern/tubman.asp or www.nps.gov/hatu. Phone: (410) 221-1871. Hours: Daily 9:00am-5:00pm, with exception of major winter holidays.*

This long-anticipated center opened to exhibit Harriet Tubman's role as a conductor on the Underground Railroad and her work as a freedom fighter, humanitarian, leader and liberator. The surrounding grounds (and byway to the site, http://harriettubmanbyway.org/) and marshes are some areas where Harriet repeatedly risked her life to guide nearly 70 enslaved people north to new lives of freedom. Walk into the Museum and step back into recreated scenes and an introductory film.

HYATT REGENCY CHESAPEAKE BAY RESORT

Cambridge - 100 Heron Blvd @ Rte. 50 21613. (410) 901-1234 www.chesapeakebay. hyatt.com. Discover an authentic Chesapeake Bay experience in a spacious 350-sq.-ft. room featuring neutral decor reflective of the area's maritime past. Luxurious amenities include step-out balcony, two plush double beds, refrigerator, coffeemaker, generous work area, wireless high-speed Internet access, marble bath with Portico products, vanity mirror, and cozy robes. Many of the 400 rooms face the river. A focal point of the resort, the 150-slip River Marsh Marina offers guests a variety of activities. Pirate's Cove offers a fun-filled activities program where kids can make new friends and learn new skills and crafts. Parents... head off on your own adventures (golf) or enjoy some quiet time (spa) while your kids learn and discover experiences only found here on the Eastern Shore (available Summers, holidays and weekends for a fee). Daily activities are offered poolside like water games, crafts, contests and fireside smores. The Winter Garden area pool is open year-round in a climate-controlled, glass-enclosed area. Large outdoor swimming pools include the Activities Pool with waterslide (a little on the cold side), a children's pool and Infinity Pool. Several restaurants, snack bars and grill for dining. Johnny Venture Kids Menu has a wide variety of kids favorites (~$7.00).

RICHARDSON MARITIME MUSEUM & BOATWORKS

Cambridge - *401 High Street, downtown 21613. www.richardsonmuseum.org. Phone: (410) 221-1871. Hours: Boatworks-Monday, Wednesday, Friday 11am-3pm. Museum - Saturday 10am-4pm, Sunday 1:00-4:00pm.*

Walk into the Museum and step back into the rich history of Dorchester County's influence on Chesapeake Bay traditional wooden sailing vessels. Bordering the Bay, bounded by broad rivers and laced with countless waterways, the County has been home to hundreds of boatyards since its early settlement. Chesapeake bay ship models and waterman artifacts honor the craftsmen and culture of Eastern Shore boat building. Just down the street, watch traditional wooden boat building in action at the Boatworks (Corner of Maryland Avenue & Hayward Street). Suggested donation is $3.00.

SKIPJACK NATHAN OF DORCHESTER

Cambridge - *526 Poplar Street (All Public Sailings depart from Long Wharf) 21613. Phone: (410) 228-7141. www.skipjack-nathan.org. Tours: All sailings subject to prevailing weather conditions. Contact them for reservations / availability or just come to the pier at the foot of High St. prior to departure time. (Maximum 25 passengers). $30.00 adult, $10.00 child (6-12). Saturday afternoons late May thru October. Reduced one hour sails on Sunday afternoons.*

Skipjack boat sailing cruises on the Choptank River. Help raise her sails or take a turn at the helm, and hear stories of the working watermen. One of the last skipjacks built, it is meant to preserve the nautical heritage of the county and a way of life.

FLY IN

Cambridge - *Horn Point Aerodrome. www.antiqueairfield.com/flyins/schedule.html Antique aircraft fly-in, aircraft judging, meet pilots, examine planes, food-on-site, aviation vendors. (Memorial Day week)*

C & D CANAL MUSEUM

Chesapeake City - *815 Bethel Road 21915. Phone: (410) 885-5622. www. nap.usace.army.mil/Missions/Civil-Works/Chesapeake-Delaware-Canal/Canal-History/ Hours: Monday-Friday 8:00am-4:00pm (except government holidays). Admission: FREE. Note: a full-sized replica of the 30-foot Bethel Bridge Lighthouse is nearby. The original was one of the many wooden lighthouses used to warn vessels of locks and bridges in the days before the 1927 canal changes made it sea level. The lighthouse is located on Corps property, a short walk from the museum.*

The Chesapeake and Delaware Canal is unique as the sole major commercial navigation waterway in the United States built during the early 1800s still in use. The C&D Canal Museum - provides visitors with a glimpse of the canal's early days. The waterwheel and pumping engines remain in the original pumphouse (now the museum). These steam engines are the oldest of their type in America still on their original foundations. Other artifacts and exhibits in the museum detail and illustrate the canal's history. New exhibits include interactive videos and a television monitor which gives visitors up-to-the minute locations on ships as they travel through the canal.

CHESAPEAKE FARMS

Chestertown - *7319 Remington Drive 21620. Phone: (410) 778-8400. www. dupont.com/products-and-services/crop-protection/chesapeake-farms/ conference-center.html Tours: The driving tour is free and opens in the spring and closes mid-October.*

Chesapeake Farms is a showcase for advanced agriculture and wildlife management. The guide-booklet leads you through the Farms and points out or explains many of the agricultural and wildlife practices being applied there. Some of these techniques you might use on your own land when you get home. There are 16 stops on the driving tour. Each stop is marked by a sign bearing a number. The tour begins at the Farms' main waterfowl rest area and passes many areas of interest such as: Sunflowers, Farm ponds, Deer food plantings, Nesting structures and a Cottontail rabbit habitat.

SCHOONER SULTANA

Chestertown - *105 S Cross Street, dock at end of Cannon Street (Rte. 213 for about 20 miles to the Chester River Bridge. Go over the bridge and into Chestertown. Turn left at the first traffic light onto Cross St) 21620. Phone: (410) 778-5954. www.schoonersultana.com. Note: Public sails also available. Passengers are encouraged to help raise the sails, steer using Sultana's 7-foot long tiller and explore the authentically reproduced crew's quarters below-decks. Sultana offers two-hour sails far families ($15.00-$30.00 per person, must be age 6+). Reservations please.*

Schooner Sultana, school-ship of the Chesapeake, sails the bay to teach bay ecology and Colonial maritime history to thousands of students each year. Activities include but are not limited to: Raising sails and steering the schooner; Using maps, charts and electronic equipment to examine the geology, hydrology and physical characteristics of the Chesapeake and its watershed;

Collecting and examining live fish, crabs and oysters to study their life cycles and physical adaptations; Collecting and examining zooplankton and phytoplankton with the use of a high powered video microscope while discussing the concept of food chains/webs; Performing water quality tests, including: turbidity, salinity, dissolved oxygen, phosphorous, nitrogen and pH; Employing reproduction 18th century navigational equipment to determined speed, depth and latitude; Using historic maps and charts to explore 18th century geopolitics and to discuss the Atlantic triangular trade route; Exploring Sultana's authentic below decks area, including the surgeon's cabin and galley, to learn about everyday life in 18th century America.

DOWNRIGGING WEEKEND SULTANA

Chestertown - *Chestertown Town Dock. Sultana's Downrigging weekend with a tall ships parade of sail; cruises on the Chester River; tours of tall ships. Admission. (late October or early November weekend)*

CHESTERTOWN TEA PARTY

Chestertown - *Chestertown historic district. www.chestertownteaparty.com. Re-enactment of 1774 Tea Party; crafts, Colonial parade, art show and entertainment all day. Sultana Schooner. Highlight is the homemade raft race on the Chester River where everything that floats can enter. (Memorial Day weekend)*

CRISFIELD WALKING TOURS

Crisfield - **3 Ninth Street (depart from Crisfield Visitors Center, Somers Cove Marina) 21817. Phone: (410) 988-2501. www.crisfieldheritagefoundation.org. Hours: Center open daily 9:00am-5:00pm (summer). Closed Sundays rest of year.**

While visiting the "Crab Capital of the World", why not really get some insights into what gave the area that title? Did you know this town was built on top of oyster shells? Now that oyster and crabbing are dwindling, what is the town's new market - tourism and condos.

- WALKING TOUR: The Port of Crisfield Tour takes each patron through the port area of the city.

-

A classic example of a waterman's boat

- One of the highlights of the tour is a visit to a modern crab and oyster processing facility where you can see, first hand, how the products of the Chesapeake are made ready for market. (small fee, Monday-Saturday at 10:00am)

NATIONAL HARD CRAB DERBY AND FAIR

Crisfield - Somers Cove Marina. http://nationalhardcrabderby.com/ This tiny town and its waters are responsible for supplying much of the world with crabs. Crabs representing all 50 states try to skittle to glory in the crab race; parade, crab cooking and picking contests, fireworks, games, amusement rides, boat docking, fireworks. Admission. (Labor Day weekend)

JANES ISLAND STATE PARK

Crisfield - 26280 Alfred Lawson Drive (MD RT 13 to Westover; RT 413, approximately 11 miles to Plantation Road) 21817. Phone: (410) 968-1565. http:// dnr2.maryland.gov/publiclands/Pages/eastern/janesisland.aspx Note: Janes Island is part of the Beach to Bay Indian Trail. This trail recognizes travel patterns established by the American Indians and later followed by the first European settlers. For more information about the trail, contact Somerset County Tourism at (800) 521-9189.

Janes Island State Park is nearly surrounded by the waters of the Chesapeake Bay and its inlets. It has rental cabins, camping and miles of isolated shoreline and marsh areas. Historic artifacts that can be found along the shoreline of Janes Island provide evidence of activities by primitive man, from hunting mammals to shucking oysters. In a sense, native people living on Janes Island were practicing a lifestyle very similar to the modern watermen surviving off the bounty of the Chesapeake Bay. If you are looking for a few hours of tranquil canoeing or kayaking in a natural paradise with few signs of civilization, you'll find it at Janes Island State Park. The approximately 2,900 acres of marsh, beach and high land offers paddlers an outdoor adventure through small waterways within the island. Most of the waterways are protected from wind and current providing ideal conditions for the novice as well as the experienced canoeist. Features: Boat launch, boat rental, fishing and crabbing, swimming, and a visitor's center. FREE park admission.

> Janes Island State Park is a Chesapeake Bay Gateway, one of over 100 special places to experience the Chesapeake. Visit www.baygateways.net to find more Bay Gateways.

SMITH ISLAND CRUISES & SMITH ISLAND

Crisfield - *4065 Smith Island Road (depart from Somers Cove Marina) 21817. www.smithislandcruises.com. Phone: (410) 423-2771. Hours: Center: Daily Noon-4:00pm (May-October). Wednesday and Saturday only (weather dependent, rest of year). Tours: Depart Crisfield at 12:30pm daily (Mid-June to mid-October). $26.00 adult, $13.00 child (3-11).*

Join Captain Tyler for a delightful cruise across the Tangier Sound to Smith Island. Enjoy looking around Smith Island on a self-guided walking tour, or rent a golf cart or a bicycle. There are gift shops to browse in, the **SMITH ISLAND CENTER** (20846 Caleb Jones Road, 410-425-3351 or www.smithisland.org), and plenty of narrow streets to stroll and meet native islanders. Smith Island is Maryland's only inhabited island accessible exclusively

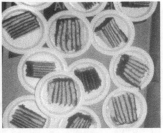

Smith Island Cake... so yummy!!

by boat. There are three separate villages on the island and an Interpretive center about the island community where lifestyles change slowly with time. While wandering around, notice dozens of cats. Why? They LOVE the crab scraps!

SMITH ISLAND CENTER: A small museum ($2.00 admission ages 12 and older) with permanent exhibits related to the history of the Island, working on the water and the interaction of people and the Chesapeake Bay. It explores the role of women in Island life, and distinctive speech patterns which

Piles and piles of crab pot marker buoys...

have developed on the Island. Do you know what "peelers" or "Christmas Give" means? The Film, "*Land and Water, People and Time*" runs about 20 minutes and shows the history of the land and its people, their life on the water and in the community...a good way to hear some of their typical stories. The Center really gives you the "feel" of the Island - how the people work, cope and eat. Can you figure out what is most important to them? Food, family and church. So real. www.smithisland.org/museum.html. Open daily Noon-4:00pm (May-October).

BAYSIDE INN

Smith Island (Ewell) - *4065 Smith Island Road 21824. (410) 425-2771. Bayside Inn restaurant is a favorite lunch spot. Order individual entrees or family-style meals. Most seafood lovers order the meal ($19.00) with crab cakes, clam fritters, baked ham, green beans, corn pudding, macaroni salad, coleslaw, stewed tomatoes and the famous Smith Island Cake. (8-10 thin layers of moist, creamy cake between layers of fudge icing). Their soup is really good, too. No matter what you order, you must try the Smith Island Cake!*

TAWES, J. MILLARD, HISTORICAL MUSEUM

Crisfield - *3 Ninth Street, Somers Dove Marina 21817. Phone: (410) 968-2501. www.crisfieldheritagefoundation.org/ Hours: Monday-Friday 10:00am-4:00pm; Weekends 11:00am-3:00pm (Memorial Day - October). Closed weekends (rest of year). Admission: $3.00 per person (over age 12). Note: Pop over to Gordon's for a cheap bite or ice cream. Linger there a while and listen in on the watermen chatter.*

The museum traces the history of the Lower Shore with exhibits on the beginnings of the Chesapeake Bay, the influence of the Native-Americans on the early colonists, seafood harvesting and processing, and the evolution of that truly American art form, decoy carving and painting. The Ward Brothers only had a fourth grade education but they learned to turn scrap wood into useful decoys and then works of art commanding huge amounts of money. Learn about how the Indian inhabitants showed colonists how to build eel pots, tong for oysters and most importantly, how to build the famous Chesapeake Bay Log Canoes. Wonder who brings the seafood you love to the table? Those hardy Chesapeake watermen harvest oysters and crabs by the millions. The museum tells their story and the story of the processing and marketing of seafood throughout the United States and the world. Learn how to use crab pots and look at pictures of ladies crab picking. Finally, view the "Shanty" exhibit where visitors can see a working waterman's crab shanty. Compare this to the different methods of soft shell crabbing and floating peelers.

SKIPJACK RACE AND LAND FESTIVAL

Deal Island Harbor - *Deal Island Harbor. Skipjack race. Car show, concerts, vendors, events. Home to still active commercial skipjacks. http://dealislandchancelionsclub.org/ Admission. (Labor Day weekend)*

PICKERING CREEK AUDUBON CENTER

Easton - *11450 Audubon Lane 21601. www.pickeringcreek.org. Phone: (410) 822-4903. Hours: Monday through Friday 9:00am-5:00pm. Trails and viewing areas are free and open to the public from dawn to dusk daily.*

The four-hundred acre farm and science education center features 2 lab classrooms (including live reptiles and amphibians); Nature Trails; One mile of shoreline; Freshwater Pond; Children's Imagination Garden; 100 acres of hardwood forest; a Canoe fleet; Live Reptile and Amphibian Displays; Mounted Bird and Mammal Displays and an Eastern Shore Tool Museum.

TUCKAHOE STEAM AND GAS SHOW

Easton - Tuckahoe Showgrounds. www.tuckahoesteam.org. Antique steam engines, gas engines, blacksmith, museum, railroad, horse pull and auction. Children under 12 are FREE. (first full weekend in July)

MILBURN ORCHARDS

Elkton - *1495 Appleton Road 21921. www.milburnorchards.com. Phone: (410) 398-1349. Note: Orchard View Ice Cream and Lunch Deck.*

Family owned and operated since 1902, Milburn Orchards provides your family with high quality farm fresh fruits and vegetables: Peaches, cherries, apples, blackberries, raspberries, blueberries, grapes, nectarines, plums, pumpkins and gourds are grown here. They make country fresh, delicious pies, famous apple cider donuts, giant Royal Gala caramel apples and other baked goods.

- TOURS - Tours are different according to the season, but fall tours include: A Hayride, A Tour of Packing House and Equipment (apples are washed, sorted, and packaged), Demonstration of an apple picking bucket, Chilling walk through gigantic Cold Storage, Walk through the farm market and donut kitchen, Pumpkin House, Johnny Appleseed Schoolhouse (Johnny Appleseed Tutorial), Pick out an apple and a munchkin gourd for your "Goodie" bag! Visit to the Barnyard Buddies, Includes one free gallon of cider and pumpkin (if harvested) per class. Your group is welcome to bring bagged lunches and use their picnic areas after the tour to play in the FarmYard Playground. Tours available Monday-Friday, 9:30am, 11:00am, and 1:00pm. Fee per person.

- FALL - U-pick apples and raspberries; Barnyard Buddy demos, hayrides, corn mazes, boo barn, bale trail, tunnel, cycle circle, straw jump, Playbarn, petting zoo, magic shows, entertainment, games. (weekends in September thru October)

WHEAT THRESHING, STEAM & GAS ENGINE SHOW

Federalsburg - *Rte 313 between Denton & Federalsburg. www.threshermen.org. See antique farm equipment in operation; flea market, steam engines, antique tractors. (first weekend in August)*

CHESAPEAKE BAY ENVIRONMENTAL CENTER

Grasonville - *600 Discovery Lane 21638. www.bayrestoration.org. Phone: (410) 827-6694. Hours: Daily 9:00am-5:00pm. Admission: $5.00 adult - $4.00 senior (55+) - $2.00 youth (5 to 8).*

The Wildfowl Trust of North America operates the Chesapeake Bay Environmental Center, a 500 acre preserve surrounded by the waters of the Chesapeake Bay and comprised of several distinct habitats. Visitors can explore over 4 miles of wetland and woodland trails, collections of live waterfowl and non-releasable raptors, an aviary and visitors center. Rental canoes are available for exploring the surrounding waters and wetlands. Monthly programs called Marsh Muckers and Creepy Crawlers are held for specific, naturalist led, hikes and exploration (small fee). The Center is an excellent place to see the Chesapeake's wintering population of waterfowl including: Canvasback, American Black Duck, Shoveler, Ruddy Ducks, Redhead, Canada Goose and Tundra Swan. Shorebirds make a strong showing in May and late summer, when hundreds can be seen.

CHOPTANK RIVERBOAT COMPANY

Hurlock - *6304 Suicide Bridge Road 21643. www.choptankriverboat.com. Phone: (410) 943-4775. Tours: Sightseeing: Individual Rate - $20.00 per person. (Sightseeing cruises are for 1 1/2 hours). Lunch Cruise: Lunch cruise consists of a 2-hour cruise, meal & tax & gratuity. Individual Rate: $42.00 per adult/$18.00 per child. Generally one cruise 3 to 6 days per week. (April-December).*

The Choptank River Boat Company operates The Dorothy & Megan and The Choptank River Queen. They are reproductions of authentic 80-foot turn-of-the-century paddlewheeler river boats. Fully enclosed with heating and air conditioning. Savor the scenery along the Choptank River on a sightseeing cruise or enjoying a delicious lunch or dinner prepared by the Suicide Bridge Restaurant, the home harbor and embarkation point of their river-boat cruises. Dine on the area's seafood as you watch the waterfowl dine with you. You may also see watermen returning, aboard their workboats, with their daily catch of fish, crabs or oysters fresh from the Choptank River.

DAY BASKET FACTORY

Elkton - *1855 Old Elk Neck Rd (I-95 North, to Exit 100, MD-272 South Proceed 2.4 miles) 21921. Phone: (410) 398-5150. www.daybasketfactory.com. Hours: Wednesday-Saturday 11:00am-5:00pm (May-December). Tours: call ahead to schedule.*

This local industry makes hand-made white oak baskets. The brothers, who had been supplying the southern market with baskets, set-up shop in the North East - partly to save on transportation costs, also because the forests along the Susquehanna River were full of White Oak, the best kind of wood for baskets. Craftsmen carefully select and split each piece of oak used by skilled weavers, who produce baskets using techniques passed down by generations for over 128 years.

TOUR: After the sides are woven, the weaver wraps an outside hoop around the inside hoop and nails through both hoops with brass nails. Some baskets are also fitted with handles of different types. How do they get the wood to bow like that? The production of a basket is a three to four day process. After drying overnight the basket is trimmed, sanded and finished. Four different sizes of market baskets, round farm baskets with bentwood handles or rope handles, picnic baskets with lids, laundry baskets, fish or firewood baskets, berry baskets, picking baskets with drop handles, and eel pots (yes, a popular waterman activity around these parts!).

ELK NECK STATE PARK AND FOREST

North East - *4395 Turkey Point Road (10 miles south of the town of North East on MD 272) 21901. http://dnr2.maryland.gov/publiclands/Pages/central/elkneck. aspx Phone: (410) 287-5333. Admission: $4.00-$6.00 per person (summers and holidays); $3.00-$5.00 per vehicle (all other times).*

Sandy beaches, marshlands and heavily wooded bluffs comprise the peninsula formed by the North East and Elk Rivers, and the Chesapeake Bay, where this park is located. Several trails meander through the diversified topography, revealing the great variety of plant and animal life. An easy walking trail to Turkey Point Lighthouse (www.tpls.org) provides a view of the Elk River and the Chesapeake Bay. Features: Boat launch, cabins, campfire programs, campsites, campstore, fishing, flatwater canoeing, hiking trails, historic interest, swimming, and visitor center.

ASSATEAGUE ADVENTURE

Ocean City - *(Talbot Street on the Bay, downtown) 21842. Phone: (410) 289-3500. www.assateagueadventure.com. Admission: $16.00 adult, $12.00 senior (65+), $8.00 child (5-12). Tours: 2 to 6 times/day, mornings and afternoons (late May-October). Note: Sodas and Bottled Water Available.*

A great way to visit Assateague Island when you don't want to overnight and camp. The ride over and back is comfortable and you can leisurely observe the fishing boats go by and learn about the area's ecosystem. Once you land on the Island, everyone disembarks to explore. Search for Wild Ponies or dredge for clams. They even do a hands-on crab and crab pot demonstration.

JOLLY ROGER AMUSEMENT PARKS

Ocean City - *2901 Coastal Highway. 30th Street & Coastal Hwy or the Boardwalk 21842. Phone: (410) 289-4902. www.jollyrogerpark.com. Hours: Summers open daily 11:00am-1:00am. Admission: per ride or purchase wristband. FREE admission and parking.*

With 35 rides for the whole family, Ocean City's largest family entertainment center includes SPLASH MOUNTAIN WATER PARK and SPEEDWORLD, plus miniature golf, traditional boardwalk rides, games and concessions. Don't forget to ride the World Famous Wild Mouse Coaster.

OCEAN CITY BOARDWALK

Ocean City - *21842. Phone: (800) OC-OCEAN. www.ococean.com. Note: Just one block off the boardwalk is the OCEAN CITY TRAIN GARDEN (109 Dorchester St, http:utzjr.home.mchsi.com) open most Friday and Saturday afternoons in the spring and summer, plus Sundays during summer school break. Free. Bayside at 65th Street is the SLIDE N RIDE water & dry amusements (www.slidenride.com) Admission.*

Be sure to visit Ocean City's world-famous Boardwalk during your stay at the beach. From the tiny train that chugs along the three-mile promenade to the antique carousel that dates back to 1902, visitors realize the charm of the traditional wood walkway.

See incredible sand carvings...what an inspiration!

An early morning bicycle ride (only until 10:00am in summer, til noon off-peak) along the Boardwalk is a great way to start every day in town. Numerous bicycle rental shops are conveniently located to get you on your way. Next, splash in the surf, boogie board (excellent here), or sit back and watch the waves roll in. Paddle a canoe or kayak. Fly a kite or build a sandcastle. Cast a line from one of several fishing piers or from the beach (rentals available).

Although we suggest walking the beach/boardwalk during the day, a small fee boards a tram anywhere on the strip. Enjoy browsing through the Boardwalk shops for that perfect souvenir. Bring your appetites along with you. Boardwalk eateries serve a delicious assortment of treats. Eastern Shore seafood including crab cakes, Maryland fried chicken, pit beef barbeque (Boogs), and famous french fries (Thrashers) are just a few of the offerings. Satisfy that sweet tooth with saltwater taffy, caramel popcorn, frozen custard swirl (Kohrs), funnel cakes, cotton candy, and creamy fudge. Children (of all ages) enjoy the Boardwalk's amusements and arcades. Get a bird's eye view of the barrier island from atop the Ferris wheel. Then take a seat on a bench overlooking the inlet and watch the boats come and go or listen to the nightly street musicians. Near 2nd Street, you can't miss two works of art - the **OCEAN GALLERY** folkart store where you have free admission to a spectacle (really, the fun

The Ocean Gallery...an art store oddity

art to look and PLEASE TOUCH is on the outside wall of the shop) and Randy Hofman's (www. randyhofman.com) amazing Biblical sand sculptures. They get your attention! Each summer, they offer free family activities like evening Bonfires and Sundaes in the Park plus many free concerts on the weekends.

MARYLAND INTERNATIONAL KITE EXPOSITION

Ocean City - *Boardwalk area. Kite competition consisting of multi-level precision flying events. Internationally known kite flyers show unique displays. (last long weekend in April)*

CRUISIN' OCEAN CITY

Ocean City - *Inlet parking lot. 3,500 street rods and classic cars cruisin' the boardwalk and the city; boardwalk parades, competition, styling and profiling. Admission. (third long weekend in May)*

OCEAN CITY FOURTH OF JULY JAMBOREE AND FIREWORKS JUBILEE

Ocean City - Northside Park (127th Street bayside), on beach and Boardwalk. Music, arts and crafts, food, family games, free concerts on beach, fireworks over the ocean. (July 4th)

SUNFEST

Ocean City - Boardwalk, Inlet lot. Ocean City's biggest festival with fine art, crafts, performers on two stages and a variety of food vendors. Fall Children's activities include pumpkin decorating and scarecrow making. The Kite Festival includes a kids workshop, kite battles and the East Coast's premier sport kite competition. Evening headline entertainers. Admission. (fourth long weekend in September)

WINTERLAND OF LIGHTS

Ocean City - Townwide, Inlet Lot; Northside Park. Dazzling lights on cold winter nights put everyone in a holiday mood. Tour the tunnel of lights and the Inlet where you'll find the beach filled with lights boasting a nautical theme. Travel the avenues of Ocean City to see the old-fashioned lighted wreaths, then on to Northside Park to see hundreds of animated lighted displays. Browse the gift shop, have a photo taken with Santa and enjoy hot chocolate in the heated, decorated tent while you wait to board the Winterfest Express to tour the lights. Small Fee to ride Tram. (evenings mid-November to New Years Day)

OCEAN CITY BOAT TOURS

SEA ROCKET - downtown at 700 S. Philadelphia Ave. (410) 289-5887 or www.searocket.com. Enjoy safe, affordable family fun onboard Ocean City's original and largest speedboat. Music and frequent encounters with playful dolphins. $22.00 adults, $13.00 seniors, $7.00 child (12 and under). 50 minute tour leaves two to six times each day (seasonally).

OC ROCKET - Talbot Street Pier. www.talbotstreetwatersports.com. (410) 289-3500. Leaving two-eight times per day each summer, this is OC's fastest speed boat ride. They claim to see the most dolphins and have raised, comfortable cushion seating for the best ride. 50 minute tour. $18.00 adult, $12 senior, $6.00 child (5-12)

DUCKANEER - Talbot Street Pier. Same contact info as OC Rocket. The call is out to brave treasure hunters of all ages. Ye best be ready for a magical pirate journey with buccaneer battles (water guns) and sunken treasure (everyone gets some). Plan to get wet in the heat of battle. Weekends (May & September), several times daily each summer. $20 (age 4 and up). $10.00 younger.

OCEAN CITY LIFE-SAVING STATION MUSEUM

Ocean City - *813 S. Boardwalk 21842. www.ocmuseum.org. Phone: (410) 289-4991. Hours: Daily 10:00am-6:00pm (June-September). Only open until 4:00pm (May & October), Wednesday-Sunday 10am-4pm (April & November). Admission: $1.00-$3.00 per person. FREEBIES: To engage your children in learning some history of the beach (instead of just the amusements, food and surf fun), try doing the Scavenger Hunt worksheet. If your child completes it, they receive a prize. Click on their online Kids Corner for games and puzzles.*

Shipwrecks, Life-Saving & Rescue, History, Swimwear, Sealife, & More! This very building once housed the surfmen charged with rescuing shipwrecked mariners from the sea, and later, the U.S. Coast Guard. One room is devoted to lifesaving stories and techniques. Notorious keepers give written and verbal accounts of heart-breaking rescues. The Beach Room houses a large collection of bathing fashions, beach toys, and accessories worn by Ocean City beach goers during the past century. Look for the Paper Blend Bikini available in vending machines in 1971. Kids think this room is very funny. The Aquarium Room contains two 250 gallon saltwater aquariums and several smaller tanks filled with interesting creatures indigenous to the Ocean City waters. Sands From Around the World is a unique collection of over 200 samples of sand collected by friends of the museum. Can you find sand from your region of the country? Davey Jones' Locker - always wondered what it is? Deep-sea divers share with you unusual objects that have been

Learning rescue techniques of the past...

recovered from the shipwrecks off of Ocean City and the surrounding area. Another room is dedicated to Mermaids. Several unique dolls' houses depict the once gracious hotels and notable businesses of Ocean City's past. Hear Sal laugh (an animated mannequin from Jester's Fun House). You'll catch yourself laughing outloud, too.

PRINCESS ROYALE RESORT HOTEL

Ocean City - *9100 Coastal Avenue (91st Street on the Ocean) 21842. (800) 4-ROYALE or www.princessroyale.com. The all-suite hotel (separate bedroom and living room and* *kitchenette) is in a quieter part of the "strip" yet right on the beach and just minutes away from the busy boardwalk area. Besides being right on the waterfront, families also love the four-story oceanfront glass atrium with Olympic-sized indoor pool, hot tub, and arcade games. Up on the roof you can pay a small fee to play tennis, deck tennis or mini-golf - on the roof! Schooners restaurant and Atrium Café serve food and entertainment and in-house, they have a convenience store and gift shop. A grocery store is across the street for other supplies as you have a small kitchen in your suite for cooking or reheating leftovers. $100-$300 per night depending on season and number of bedrooms.*

RIPLEY'S BELIEVE IT OR NOT!

Ocean City - *401 S Atlantic Ave. Wicomico Street & Boardwalk 21842. http:// oceancity.ripleys.com/. Phone: (410) 289-5600. Hours: Daily 9:00am-1:00am (summer). Daily 10:00am-5:00pm (rest of year). Admission: $14.99 adult, $8.99 child. Discounts online. Note: on site, Mirror Maze & Laserace. Combo tickets offered.*

Discover the museum full of the bizarre and exciting objects you won't see in any other museum. 14 theme galleries showcase everything from a rock from Mars to shark attack stories. Look for the world's only 40-foot animated shark crashing through the pier building. From shrunken heads to modern weirdness, always unusual. Probably best for the older kids in your party.

EASTER KIDS FAIR

Ocean City - *Convention Center. www.oceanpromotions.info Continuous events, activities and entertainment including Beanny the Easter Bunny, egg hunts, coloring tables, magic and puppet shows, clowns and contests. Admission. (Easter)*

FRONTIER TOWN WESTERN PARK

Ocean City, West - *(Rte. 611 west) 21811. www.frontiertown.com. Phone: (410) 641-0057. Hours: Daily 10:00am-6:00pm (mid June to Labor Day). Admission: Packages for Western Park, waterpark, other rides. See website for current packages. $12.00-$14.00 per person Frontier Town park alone (includes rides & shows). Many discounts offered in OC coupon books. Note: FREE parking, waterpark changing rooms and lockers. Miniature golf course.*

"C'mon down folks"...to this replica western town circa 1860 situated alongside of Frontier Town Campground (sites rented with reservations). Return to "them

days of yesteryear" and live a day In the life of a rootin' tootin' cowboy, an earth-poundin' Indian Chief or a high steppin' Can Can gal. Most young deputies want to spend their allowance purchasing cap guns and cowboy apparel to pretend shootin' at the OK Corral (before and after the show). Besides the dispersed schedule of live shows, try to take in a steam train ride, stagecoach ride, pan
for gold, paddle boats, trail rides and such. Be careful the outlaws don't get you out on the trail.... The Waterpark has a western theme, too. Slide down Red Bird's Mountain, a giant water slide, and splash into the catch pool. Their Lazy River will have ya wishin' you'd "growed fins instead of feet". Designed for kids (with parents in mind) The Waterin' Hole, a family activity pool, features a huge shallow wadin' pool with covered wagon mini-slides, cactus fountains, water sprays and more.

DELMARVA DISCOVERY CENTER

Pocomoke City - *6 Market St, riverfront 21851. www.delmarvadiscoverycenter.org. Phone: (410) 957-9933. Hours: Monday-Saturday 10:00am-4:00pm & Sunday Noon-4:00pm. Admission: $10.00 adult, $8.00 senior & student, $5.00 child (4-17) Note: Pocomoke River Package includes the center's exhibits and a guided cruise on the Pocomoke River with the Bay Queen.*

Located on the banks of the slow-moving Pocomoke River, this museum explores river ecology and the town's evolving relationship to the river. Sound recordings, full-size dioramas, an aquarium, touch tanks, animal tracks, ships models, dugout canoes and duck decoys are just a few of the items used for interpretation of the following themes: Beaver Lodge, the Cypress Swamp, Birds, Native People, Colonial America, The Wharf & The Steamer, Shipbuilding & Woodworking, Fishing & Industry. The modern interior space also houses an introductory theatre, and future plans include an on-site restaurant.

STURGIS ONE ROOM SCHOOL MUSEUM

Pocomoke City - *209 Willow Street 21851. Phone: (410) 957-1913. Hours: Tuesday - Saturday from 1:00-4:00pm (May-October). Admission: Donations.*

www.octhebeach.com/museum/Sturgis.html

Sturgis One Room School Museum, formerly known as Sturgis School, is the only African American One Room School in Worcester County retaining its original integrity. It is a small structure built about 100 years ago on Brantley Road on land that was purchased by William Sturgis in 1888. Sturgis One Room School operated as a school for 37 years. Grades 1 - 7 were taught by one teacher until it closed its doors in 1937. Next door is a Heritage House used to display local artifacts.

TUCKAHOE STATE PARK

Queen Anne - *13070 Crouse Mill Road 21657. Phone: (410) 820-1668. http:// dnr2.maryland.gov/publiclands/Pages/eastern/tuckahoe.aspx. Day Use FREE.*

Tuckahoe Creek, a quiet country stream bordered for most of its length by wooded marshlands, runs through the length of the park. A 60-acre lake offers boating and fishing. The park offers 20 miles of scenic hiking, biking and equestrian trails, flat water canoeing, hunting, picnicking, as well as a recycled tire playground for children. The **ADKINS ARBORETUM** (410-634-2847, 12610 Eveland Road, daily 10:00am-4:00pm) encompasses 500 acres of park land and almost three miles of surfaced walkways leading through the tagged native species of trees and shrubs through meadows and woodlands. The park offers activities and special events on a seasonal basis. Activities include day camps, Scales & Tales Program, and canoe trips.

WYE ISLAND NATURAL RESOURCES MANAGEMENT AREA

Queenstown - *632 Wye Island Road (Route 50 and turn right onto Carmichael Road. Travel 5 miles on Carmichael Road until you cross the Wye Island Bridge) 21658.   http://dnr2.maryland.gov/publiclands/Pages/eastern/wyeisland.aspx. Phone: (410) 827-7577. Hours: Dawn to dusk.*

Privately owned and farmed for more than 300 years, now the island's 2,800 acres are managed for some agriculture but mainly a habitat for wintering waterfowl and native wildlife. Wildlife viewing and hiking are the most popular activities on Wye Island's six miles of trails. The School House Woods Nature Trail takes you through a mature hardwood forest while the Ferry Landing Trail leads beneath a canopy of Osage Orange Trees. Wye Island also houses a Holly Tree that is more than 275 years old. Follow the Holly Tree Trail to visit this long-time resident. Other activities include boating, fishing, biking, equestrian trails, canoeing and kayaking. Day use park entrance is FREE.

GRAND ILLUMINATION AND CANDLELIGHT CAROLING WALK

Ridgely - Adkins Arboretum. The Arboretum's holiday decorations are illuminated, carolers lead visitors along lighted paths through the forest and Santa pays a visit. Admission. www.adkinsarboretum.org. (first Saturday in December)

PLUMPTON PARK ZOO

Rising Sun - *1416 Telegraph Road (10 minutes off I-95 and 5 minutes off Route 1) 21911. Phone: (410) 658-6850. www.plumptonparkzoo.org. Hours: Open daily 10:00am-5:00pm, weather permitting. Admission closes 1 hour prior to closing. Admission: $12.95 adult, $10.95 senior (60+), $8.95 child (2-12). Note: Concession Stand, vending machines available for animal feed.*

Exotic animals are displayed in a pastoral country setting, including giraffes, bears, tigers, monkeys, deer and kangaroos. Other unusual adoptions are pot-bellied pigs and bearded dragon. Most of these animals come here from threatened or abandoned situations.

EASTERN NECK NATIONAL WILDLIFE REFUGE

Rock Hall - *1730 Eastern Neck Road (At the blinking red light in Rock Hall, turn left onto Rt. 445. Follow Rt. 445 about 6 miles out) 21661. Phone: (410) 639-7056. www.fws.gov/northeast/easternneck. Hours: Daily sunrise to 1/2 hour after sunset. Admission: FREE.*

Eastern Neck National Wildlife Refuge, located at the confluence of the Chester River and the Chesapeake Bay, is a 2,285-acre island refuge and a major feeding and resting place for migratory and wintering waterfowl on Maryland's Eastern Shore. It is especially noted as a staging area for tundra swans. The refuge is also home to the endangered Delmarva fox squirrel and the threatened southern bald eagle. Nearly six miles of roads and trails are open to visitors most of the year. Four wildlife trails and a handicap-accessible boardwalk and observation tower are available for those who wish to observe the varied habitats of the refuge. Trails vary 1/4 mile - 1 1/2 miles.

DURDING'S STORE

Rock Hall - *5742 Main Street, intersection of Main and Sharp in waterfront area. 21661. Phone: (410) 778-7957. http://durdingsicecream.com. Have a real milkshake from a real soda fountain! Over in the corner, the old wooden telephone booth still stands...and works. As you sit in one of the wooden booths on the Sharp Street side, look around at the charming detailing, preserved* *from an earlier time – the pressed tin ceiling, the hanging brass lamps, and the slowly rotating ceiling fan. Even the Coca Cola glasses, reflected in the plate-glass mirror behind the soda fountain, are original, dating back to the days of the five cent Coke. They serve soups, salads and sandwiches too.*

🍽 _____

ROCK HALL PARADE AND FIREWORKS

Rock Hall - The Bulkhead and Main Street. Day-long celebrations in a waterman's town. Food, music, horseshoe tournament, turtle races and a parade. Largest display on Maryland's Eastern Shore, overlooking Rock Hall Harbor. (July 3rd & July 4th)

WATERMAN'S MUSEUM

Rock Hall - 20880 Rock Hall Ave   21661. www.rockhallmd.com/watermans-museum Phone: (410) 778-6697.   Hours: Daily 10:00am-4:00pm, except major holidays. Admission: FREE. Donation box.

Locals have put together assorted artifacts on Chesapeake Bay crabbing, fishing, and oyster tonging. Crab pots, eel traps, dinghies, anchors, oarlocks, nets, buoys and knots everywhere. In winter, watermen often lived for lengthy periods of time in tiny one room shanties mounted on flat bottomed boats. Moored out on the partially or totally frozen bay, these shacks provided just enough space for a man, a few critical belongings, a potbellied stove, a bunk, a table, a chair, and of course, his dog…see a real-life sample of this. Another exhibit space details a realistic oyster harvesting station.

QUALITY INN SALISBURY

Salisbury - 2701 North Salisbury Blvd., US 13 north. 21801. Two room family suites and deluxe complimentary continental breakfast are nice features for a fair price (start around $60). Every room has a small frig and microwave. Only minutes from downtown attractions and 20 miles from Ocean City. Located right in the middle of a huge shopping complex. (410) 543-4666 or www.choicehotels.com/maryland/salisbury/quality-inn-hotels/md416. _____ 🛏

DELMARVA SHOREBIRDS BASEBALL

Salisbury - 6400 Hobbs Road (Arthur Perdue Stadium) 21802. Phone: (888) BIRDS-96. www.theshorebirds.com.

The single A affiliates for the Baltimore Orioles play home games at this modern ballpark. Come see Sherman the Shorebird and the future stars of the major leagues. While you're there, take the kids on the carousel and playground, speed-pitch machine, enjoy a buffet or occasional post-game fireworks.

PEMBERTON HALL PLANTATION

Salisbury - *5561 Plantation Lane (take Salisbury Bus. Rte 50 to Rte. 349, Nanticoke Rd, for 1/4 mile. Turn left on Pemberton Drive) 21801. www.pembertonpark.org. Phone: (410) 548-4900. Park Hours: daily sunrise to sunset. Tours: Sundays from 2:00-4:00pm from May 1 - October 1 and by appointment. Note: The 262-acre park boasts 4.5 miles of self-guided natural trails, hardwood forests, meadows, wetlands and fresh water ponds.*

Pemberton Hall, as the plantation house is known, was built in 1741 for Colonel Isaac Handy and his wife Ann. It is one of the earliest dated brick gambrel roofed houses in Maryland. The park features a historic Eastern Shore plantation house, a visitor's center, a small museum with artifacts from the plantation, and several miles of nature trails spread throughout the 207 acre property. Settlers discovered that Maryland's Lower Eastern Shore offered many advantages: level expanses of sandy soil favorable for growing tobacco, grain and other crops; abundant streams to power mills; and protected inlets and coves suitable for boat landings from which plantation goods could be shipped overseas. Along with viewing the house and enjoying the trails and property, participate in organized educational programs.

SALISBURY ZOO

Salisbury - *755 S Park Drive (City Park, Rte 50 into town, left on Civic Avenue, right at end, next left onto Memorial Plaza) 21802. www.salisburyzoo.org. Phone: (410) 548-3188. Hours: Daily 9:00am-4:30pm. Closed Thanksgiving and Christmas. Admission: FREE.*

Long touted as one of the finest small zoos in America, the zoo houses more than 400 species of animals and wildfowl native to North, Central and South America. From bears hanging out in a hammock to curious prairie dogs or elegant flamingos. Unusual Cavys look like a sort of kangaroo deer. Spider Monkeys like to play. Over by the sloth, try hanging upside down like the sloth. Because they're in the middle of decoy art country, they have a wonderful display of live wildfowl. Compare it to the decoys you've seen around town. Set inside City Park, located on the Wicomico River, the area also offers sport courts, paddle boat rentals and more than three miles of trails. The park also has a large, sturdy "Castle" playground and a huge misting station to cool off.

For updates visit: www.KidsLoveTravel.com

SALISBURY PEWTER OUTLET

Salisbury - *2611 N. Salisbury Blvd. (Rte. 13 north) 21804. Phone: (410) 546-1188. Hours: Monday-Friday 9:30am-5:30pm, Saturday 10:00am-5:00pm. Some Sundays. Admission: FREE. http://salisburyinc.net/salisbury-fine-metal-artisans/*

The company continues the tradition of handcrafted American products. Watch a short video of the process - then see them do it, live! Look directly into the factory from an observation window to watch items being made. They start with a thin pewter disk or flat and model and shape it around a form on a lathe. As it's spinning, the crafter uses hands and old tools to scrape, shape, shave and sink

metal formed into art...

designs into the pewter piece. Another window reveals the ladies polishing and engraving. Then, browse in the elegant showroom featuring gift items of pewterware at factory seconds and overrun savings. This is a great tour as you don't have to worry about safety, noise or reservations.

WARD MUSEUM OF WILDFOWL ART

Salisbury - *909 S Shumaker Drive 21804. www.wardmuseum.org. Phone: (410) 742-4988. Hours: Monday-Saturday 10:00am-5:00pm, Sunday Noon-5:00pm. Closed major winter holidays. Admission: $7.00 adult, $5.00 senior, $3.00 student or child. School group tours are $3.00-$4.00 per person. Note: Classes on elementary carving (with soap) for kids are held often with master carvers assisting. A beginners decoy painting kit is available in the gift shop, too. The Nature Trail is 2 miles long and hooks up with the zoo. Plaquards along the way detail flora and fauna.*

This museum has the largest collection of bird carvings in the world! Antique decoys and modern carvings are displayed along with waterfowling history interpretations and development of decoy carving. By now, you've probablyheard of the Ward Brothers who started this new art form. The Ward Brothers Workshop is a stylized recreation of their workshop and contains examples of their carving, painting and poetry used as work or inspiration. Begin in The Decoy in Time Hall which focuses on the history of the decoy as a hunter's tool. The Habitat Theatre takes a detailed look at natural wildfowl environments. To engage the kids interest, ask for an Activity Sheet to complete. Look for decoy ducks; birds nesting in a tennis shoe; American Indian primitive decoys and the many ways hunters hide to trick the waterfowl.

CHESAPEAKE WILDFOWL EXPO

Salisbury - *Ward Museum of Wildfowl Art. Shootin' stool competition, old decoy contest, auction, search/rescue dog demos, pig roast, water fowling, cooking demonstrations. (second long weekend in October)*

FURNACE TOWN LIVING HERITAGE MUSEUM

Snow Hill - *3816 Old Furnace Road (SR 12, 14 miles south of Salisbury) 21863. Phone: (410) 632-2032. www.furnacetown.ocom. Hours: Daily 10:00am-5:00pm (April-October). Admission: $3.00-$5.00 (age 2+).*

This is an iron manufacturing village from long ago located in Pocomoke Forest. The interpretive program at Furnace Town is an effort to bring to life the

daily life activities of this 19th century village. Highlights of the self-guided tour include: the organ playing in the old church; the Charging Ramp (imagine filling the carts and then hauling them up the ramp to pour into a 3000 degree furnace hole!); and artifacts found on

the property displayed in the museum

up and down the charging ramp...

inside a furnace...

(many you can touch). Also, artisans recreate the various crafts and professions that were part of Furnace Town during its life. We met the town weaver and a kitchen gardener harvesting peanuts. The 35' high furnace was designed to smelt bog ore found in the swamp just behind the structure. Later, it had a heating element added to make pig iron. Pig iron bars were sold and melted to make iron artillery, stoves, nails, well pumps, skillets, etc. Their models of an iron furnace are the best interpretation we've seen anywhere.

CHESAPEAKE CELTIC FESTIVAL

Snow Hill - Furnace Town Living Heritage Museum. www.celticfest.net. Bagpipe bands, sheep herding, Celtic music & dance on three outdoor stages, medieval encampment, ethnic foods, marketplace & more. Admission. (first weekend in October)

19TH CENTURY CHRISTMAS

Snow Hill - Furnacetown. Open house with the village trimmed for Christmas. Animals, crafts and shopping. Admission. (first two Saturdays in December)

MT. ZION ONE-ROOM SCHOOL MUSEUM

Snow Hill - *117 Ironshire Street (Ironshire and Church Streets) 21863. Phone: (410) 632-0669. www.octhebeach.com/museum/Zion.html. Hours: Tuesday-Saturday 1:00-4:00pm (mid-June thru 1st week of September). Admission: $0.50-$2.00 per person.*

The Mt. Zion One Room School House was used as a school until 1931. Years later, a school superintendent moved and restored the school and it has since demonstrated to students and visitors how their forebears were taught in the days of one room schools. McGuffy readers, quill pens, inkwells, slates and a water bucket are in place just as if the students had been dismissed yesterday.

POCOMOKE RIVER STATE PARK & FOREST

Snow Hill - *3461 Worcester Hwy 21863. Phone: (410) 632-2566. http://dnr2. maryland.gov/publiclands/Pages/eastern/pocomokeriver.aspx. Day use FREE.*

The scenic Pocomoke River is the setting for the Pocomoke River State Forest and Park, Shad Landing, and Milburn Landing areas. (Note: Shad Landing is on the south side of the Pocomoke River off Route 113. Milburn Landing is on the north side of the river on Route 364. It is a 25 minute drive between the two areas of Pocomoke River State Park). With 14,753 wooded acres in the Southwestern section of Worcester County, between Snow Hill and Pocomoke City, the state forest is famous for its stand of loblolly pine and for its cypress swamps which border the Pocomoke River. Pocomoke means black water, and there is good fishing in these waters. The river originates in the Great Cypress Swamp in Delaware and flows southwesterly 45 miles to the Chesapeake Bay. Recreation features include: biking trails, boat launch, boat rental, camp fire programs, camp sites, camp store, fishing, flat water canoeing, hiking trails, picnic shelters, swimming pool (seasonal) and center.

PURNELL MUSEUM

Snow Hill - *208 West Market Street 21863. www.purnellmuseum.com   Phone: (410) 632-0515. Hours: Tuesday-Saturday 10:00am-4:00pm, Sunday 1:00-4:00pm. Admission: $3.00 adult (age 13+).   Note: Ask for the History Hunt Scavenger hunt worksheet from the cashier. They usually have some around for school group tours.*

The Julia A. Purnell Museum offers interpretive exhibits of many aspects of the lives of Snow Hill and Worcester Countians. A time-line parallels the history of Worcester County with the history of the United States. Kitchen and hearth exhibits show visitors the utensils and methods used to keep a happy home during the 18th and 19th centuries. A "general merchandise" welcomes browsers back to a time when communities were built around the local general store. The Victorian era is also represented, complete with clothing, jewelry and everyday items made of silver and exquisitely carved ivory. Machines and tools show the many "modern" improvements Mrs. Purnell experienced. Kids like the display of toys, games and bicycles.

VICTORIAN CHRISTMAS CELEBRATION

Snow Hill - Julia A. Purnell Museum, Attend an old-fashioned holiday party with Victorian music, decorations & refreshments. Admission. (first Saturday in December)

CHESAPEAKE BAY MARITIME MUSEUM

St. Michaels - *Waterfront Park, St. Michaels Harbor, Navy Point (Rte. 50 to Easton, right on Rte. 322, right on Rte. 33) 21663. www.cbmm.org. Phone: (410) 745-2916. Hours: Daily 9:00am-5:00pm (May-October); 10:00am-4:00pm (November-April). Admission: $15.00 adult, $12.00 senior (62+) and college students, $6.00 child (6-17).   Educators: Download Oystering or Crab Cakes Curriculum: www.cbmm.org/l_ educators.htm. Note: Lighthouse Overnights for groups and families (run around $35+ per person) can be arranged. Museum admission is included. Bring picnic foods and coolers - a campout in a real lighthouse!*

Situated on the harbor in historic St. Michaels, the Chesapeake Bay Maritime Museum brings to life the story of the Bay and the people who have lived and worked around it. Explore its many exhibit buildings, the world's largest collection of traditional Bay boats, and its fully restored 1879 Hooper Strait Lighthouse. Try on some daper yacht clothes and then climb on board a cruiser and pretend to drive. Listen in on advice at the tackle shop or oyster boat. Young kids may want to "Rub-a-dub-dub" at rubbing stations or read a storybook "My Life as an Oyster." Meet local crafters; pull up crab pots and nipper for oysters; and enjoy interactive exhibits exploring the Bay's role in our nation's history: the sport and art of Chesapeake decoys, the golden age of steamboats, and oystering on the Chesapeake. Unlike most museums, the Chesapeake Bay Maritime Museum offers you the real thing: people who actually live the story they tell. In the Museum's working Boat Yard, you can watch the restoration of the Bay's traditional vessels and go talk with the shipwrights, apprentices, or a visiting captain or boat builder. Lots to do and see. Nicely done, plan on a few hours here.

MID-ATLANTIC SMALL CRAFT FESTIVAL

"Thor" was a sunken old workboat, now a playground...how cool!

St. Michaels - *Chesapeake Bay Maritime Museum. www.cbmm. org. Amateur and professional boat builders and enthusiasts bring their kayaks, canoes, and skiffs to show and race. Museum open too. Admission. (first Saturday in October)*

OYSTERFEST

St. Michaels - *Chesapeake Bay Maritime Museum. Shucking, tonging, nippering, children's activities, live music, boat rides and purchase raw, steamed and fried oysters. Admission. (first Saturday in November)*

You will be surprised to learn that in 1608, it took only three days for oysters to clean the bay water; now it takes a year or more.

TILGHMAN ISLAND DAY FESTIVAL

Tilghman Island - www.tilghmanmd.com. Local seafood, live music, watermen contests, artisans, championship docking, oyster shucking, crab picking contests and an auction. Admission. (third Saturday in October)

TILGHMAN ISLAND SUMMER SEAFOOD FESTIVAL

Tilghman Island - Fire Station & Kronsberg Park. www.tilghmanmd.com. Local seafood, live music, crab races, crafts and fireman's parade. (fourth Saturday in June)

WYE GRIST MILL AND MUSEUM

Wye Mills - 900 Wye Mills Road (Rt.662) (Rte. 662 off Rte. 50) 21676. Phone: (410) 827-6909. http://oldwyemill.org. Hours: Friday & Saturday 10:00am-4:00pm, Sunday 1:00-4:00pm (April-November). Grindings the 1st and 3rd Saturday of the month.

General George Washington and his troops owed a debt of gratitude to Wye Mills. During the Revolutionary War, the Wye Grist Mill supplied flour to the Continental army - helping this area earn the reputation as the "breadbasket of the Revolution." Today, the 1681 mill operates as a living museum and houses an exhibit titled, "Wheels of Fortune," which tells the story of the Shore's agricultural history. Every other Saturday, the mill comes to life when volunteers demonstrate how the massive steel water wheel, the grinding stones, and maze of chutes and elevators were used to grind wheat and corn. Did you know this Mill is the beaten biscuit capital of the world? Leavening agents were rare in Colonial times so bakers discovered that biscuits would rise if the dough was beaten for thirty minutes with a hammer or back of an axe. The Orrell family mill in town has been making the round, dense biscuits and today operates the world's only commercial beaten biscuit business. Stop by for a bag to go. $2.00 donation requested.

Chapter 5
Southern
Area

Chesapeake Beach
- Beach Trolley
- Breezy Point Beach
- Chesapeake Beach Railway Museum
- Chesapeake Beach Waterpark

Colton's Point
- St. Clements Island Museum

Hollywood
- Greenwell State Park
- Sotterley Plantation

Leonardtown
- St. Mary's River State Park
- Oyster Festival

Lexington Park
- Hampton Inn - Lexington Park
- Linda's Café
- Patuxent River Naval Air Museum

Lusby
- Calvert Cliffs State Park
- Flag Ponds Nature Park

Marbury
- Smallwood State Park

Mechanicsville
- Crazy Corn Maze

Piney Point
- Piney Point Lighthouse Museum & The Black Panther Shipwreck Preserve

Port Republic
- American Chestnut Land Trust
- Calvert County Jousting Tournament

Port Tabacco
- Thomas Stone National Historic Site

Prince Frederick
- Battle Creek Cypress Swamp Sanctuary

Scotland
- Point Lookout State Park

Solomons
- Annmarie Garden
- Calvert Marine Museum

Solomons Island
- Chesapeake Biological Lab Visitors Center
- J.C. Lore & Sons Oyster House
- Stoney's Kingfishers Seafood House

St. Leonard
- Jefferson Patterson Park & Museum

St. Mary's
- World Carnival
- Historic St. Marys City

Waldorf (Beantown)
- Dr. Samuel Mudd Home

A Quick Tour of our Hand-Picked Favorites Around...

Southern Maryland

Escape to **Solomons** at the confluence of the Patuxent River and the Chesapeake Bay. When commercial oyster canning was big business, the village of Solomons was a bustling place.

Start the day with a visit to the **Calvert Marine Museum**, which traces the rich maritime history and diversity of the Chesapeake Bay. Climb to the top of the Drum Point Lighthouse, touch some sea creatures, dress up and captain a skiff or watch as paleo fossils are dug up. To truly appreciate the setting and Solomons, take a leisurely cruise around the island in the Calvert Marine Museum's "bug eye", the Wm. B. Tennison. Back on shore, walk into the village for lunch at a waterside restaurant, then stroll along the Riverwalk that borders the Patuxent and wander through the gift shops or around the Lore Oyster House historical museum. You can stand on the same floorboards used by many an oyster picker back in the day. Because of the quality of the restorations and the modern, kid-friendly exhibits, this is truly our favorite Marine town in the state.

If you want more adventure, nearby **Calvert Cliffs State Park** invites curious kids to find prehistoric treasure (fossils) or just skip along the water.

And, if your kids are really into archaeology, the State Museum of Archaeology is found at **Jefferson Patterson Park & Museum** (St. Leonard). The park is a place full of secrets waiting to be unearthed. Whether you hike miles of trails, explore the interactive Visitor Center, or enjoy one of their special events, you'll leave with a great appreciation for the land and the people who once lived here. As you view artifacts from every county in Maryland, exhibits answer common questions such as, "How do you know how deep to dig?" and "What's the coolest thing scientists have ever found?" There's a Discovery Room full of dress up and old-fashioned toys and tools, too.

After lunch, proceed north to Waldorf (Beantown) and the **Dr. Samuel A. Mudd House**, home of the physician who set the leg of John Wilkes Booth, assassin of President Lincoln. Docents on site stress Mudd's side of the story. Did he deserve to garner the quote we use, "Your name is Mud(d)!" to describe someone who's name is no longer honorable? You decide.

Start another day trip with a visit to **Historic St. Mary's City**, Maryland's premier outdoor living history museum. While there, board the Maryland Dove, for a working lesson on colonial seamanship. The original Dove carried the first colonists from England to Maryland. Experience the life and daily concerns of an early colonial family at the Tobacco Plantation and learn how colonists interacted with Native Americans at the Indian Hamlet. Don't miss the great new exhibits including the Print Shop, St. John's Site Museum and the 1667 Brick Chapel. End you visit to the 17th century with a stop at Farthing's Ordinary Shop. Stop in historic Leonardtown or Lexington Park for lunch at one of the several portion-friendly restaurants.

Sites and attractions are listed in order by City, Zip Code, and Name. Symbols indicated represent:

 Restaurants   Lodging

CALVERT COUNTY FARM TOUR FESTIVAL

County-wide, various farms. www.calvertag.com. Six working farms have demos, hayrides, corn maze, pumpkins, animals, music, food, children's activities, produce, and pony rides. Rain or shine. (third Sunday in October)

BREEZY POINT BEACH

Chesapeake Beach - *Breezy Point Road (Rte. 4 south to MD 260 to Chesapeake Beach. Right on MD 261) 20732. www.co.cal.md.us/residents/parks/getinvolved/. Phone: (410) 535-0259. Hours: Daily daylight hours May - October. Admission: $4.00-$10.00 (age 3+).*

A bayfront park featuring swimming, fishing, picnicking and seasonal camping. Explore the beach, swim in the Bay (nettle nets provided), fish for your dinner or picnic in the shade.

CHESAPEAKE BEACH RAILWAY MUSEUM

Chesapeake Beach - *4155 Mears Avenue (next to parking lot of resort area) 20732. Phone: (410) 257-3892. www.cbrm.org. Hours: Daily 1:00-4:00pm (May-September), Weekends only (Spring and Fall). Admission: Small fee charged seasonally. Note: Summer Children's Programs and evening concerts on summer Thursdays.*

Opened in 1900, this building was the station for a standard gauge railway operating between the District line and Chesapeake Beach. The station service ended in 1935. The site now houses a museum of bay resort and railroad memorabilia. Some rail cars are parked outside and open to look through. Because this is right in the midst of the "action" attractions of town, it's an easy stop to fit into your visit.

CHESAPEAKE BEACH WATERPARK

Chesapeake Beach - *4079 Gordon Stinnett Avenue (Rte. 261, right on Gordon Stinnett) 20732. Phone: (410) 257-1404. www.chesapeakebeachwaterpark.com. Hours: Weekends May-September. Daily 11:00am-7:00pm, when county school is out. Weather permitting. Admission: $19.00-$21.00 (age 2+). Good discounts for county and city residents.*

Eight water slides, fountains, waterfalls, a lagoon, kids' activity pool, water volleyball area, and more treat everyone to a cool time. The adjacent recreational center houses a gym for casual games of basketball or dances, a game room with pool table, meeting rooms with windows over-looking the water, and much more.

ST. CLEMENTS ISLAND MUSEUM

Colton's Point - *38370 Point Breeze Road (Rte. 5 to Morganza and turn west onto Rte. 242. On the mainland overlooking the island) 20626. Phone: (301) 769-2222. www.co.saint-marys.md.us/recreate/stclementsisland.asp. Hours: Daily 10:00am-5:00pm; closed January-late March. Admission: $1.50-$3.00 (age 6+). Tours: Water Taxi tours to St. Clement's Island are available weekends 12:00 noon to 4:00pm from Memorial Day weekend through the end of October (weather permitting). $5.00 per person fare. See the cross on the site of the landing and the Blackistone Lighthouse.*

The museum rests on the east shore of the Potomac River overlooking **ST. CLEMENTS ISLAND STATE PARK**, the "Birthplace of Maryland."(www.dnr.state.md.us/publiclands/southern/stclements.asp). Once on land, you can tour the ecology of the area and peak inside Blackistone Lighthouse.

The Birthplace of Maryland

The Museum itself focuses on the English history that preceded the voyage to Maryland - mostly for political and religious issues. Discover the vision of George Calvert, the First Lord Baltimore, to begin a colony of religious tolerance and his sons' implementation of this plan (he died before they set sail). Learn about the voyage of the Ark and the Dove departing from the Isle of Wight in England on the feast day of St. Clement, the patron saint of mariners. Dress up in Colonial clothes to pose with Lord Baltimore. You'll view a priest's written account of the voyage and landing on the Island - even the early negotiations with the Native Americans for a permanent settlement. How was the yucca plant used as detergent? The Potomac River portion shares the heritage of industries in hunting, crabbing, fishing and oystering. Also on the grounds, the Little Red Schoolhouse is an authentic 19th century one-room school for viewing, set up as if students were out on recess. A dory boat watercraft is on display and the fishing dock outside lures many fishermen. Look for unusual marine life like skate and jelly fish – or maybe try to catch the infamous blue crab swimming by.

BLESSING OF THE FLEET

Colton's Point - *St. Clement's Island/Potomac River Museum. Seafood demos, rides for kids, parades and food. www.blessingofthefleetmd.com. Admission. (first weekend in October)*

GREENWELL STATE PARK

Hollywood - *(Rte. 245 to Steerhorn Neck Road) 20636. Phone: (301) 373-9775. http://dnr2.maryland.gov/publiclands/Pages/southern/greenwell.aspx.*

The park consists of land along the Patuxent River and features ten miles of hiking, equestrian and cycling trails, as well as a fishing pier. The focal point of the park is Rosedale Manor House with spectacular river views. The Francis Knott Lodge offers overnight accommodations for groups. There's a beach and swimming. Day use park entrance is $3.00-$4.00 per vehicle.

SOTTERLEY PLANTATION

Hollywood - *44440 Sotterley Wharf Road (Rt. 4 to Solomons, cross the Thomas Johnson Bridge, go to Rt. 235 and turn right heading north 4-5 miles to Rt. 245) 20636. Phone: (301) 373-2280. www.sotterley.org. Hours: Tuesday-Sunday 10:00am-4:00pm (May-October). Admission: Tours: $5.00-$10.00 per person (age 6+). Self-guided tours are $3.00-$5.00 per person.*

Located on the banks of the Patuxent River, this very early 18th-century Tidewater Plantation features an architecturally significant manor house of unique post-in-ground construction and fine Georgian woodwork. Sotterley was home to generations of prominent families including that of the third Governor of Maryland, and later, that of financier J.P. Morgan. It was also home to hundreds of anonymous slaves. The 90-acre site includes gardens with panoramic views of the river, a smokehouse, a "necessary", a 1757 Customs Warehouse, a rare extant slave cabin and nature trails.

FAMILY PLANTATION CHRISTMAS

Hollywood - *Sotterley Plantation. Special tours by candlelight; historical drama; live seasonal music, food and drink available; reservations required. Petting zoo. Carriage toys. Admission. (first weekend in December)*

ST. MARY'S RIVER STATE PARK

Leonardtown - *(Rte. 5 to Camp Cosoma Road) 20634. Phone: (301) 872-5688. http://dnr2.maryland.gov/publiclands/Pages/southern/stmarysriver.aspx Hours: Dawn to dusk.*

Situated at the north end of the St. Mary's River watershed, evidence indicates that Indians lived in the region dating back to 3,000 BC. Arrowheads, axe heads, and pottery can still be found along the stream banks. In 1634, English settlers founded the first colony, named St. Mary's City, near the mouth of the St. Mary's River. At the time of the industrial era, the nearby town of Great Mills relied on the river for power. Birding, fishing and trails are on the developed side of the land. Day use park entrance is $3.00-$4.00/vehicle.

OYSTER FESTIVAL

Leonardtown - St. Marys County Fairgrounds. www.usoysterfest.com. National shucking contest and oyster cook-off, lots of other seafood, exhibits, arts and crafts and live entertainment. Admission. (third weekend in October)

HAMPTON INN

Lexington Park - 22211 Three Notch Road, Route 235 20653. (301) 863-3200 or http:// hamptoninn3.hilton.com/en/hotels/maryland/hampton-inn-lexington-park-LPKMDHX/ index.html. The Hampton Inn Lexington Park hotel is located across from the Patuxent River Naval Air Station Gate 1 in Lexington Park, Maryland. The hotel is about one mile north of the Central Business District and 8 miles southwest of Solomon's Island. Clean, spacious rooms and wonderful beds. Guests also enjoy the following complimentary items: On the House™ hot breakfast, Hampton's On the Run™ breakfast bags (Monday-Friday), high speed internet access in every room, wireless internet access in the lobby. Their breakfast bars are so fresh and plentiful! Outdoor pool, too.

LINDA'S CAFÉ

Lexington Park - 21779 Tulagi Pl, 20653. Route 235. (301) 862-3544 or Leonardstown Town Square, Rte. 245, (301) 475-5395. www.facebook.com/lindascafelpcity Home cooked meals - their specialty is stuffed ham steak or something with scrapple gravy. Lots of flavor. Very fair pricing and large servings. Breakfast all day. Lunch and dinner.

PATUXENT RIVER NAVAL AIR MUSEUM

Lexington Park - *22156 Three Notch Road (intersection of Rte 235 & Pegg Road, Gate 1 of the Warfare Center) 20653. Phone: (301) 863-7418. www.paxmuseum.com. Hours: Tuesday-Saturday 10:00am-5:00pm, Sunday Noon-5:00pm. Admission: $5.00 adult, $3.00 active military, students, senior (65+), child (6-17).*

Indoor exhibits specialize in aircraft models, propulsion systems, the development of the helmet and simulator flight trainers. Kids especially like the history of the ejection seat display. The Flight Deck outside displays actual modern aircraft - so many familiar planes lined up, it looks like a movie scene. With names like Hornet, Tomcat and Stallion, your kids may want to guess names or create new ones. If you wonder what they really do here - the process of testing new equipment is broken down for you. Some tests are ground-based and some are in-flight activities. A trained Navy or Marine Corps test pilot, who has graduated from the US Navy Test Pilot School at Patuxent River, is assigned to fly the test missions. The test team plans for, collects and evaluates Test Data. Not as glamorous inside, the outside display is probably the most fun for kids to look at.

CALVERT CLIFFS STATE PARK

Lusby - *9500 HG Trueman Hwy (Rte 4 south, 14 miles south of Prince Frederick look for the park sign off HG Trueman Hwy) 20657. Phone: (301) 743-7613. http://dnr2.maryland.gov/publiclands/Pages/southern/calvertcliffs.aspx Hours: Daily sunrise to sunset. Admission: $5.00-$6.00 day use park entrance fee per vehicle. Note: Don't want to hike the trail and hunt for fossils? An indoor replica exhibit is at the Calvert Marine Museum.*

A hike through this wooded state park brings you to the majestic Calvert Cliffs on the Chesapeake Bay. Formed in ancient times, the cliffs contain more than 600 species of fossils. The park is ideal for hiking and walking, picnicking, fishing, and fossil hunting. At the entrance there is a wonderful tire park for children and a pond for fishing. There is a 45-minute walk one-way (two miles) to the beach. Fossil collecting can still be done along the open beach near the cliffs. The beach area is small and you need to be watchful of falling clay from the cliffs - especially after heavy storms. Many areas may be off limits.

FLAG PONDS NATURE PARK

Lusby - *(N. Solomons Island Road, Rte. 2 & 4 south, 10 miles past Prince Frederick) 20657. Phone: (410) 586-1477. http://calvertparks.org/fpp.html Hours: Daily 9:00am-6:00pm, weekends until 8:00pm (summer). Weekends only (rest of year). Admission: $5.00-$8.00 per vehicle.*

Visitors frequently find ancient fossils deposited from the Calvert Cliffs. Several miles of trails lead you through a variety of habitats from upland forest, wooded swamps, open marshes and to the beach dune community typical of the Eastern Shore or the Carolinas. The half-mile walk to the beach takes you past relics of a pound net fishery operation from the early 1950s.

The Museum has a Pound-Net Fishing Exhibit interpreting the fishery camp. A fisherman's shanty, the "Buoy Hotel No. 2," clearly demonstrates the camp. From there a "Fisherman's Trail" leads to other historical sites in the park.

SMALLWOOD STATE PARK

Marbury - 2750 Sweden Point Road, off MD 224 20658. Phone: (800) 784-5380. http://dnr2.maryland.gov/publiclands/Pages/southern/smallwood.aspx   Hours: Sunday 1:00-5:00pm (May-September). Admission: Day use park fee is $3.00-$4.00/person.

This is the site of General William Smallwood's Retreat home. Smallwood was a Revolutionary War officer and fourth governor of Maryland. Guided tours by costumed docents or attend a Military exhibition. Marina has great access to the Potomac River. Nearby is the **PURSE STATE PARK** (Rte. 224 on Riverside Road, 301-743-7613) where fossilized sharks teeth, bones and shells are often found along the water's edge during low tide. The beach is basically nonexistent during high tide. Be sure to venture out during low tide.

CRAZY CORN MAZE

Mechanicsville - Forrest Hall Farm & Orchard. www.forresthallfarm.com. More than two miles of trails through a five-acre maze. Ticket includes hayride, visit with farm animals, maze and a pumpkin. Admission. (open to general public on weekends, by appointment on weekdays in September/October)

PINEY POINT LIGHTHOUSE MUSEUM & THE BLACK PANTHER SHIPWRECK PRESERVE

Piney Point - 44701 Lighthouse Road (SR 5 south to Waldorf, thru to Calloway. Turn

a huge bell, and a rubber hami who could resist?

right on Rte. 249, then right at the lighthouse) 20674. Phone: (301) 769-2222. www.co.saint-marys.md.us/recreate/PPL.asp.   Hours: Museum open daily from 10:00am-5:00pm (April-December). Shipwreck preserve open Friday-Monday only (October - early January). Admission: $3.50-$7.00 (ages 6+).

Exhibits now focus on the construction and operation of the lighthouse, the role of the United States Coast Guard, and the attraction of the Piney Point area as a get away for the social elite. Divers are interested in the story of the Black Panther U-1105 German submarine sunk in the Potomac that now serves as Maryland's first historic shipwreck dive preserve. Also on campus is the building that houses the collection of four historic wooden vessels: a skipjack, a bugeye, a log canoe, and a Potomac River dory boat - all used on this River over time. Exhibits focus on the life of the watermen who sustained a livelihood working the waters of the Potomac for crabs, fish and oysters. The Lighthouse grounds and pier are designed for exploring and the lighthouse itself is open to climb during museum hours. Perfect time to come and wander the grounds is near sunset. Known as the "Lighthouse of Presidents", James Madison, Abraham Lincoln and Theodore Roosevelt were among the Presidents who visited Piney Point in its days as a resort for Washington dignitaries.

AMERICAN CHESTNUT LAND TRUST

Port Republic - *20676. Phone: (410) 586-1570. www.acltweb.org. Hours: Dawn to dusk.*

Fifteen miles of serene hiking trails open to the public in two locations. Port Republic (South Trail) and Prince Frederick (North trail). Much of this land was once rich tobacco and crop farming acreage. The cash crop was supplemented by hunting, trapping, and fishing that was easily supported by nearby woods, marshes, and waterways. Guided canoe trips are on the beautiful Parker's Creek, spring through fall. FREE.

CALVERT COUNTY JOUSTING TOURNAMENT

Port Republic - Christ Episcopal Church grounds. www.christchurchcalvert.org. Oldest tournament of Maryland's official state sport; crafts, bazaar, organ recitals and country supper. Admission. (last Saturday in August)

THOMAS STONE NATIONAL HISTORIC SITE

Port Tabacco - 6655 Rosehill Road 20677. www.nps.gov/thst. Phone: (301) 392-1776. Hours: Thursday-Sunday 10:00am-4:00pm (March-December). Admission: FREE. Tours: last approximately 30 minutes. Educators: Lesson Plans & Teachers Guides on the Declaration & Revolution plus post-visit games: www.nps.gov/thst/ learn/education/park/curriculummaterials.htm.

Ranger-Led tours of Haberdeventure, Thomas Stone's home, are offered as insight into the sacrifices of a signer of the Declaration of Independence. In 1770, when Thomas Stone began the construction of his home, he was a modest family man with a career as a lawyer and local political figure.

Haberdeventure, which literally translates as a "dwelling place of or in the winds", was built by Thomas Stone to be the home from which he would raise his family.

But, in 1776, Thomas Stone's world changed, no longer just a country lawyer, by signing the Declaration of Independence he had literally written himself into American History. Thomas Stone spent the rest of his life in public service which necessitated moving his family to Annapolis. The home remained in the family. Visitors are also welcome to experience the park at their own pace to stroll across the park grounds amidst the farm buildings or travel old farm trace roads and imagine the past. The park contains the restored home of Thomas Stone, outbuildings and family cemetery. Both Stone and his wife are buried here. A Visitor Center features exhibits, an orientation film, sales area and restrooms.

BATTLE CREEK CYPRESS SWAMP SANCTUARY

Prince Frederick - *Grays Road (Rte. 4 south, right on Sixes Rd (MD506), turn left on Grays Rd, 1/4 mile on right) 20678. www.calvertparks.org/bccss.html. Phone: (410) 535-5327. Hours: Monday-Friday 9:00am-4:30pm, Saturday 10:00am-4:30pm, Sunday 1:00-4:30pm. Closes later summer weekends. Admission: FREE.*

This unique ecological area is the northernmost naturally occurring stand of bald cypress trees in America. A sub-tropical tree found mostly in the Carolinas and Southeast, cypress stands are unusual this far north. This stand is believed to have established itself sometime in the last 10,000 years. Early settlers in the county, especially boat builders, discovered that cypress wood does not break down readily from bacterial or fungal infection and is virtually rot resistant underwater. A 1/4 mile elevated boardwalk trail meanders through the 100-foot canopy of trees that can reach an age of over 1,000 years. Such swamps were prevalent during the age of mammoths. The Nature Center contains live animals and exhibits about their environment. Live animal demonstrations are often offered. Their cute reading Nook was created from a hollow stump from a tulip tree that blew down. Cute!

POINT LOOKOUT STATE PARK

Scotland - *(junction of Chesapeake Bay & Potomac River, Rte. 5) 20687. Phone: (301) 872-5688. www.dnr2.maryland.gov/publiclands/Pages/southern/pointlookout. aspx. Hours: Dawn to dusk. Admission: $3.00-$5.00 per vehicle (October-April) or $5.00-$7.00 per person (peak weekends).*

Point Lookout lies at the tip of the county peninsula at the confluence of the Potomac River and the Chesapeake Bay. In addition to its historic Civil War Museum (Point Lookout sponsors historic programs and demonstrations throughout the year) and a Nature Center, the park offers abundant recreational opportunities for canoeing, kayaking, and boating, fishing and crabbing, beaching and swimming, cycling and hiking. The site offers camping and cabins for rental. <u>**LIGHTHOUSE & CIVIL WAR MUSEUM**</u>: Point Lookout served as a watch post to warn of British ships traveling the Chesapeake Bay during the Revolutionary War and the War of 1812. Point Lookout Lighthouse was built in 1830 to aid in navigating the Chesapeake Bay (access to the lighthouse is very limited). During the Civil War, Point Lookout served as a Union hospital and a prison camp for captured Confederate soldiers. The site features a Civil War museum and the remains of Fort Lincoln.

EASTER SUNRISE SERVICE

Scotland - *Point Lookout State Park picnic/beach area. Non-denominational service beginning at sunrise. Admission. (Easter Sunday)*

BLUE AND GRAY DAYS

Scotland - *Fort Lincoln within Point Lookout State Park. Civil War living history demos, military and civilians of Point Lookout, no reservations required. Admission. (second weekend in June)*

ANNMARIE GARDEN

Solomons - *13480 Dowell Road (Rte. 4 south, left on Dowell Rd. at Solomons Firehouse) 20688. Phone: (410) 326-4640. www.annmariegarden.org. Hours: Daily 9:00am-5:00pm. Pets allowed except during special events. Admission: $3.00-$5.00 (age 6+).*

This garden is a 30-acre public sculpture park featuring an inviting paved path through the woods past works of outdoor sculpture. Notice the seasonal changes reflected in outdoor art. Some sculptures are gates or ramps. Two favorite works, The Council Ring and A Surveyor's Map invite the guest into the art to walk on, touch, read, and explore how art and nature complement each other. The Tribute to the Oyster Tonger piece is a local heritage favorite. Kids will gravitate to the Childrens Discovery Garden and the Butterfly Garden. Many families like biking, picnicking or walking the trails.

GARDEN IN LIGHTS

Solomons - *Annmarie Garden. Delightful holiday light show full of imaginative creations and "Holiday I Spy" game for kids. Admission. (nightly from second Friday thru New Years Day, except Christmas Eve)*

CALVERT MARINE MUSEUM

Solomons - *14200 Solomons Island Road (Rte 4 south, take the right lane exit just before the Bridge, go left at the stop sign and drive 1/2 block) 20688. Phone: (410) 326-2042. www.calvertmarinemuseum.com. Hours: Daily 10:00am-5:00pm. Admission: $9.00 adult, $7.00 senior (55+), $4.00 child (5-12) - Museum and outdoor exhibits. $7.00 adult and $4.00 child for boat ride. Oyster House viewing is FREE. Tours: The only Coast Guard-licensed log hulled vessel in the US, the WM. B. TENNISON, boards for leisurely one-hour cruises around Solomons Harbor, Biological Research Center, the long span bridge, and the Patuxent River from here. Built in 1899, this Landmark was later converted from sail to power and served as an oyster buyboat until 1978. Cruises are Wednesday-Sunday at 2:00pm (May-October) with weekend additional cruises at 12:30 and 3:00pm (July, August). Note: The COVE POINT LIGHTHOUSE is accessible via a shuttle bus from the Museum, or a drive a few miles north. Tour a piece of history at the oldest continuously working lighthouse in Maryland. Built in 1828, the forty-foot brick tower is surmounted by an iron lantern containing a fourth-order lens. In addition to the light tower and keeper's house, buildings at the station include a 1901 fog signal building, a brick generator/fog signal building and a two-bedroom cottage. Tours seasonally are $3.00 per person. Self-guided tours are free. Groups can overnight here.*

The rich maritime history and diversity of life found in the Bay come alive in this wonderful museum set on land and water. Inside the museum, you'll find boats, models, woodcarvings, oysters and crabbing history, fossils and the incredible Skates and Rays exhibit. Do you know what a Mermaid's Purse is? See live skate embryo in various stages of development inside the purses and a new baby skate, too!

A "hands-on" Discovery Room for children of all ages (preschool to adult) features a touch tank housing creatures from the Chesapeake Bay. The plumbing and systems required to operate the tank and keep the creatures alive are in plain view, allowing interpreters to explain how they work to mimic the natural environment. One of the exciting features is a model of the Cove Point Lighthouse. Visitors are able to climb inside to activate the light, or dress as lighthouse keepers and enter the keeper's cottage. A boat made especially for kids is here for children to practice

their voyaging skills as they climb aboard, raise and lower the sail, or steer.

In the paleontology zone, a segment of the Calvert Cliffs emerge from the mural that decorates the entire wall. At the foot of the cliff, visitors can search for fossils in the beach box and then take their treasures to a fossil identification station to learn about the creature it came from in prehistoric times. And the best part, you get to take your fossil find home as a souvenir!

Another "Wow" area is the Paleo Hall! The prehistoric skeleton of a shark

greets you as you try to place clues together to determine how the animals died. The Treasure From the Cliffs area is where trained scientists are working on current specimens for display.

Outdoors find a boat basin, River Otter habitat, and a recreated salt marsh, complete with a boardwalk over to **DRUM POINT LIGHTHOUSE**. Climb up through the hatch of the Lighthouse constructed in 1883 at Drum Point to mark the entrance to the Patuxent River. This screwpile, cottage-type light is one of only three remaining that once served on the Chesapeake Bay. Beautifully restored, complete with furnishings of the early 20th century, it has become a popular attraction.... probably because the keeper's house is actually part of the tower. By far, this is the most family-friendly maritime museum we have ever visited!

MARITIME FOLKLIFE FESTIVAL

Solomons - *Calvert Marine Museum. Visit the antique boat & marine engine show; taste traditional foods; learn crab picking, oyster shucking and fish filleting; enjoy Gospel and Old-time music; children's games and races; rides on bugeye and draketail work boats; talk with carvers, crab pot makers, watch model boat demos, test your dog in the Chesapeake Bay Retriever Trials; build a toy boat in the boat shed. Admission. (first Saturday in May)*

CHESAPEAKE BIOLOGICAL LAB VISITORS CENTER

Solomons Island - *Charles Street (Rte 4 south, take the right lane exit just before the Johnson Bridge. Left at stop sign, right at MD 2) 20688. Phone: (410) 326-7443. www.umces.edu/cbl. Hours: Tuesday-Sunday 10:00am-4:00pm. (mid-April to mid-December). Admission: FREE. Tours: Lab tours given on Wednesday and Friday at 2:00pm. They last 1.5 hours and are not recommended for small children.*

Founded by a zoologist, now a part of the UM Center for Environmental Science, its mission is to educate college students and the community about the ongoing exploration of the natural world. Experience the true scientific atmosphere of the research facility, learn about the ecology and resources from the Chesapeake Bay and the important discoveries of CBL scientists. The Visitors center is at the end of the island, overlooking the bay. A Welcome Video briefly recounts the history of CBL's founding, introduces the exhibits in the Center, and reviews the basic principles of Chesapeake Bay ecology. A series of both permanent and changing displays highlight Ongoing Research Projects. An Oyster Reef Community Display and Aquarium illustrates marine life associated with oyster reefs. A station devoted to BAYPULSE, illustrates some of the new remote sensing and electronic technologies upon which today's scientists depend. A Research Fleet & GEAR Display focuses on an exhibit of traditional and historical sampling equipment and there's an Oyster Bar Reconstruction and Seagrass Replenishment Display.

J.C. LORE & SONS OYSTER HOUSE

Solomons Island - *14430 Solomons Island Road (just south of the Calvert Marine Museum) 20688. Phone: (410) 326-2042. www.calvertmarinemuseum. com/exhibits/lore-oyster-house.php. Hours: Daily 1:00pm-4:00pm (June-August). Weekends and holidays (May and September). Admission: FREE.*

Visit this restored 1934 seafood-packing house and learn about the boom and decline of the region's commercial seafood industries. The orientation film is made from actual pictures from the mid-1900s. Can you believe all of those shells lying around?? Imagine yourself as a shucker paid by the gallon. Now, stand in the actual workroom. We learned they liked to sing as they worked. In realistic settings, you'll see the tools and gear used by local watermen to harvest fish, soft-shell clams, eels, crabs and oysters. The boat building exhibit, located on the second level of the Oyster House, portrays the present traditions of wooden work-boat building in the region. The dock outside is teeming with boats and sea critters that summer here - jellyfish, oysters and crab. Quite interesting.

STONEY'S KINGFISHERS SEAFOOD HOUSE

Solomon's Island - 14442 Solomons Island Rd   20688. www.stoneysseafoodhouse.com (410) 394-0236. On the water in a favorite waterside town is a nice place to walk to/ from the Calvert Marine Museum. Try a Crabcake or Baby Crabcake. Babies are the size of baseballs, regular, the size of softballs - literally! Also liked the Broomes Island Crab Soup. The Kids Menu has PB&J plus shrimp or grilled cheese plates. Watching the boaters come in is a favorite pasttime while waiting for your food.

JEFFERSON PATTERSON PARK & MUSEUM

St. Leonard - *10515 Mackall Road 20685. www.jefpat.org. Phone: (410) 586-8501. Hours: Wednesday-Sunday 10:00am-5:00pm (mid-April - mid-October). Admission: FREE.*

Jefferson Patterson Park & Museum (JPPM) is a place full of secrets waiting to be unearthed. Whether you come to hike miles of trails, explore the Visitor Center full of interactive exhibits, or to enjoy one of their events, you will leave with a greater appreciation for the land and the people who once lived here.

The Visitor Center houses exhibits on the history of the JPPM property and those who lived here. "FAQ Archaeology" is an interactive exhibit focused on answering some of the most common questions that archaeologists receive, such as "how do you know how deep to dig?" and "what's the coolest thing you've ever found?" View artifacts from every county in Maryland and learn about archaeological discoveries made on Park and Museum property. There's a intro video showing in the theatre and the Discovery Room has a Colonial dress up area plus kids can play with colonial and American Indian tools or toys. Next, try your hand at being an archaeologist and identify artifacts.

The newest arrival is the Indian Village audio tour, "Walking in their Footsteps" showcases a step by step journey through signage and the recreated village itself. You can activate the tour by calling a special number on your cell phone or download the tour to your personal mp3 player.

CELEBRATE MARYLAND ARCHAEOLOGY MONTH

St. Leonard - Jefferson Patterson Park and Museum. Learn how archaeologists study cultures at the Woodland Indian Hamlet and mock archaeology sites. Adults can learn about the actual processes used to expose archaeology in daily life. FREE. (fourth Saturday in April)

CELTIC FESTIVAL & HIGHLAND GATHERING

St. Leonard - Jefferson Patterson Park and Museum. www.cssm.org. Celtic music, dance and craft demos; Highland athletic, bagpipe, and dance competitions; re-enactments, storytellers. Admission. (last Saturday in April)

CHILDREN'S DAY ON THE FARM

St. Leonard - Jefferson Patterson Park. Live farm animals, music, entertainment, scarecrow making, tractor parade, pony rides, wagon rides, story telling, puppet show and magician. Free admission, small fee for some activities. (first Sunday in June)

AMERICAN INDIAN HERITAGE DAY

St. Leonard - Jefferson Patterson Park and Museum. Everyday life as it was around the Chesapeake Bay more than 500 years ago; cultural heritage through visual and performing arts and crafts (basketry, archery, stone tool making) by American Indians from the region (some hands-on participation). Discovery Room open for exploration. Admission. (second Saturday in August)

WAR OF 1812 RE-ENACTMENT

St. Leonard - Jefferson Patterson Park and Museum. Re-enactment at the site of the Battle of St. Leonard Creek; British and American encampments, musket and cannon demonstrations, 19th century crafters and vendors. Tours of Lab offered. Admission. (last Saturday in September)

HISTORIC ST. MARYS CITY

St. Marys City - *(SR 5 & Rosecroft Road, south of Leonardtown) 20686. Phone: (240) 895-4990. www.stmaryscity.org. Hours: Wednesday-Sunday 10:00am-5:00pm (mid-June thru November). Tuesday-Saturday each Spring. Closed Thanksgiving Day and Christmastime, New Years. Admission: $10.00 adult, $9.00 seniors (60+), $6.00 ages 6-18. Audio tour rentals are an additional $3. Note: Hands-on activities are offered at most sites. Special events occur on weekends - kids have the chance to work alongside pro archaeologists (they're currently working on rebuilding original sites for a chapel and print shop), churn butter, watch a militia drill,, or shoot a bow and arrow.*

At Historic St. Mary's City, colorful costumed interpreters appear in recreated 17th-century settings to tell stories about Maryland's first years, when St. Mary's was the colony's capital. You're encouraged to interact with the first person "characters" as you discuss the 1600s and talk to colonists eager to share advice for surviving the seasons and making a new home in the Americas. Outdoor exhibits include the reconstructed State House of 1676, Smith's Ordinary (find out what colonists did for entertainment), and the Godiah Spray Tobacco Plantation, a working colonial

Splitting logs for fence slats...

farm. The wonderful plantation tour treats you, the guest, as a new colonist in this fair land. Tobacco - why was it so cool back then? - more popular than coffee or chocolate. Reenactors use the children to split logs, properly greet one another, pick herbs, or use balm as furniture polish. At the village's Woodland Indian Hamlet, visitors discover how Maryland's native population interacted positively with English Colonists.

Sailors' stories of the tobacco trade and immigration resound across the deck of the Maryland Dove, a replica square-rigged ship. What was it like? Where did you sleep? What did they eat? The site offers 5 miles of wooded and waterside trails, too. Did you know St. Marys City was the location of the first printing press in the south and the first Catholic chapel in English America? Newly discovered properties open often (ex. Personal homes). Audio, video and hands-on exhibits enhance the spaces. Very interactive, professional docents make this attraction a must family day trip.

MARYLAND DAY

St. Mary's City - *Historic Area. Celebrate Maryland's birthday with pageantry and ceremonies marking the founding of the state in 1634. Tour the living history exhibits and fly over to the kite festival – BYOK. FREE. (March 25th or close to)*

MARITIME HERITAGE FESTIVAL

St. Mary's City - *Waterfront. Big boats, little boats, work boats, play boats. Hands-on activities for children of all ages. Learn a new skill or take a cruise on the St. Mary's River. Then, cheer on your favorite contender in the model sailboat regatta. Admission. (third Saturday in June)*

TIDEWATER ARCHAEOLOGY WEEKEND

St. Mary's City - *Historic Area. Help archaeologists remove pieces of the past from excavations; watch as artifacts are identified; lab tours. Admission. (last weekend in July)*

WOODLAND INDIAN DISCOVERY DAY

St. Mary's City - *Historic Area. Explore American Indian culture and skills through demos and hands-on activities. Try a traditional dance, shoot a bow and arrow, learn to start a fire without a match. Storytelling. Admission. (second Saturday in September)*

GRAND MILITIA MUSTER

St. Mary's City - *Largest gathering of 17th century reenactment units in the nation. "Competitions! Color! Pageantry!" Visit with militia families at one of the largest gatherings of 17th-century re-enactors in the U.S. Hearth cooking, mock battle, drills, and sutlers. Admission. (third Saturday in October)*

HEARTH AND HOME IN EARLY MARYLAND

St. Mary's City - *Historic Area. Discover the ways Maryland's first citizens prepared for winter before supermarkets and department stores. Hands-on activities. Admission. (thanksgiving weekend in November)*

DR. SAMUEL MUDD HOME

Waldorf (Beantown) - *3725 Dr. Samuel Mudd Road (SR 5 South, off Poplar Hill Road) 20601. Phone: (301) 645-6870. http://drmudd.org/ Hours: Wednesday, Saturday 11:00am-4:00pm, Sunday Noon-4:00pm, last tour begins at 3:30pm. (April - late November) Admission: $7.00 adult, $2.00 child (6-12).*

After leaving the Surratt tavern, Booth arrived early the morning of April 15 at the Mudd's house. Dr. Mudd set Booth's broken leg, had crutches made andsent Booth and his friend, Herold upstairs to a bedroom to sleep. Mudd had met Booth on several occasions before - some say discussing Confederate

A house with so much important history...

matters, others claim they were social or business-related meetings.

Docents at the house, now a museum, stress Mudd's side of the story. Mudd didn't recognize Booth in the dim lighting and didn't know of the assassination until later. The original red plush couch where Booth first sat in the parlor and the bedroom where he slept can be seen on the tour. Booth left the Mudd property by horseback down a plantation road, which you can still see behind the house.

At his trial, Mudd was convicted of aiding in the death of Lincoln and received a life sentence at Fort Jefferson Prison (see *Kids Love Florida*). Articles made by Dr. Mudd while incarcerated at the Dry Tortugas prison are on view throughout the house. The game table, secretary table, and jewelry boxes (made with shells and wood from the deserted island). President Andrew Johnson pardoned Mudd in 1869, after Mudd helped save the lives of prisoners and guards during a yellow fever epidemic. Mudd returned home to his wife and they had more children.

VICTORIAN CHRISTMAS

Waldorf - *Dr. Samuel A. Mudd House Museum. Refreshments, Civil War exhibits, music entertainment, Mr. & Mrs. Claus, and walk-through tours. Admission. (first weekend in December)*

Travel Journal & Notes:

Chapter 6
Western
Area

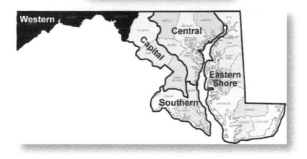

Big Pool
- Fort Frederick

Boonsboro
- Crystal Grottoes Caverns
- Greenbrier State Park
- South Mountain State Park Battlefield
- Washington Monument State Park

Burkittsville
- Gathland State Park & Townsend Museum

Cumberland
- Canal Place Heritage Area
- Gordon-Roberts House
- Western Maryland Scenic Railroad
- Heritage Days Festival

Deep Creek Lake (Accident)
- Husky Power Dogsledding
- Cove Run Farms Corn Maze

Deep Creek Lake (McHenry)
- Smiley's Funzone Pizzeria
- Wisp Resort At Deep Creek Lake
- McHenry Highland Festival
- Deep Creek Lake Fireworks Celebration

Deep Creek Lake (Oakland)
- Lakeside Creamery
- Trader's Coffee House
- Autumn Glory Festival

Deep Creek Lake (Swanton)
- Deep Creek Lake State Park & Discovery Center
- Fireside Deli

Flintstone
- Green Ridge State Forest

Frostburg

- Frostburg State University Planetarium
- Thrasher Carriage Museum

Grantsville
- Savage River State Forest / New Germany & Big Run State Parks
- Spruce Forest Artisan Village

Hagerstown
- Antietam Recreation & Wild West Shows
- Discovery Station
- Hagerstown Speedway
- Maryland Symphony Orchestra (MSO)
- Plaza Hotel, Hagerstown
- Schmankerl-Stube Bavarian Restaurant
- The Train Room
- Hagar House & Hagerstown City Park
- Hagerstown Roundhouse Museum
- Augustoberfest
- Old-Fashioned Cowboy Christmas
- Festival Of Trees

Hagerstown (Clear Spring)
- Wilson Country Store / One Room Schoolhouse

Hagerstown (Williamsport)
- Yogi Bear's Jellystone Park

Hancock
- C & O Canal Visitor Center
- Sideling Hill
- Western Maryland Rail Trail

Lonaconing
- Dans Mountain State Park

Oakland

- Cranesville Subartic Swamp
- Herrington Manor State Park
- Oakland Heritage Square
- Pleasant Valley Dream Rides
- Potomac-Garrett State Forest / Backbone Mountain
- Swallow Falls State Park

Oakland (Mountain Lake Park)

- Broadford Lake Recreation Area
- Simon Pearce Glassblowing

Sharpsburg

- Washington County Rural Heritage Museum
- Antietam Battlefield
- American Deli And Nutter's Ice Cream

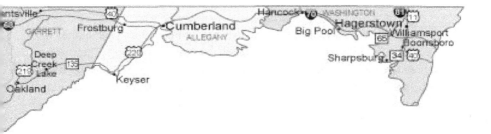

A Quick Tour of our Hand-Picked Favorites Around...

Western Maryland

Western Maryland is an escape to the mountains. Start your journey west (from the DC/Capital area) at the historic town of Hagerstown. They have an active **City Park** with festivals galore and, next-door, the interesting **Hagar House**, with its peculiar feeling - it's more about the house and its stories than the furnishings. Hagerstown also has its own children's museum, train museums and an adorable Bavarian restaurant downtown.

Antietam National Battlefield is not too far away (south) in Sharpsburg. This peaceful family town was the place where the slow moving giant armies of the Civil War exploded, leaving tens of thousands dead and wounded. Grab a map and take the driving tour alongside the battlefield, stopping at the "peace" church and the famous walk out to the Burnside Bridge.

Arrive in Cumberland at the **Western Maryland Scenic Railroad** in time to board the Steam Train or Diesel for a wonderful ride through Maryland's beautiful mountains. Have a "hobo lunch" on board or save your appetite for the various delis back at the train depot. Spend the rest of the day at the **Canal Place** attractions. Enter a re-created Paw Paw Tunnel to the exhibits related to boat building, coal mining, trains and canals. The highlight is the giant, full size replica Canal Boat you can pretend play on or move the locks and dams on the play tables.

Further west is our favorite Maryland Mountain area for families – Deep Creek Lake. With 65 miles of shoreline, **Deep Creek Lake** is Maryland's largest freshwater lake. Stay in a lakeside cabin or lodge. Take a boat tour around the lake or a carriage tour along the mountainside. You'll have plenty of choices at this four-season resort area: fishing, boating, swimming, hiking, biking, nature centers, and fun eateries lacing the perimeter among them.

Once temperatures drop, that's when skiers and snowboarders arrive at the **Wisp** at Deep Creek Mountain Resort. For something different, try snow tubing – or water-tubing slides and ski top mountain biking each summer. Wisp Resort has so much to offer, you won't be able to everything in one visit.

The outlying towns that make up the Deep Creek Lake area are full of hidden gems. Go on the dogsled ride you've dreamed of at **Husky Power Dogsledding** – they run in snow and summer trails. Once off, it is peacefully quiet, the only sounds are those of the snow or brush crunching under you, the panting of the dogs eager to run, and the musher's strong calls. You just hold on and relax! See some of Maryland's best waterfalls at **Swallow Falls State Park** where a short walk out to the observation points contains the state's most breathtaking scenery. Or, walk along a catwalk viewing providing a birds-eye view of the delicate, deliberate process of glassblowing at **Simon Pearce Glassblowing Factory**.

Sites and attractions are listed in order by City, Zip Code, and Name. Symbols indicated represent:

 Restaurants   Lodging

FORT FREDERICK

Big Pool - *11100 Fort Frederick Road (18 miles west of town - one mile south of I-70 (Rte. 56 exit 12) 21711. Phone: (301) 842-2155. http://dnr2.maryland.gov/publiclands/Pages/western/fortfrederick.aspx Hours: Daily 8:00am-sunset (April-October). 10:00am-sunset (November-March). Closed major winter holidays. Admission: $3.00-$4.00 per person. Weekends in April, May, September, October. Daily Memorial Day-Labor Day. Note: Programs include Artillery Program reenactments and Colonial Children's Day - probably the best time to visit.*

The massive stone fort, Fort Frederick, was built by the colony of Maryland in 1756 to protect the frontier settlers during the French and Indian War. It also served as a prison camp for Hessian soldiers during the Revolutionary War. Union troops used it during the Civil War as a post.

Later, for several generations, the fort was farmed by a family of free-African Americans. The nearby C&O Canal runs through the park. The visitor center offers a 10 minute orientation film, "Legacy of Fort Frederick," upon request. Exhibits highlight aspects of the park's history. Summertime and weekends, costumed interpreters orient and answer questions about life with the fort walls during 4 different time periods or wars. The park also features a boat launch, cross country skiing, camp sites, camp store, food and beverage, fishing, flat water canoeing, hiking trail, historic interest, picnic, playground, shelters, and visitor's center. The Wetlands Trail, 1/3 mile in length, passes along a wetlands area behind the campground.

18TH CENTURY MARKET FAIR

Big Pool - *Fort Frederick State Park. Witness the best 18th-century artisans, craftsmen, and sutlers amid a 1730-1740 encampment. Admission. (last weekend in April)*

CRYSTAL GROTTOES CAVERNS

Boonsboro - *19821 Shepherdstown Pike, Rte. 34 (one mile south of Alt. Hwy 40, six miles from Antietam) 21713. www.crystalgrottoescaverns.com. Phone: (301) 432-6336. Hours: Daily 10:00am-5:00pm (April-November); Weekends only 11:00am-4:00pm (December-March). Admission: $20.00 adult, $10.00 child (11 & younger). Cash only. Discount coupon online. FREEBIES: Word Search: www. crystalgrottoescaverns.com/pdf/wordsearch.pdf.*

Maryland's only commercial underground caverns feature many pure white-colored stalactites and stalagmites; natural sculptures and other formations that can be seen from illuminated walkways, including 'Old Father Time,' 'The King on His Throne,' and the cathedral ceiling chandelier in the 'Crystal Palace' room. The Lake Room contains a reflecting pool that shows off stalactites on a 16-foot ceiling that is out of the visitor's line of view. Well-informed guides explain the history, formations, and geological aspects of the caverns on a 40-minute tour. The walkways are dry with only a few stairs and a graded ramp at the exit, making Crystal Grottoes one of the easiest show caves to visit.

GREENBRIER STATE PARK

Boonsboro - *21843 National Pike (I-70 exit 42, Rte. 17 north thru Myersville. Turn left onto US 40 for 3 miles) 21713. Phone: (301) 791-4767. http://dnr2.maryland. gov/publiclands/Pages/western/greenbrier.aspx Hours: Daily 8:00am-sunset. Admission: $3.00-$5.00 per person (summers); $3.00 per vehicle (rest of year). Out-of-state residents add $2 to all day use service charges.*

Located in the Appalachian Mountains, this state park offers many recreational opportunities. The man-made freshwater lake offers swimming, sunbathing, boating and fishing opportunities. There are also hiking trails which meander through a variety of wildlife habitats and afford a view of the area's geological history. Picnic tables and grills and playgrounds are available in the day-use area.

SOUTH MOUNTAIN STATE BATTLEFIELD

Boonsboro - *Park Office is at Alt. 40 at Turners Gap @ Washington Monument (the battlefield stretches for 7 miles along the back of South Mountain between Washington & Gathland State Parks) 21713. Phone: (301) 791-4767.   http:// dnr2.maryland.gov/publiclands/Pages/western/southmountainbattlefield.aspx Hours: Daily 8:00am-4:00pm, weather permitting. Admission: FREE.*

Maryland's first battlefield! Fought September 14, 1861, the Battle of South Mountain was the first major battle of the Civil War to be fought in Maryland, three days before Antietam. The battle was the turning point of Lee's Maryland campaign with over 6,000 casualties falling in the long, one-day battle. Hiking (along part of the Appalachian Trail) and picnicking are available.

WASHINGTON MONUMENT STATE PARK

Boonsboro - *(four miles east of Boonsboro and 1 1/2 miles north of Alternate Route 40 on Monument Road) 21713. Phone: (301) 733-0462. http://dnr2.maryland. gov/publiclands/Pages/western/washington.aspx   Hours: Daily 9:00am-sunset. Admission: $2.00-$3.00/vehicle.*

Sitting atop South Mountain, this park is home to the first monument built in honor of George Washington. Locals built it from "blue stones" in the area and it is said to be a monument built with "the purest of intentions." In addition, the park offers camping for youth groups, picnicking, and shelters for a rental fee.

GATHLAND STATE PARK & TOWNSEND MUSEUM

Burkittsville - *900 Arnoldstown Rd (junction of Gapland Road, one mile east of MD 67, 1 mile west of town, off MD Route 17) 21718. Phone: (301) 791-4707. http://dnr2.maryland.gov/publiclands/Pages/western/gathland.aspx.   Hours: Park open year round; museum open weekends Noon-5:00pm (April-October). Admission: FREE. Note: Gathland State Park sponsors Civil War living history events featuring individual reenactor units on weekends throughout the year. The annual Civil War weekend, the largest living history event, features artillery firing and infantry demonstrations and is held on the second weekend in September.*

Gathland stands atop South Mountain at Cramption's Gap, one of three gaps involved in the Battle of South Mountain in September 1862, two days before the fateful battle of Antietam. George Alfred Townsend, youngest Civil War Correspondent, author and columnist, built a unique estate on the site in the late 1800s and erected a large stone arch in memory of his fellow correspondents, artists and photographers. The museum chronicles Townsend's life and touches on artifacts and replicas of Civil war weapons and uniforms. The Appalachian Trail traverses the park and nature lovers are offered picturesque hiking trails and many picnicking sites.

CANAL PLACE HERITAGE AREA

Cumberland - *Western MD Railway Station, 13 Canal Street (I-68, exit 43C, left at bottom of ramp, then straight) 21502. Phone: (301) 724-3655 or (800) 989-9394. www.canalplace.org. Hours: Daily 9:00am-5:00pm. Some aspects closed on Monday and Tuesday in winter months. Admission: FREE.*

- <u>GREAT ALLEGHENY PASSAGE TRAIL OF MARYLAND</u> is the 21 mile local section of an interstate hiker/biker trail starting in Pittsburgh and ending in Cumberland. (www.ahtmtrail.org or phone 301-777-2161)

- <u>C & O CANAL NATIONAL HISTORICAL PARK VISITOR CENTER</u>: (https://www.nps.gov/choh/index.htm) The park features an orientation area with park maps, brochures, and general C&O Canal information. Visitors enter the main exhibit area through a re-created Paw Paw Tunnel (this is a really cool illusion and a great way to get you in the mood). Once inside the main exhibit hall, kids can play in and interact with exhibits related to boat building at the Cumberland boatyards, the Alleghany County coal industry that shipped on the canal and the significance of Cumberland, Maryland as a transportation center. The highlight exhibit is the giant, full size replica Canal Boat (look for the kitchen table, even!) If

the kids don't understand how canal lock and dams work, they have an easy video along with mini-diorama to explain it simply. Lots of stations have talking phones that make it fun for kids, too. Great job on display content. (301) 722-8226.

inside the giant canal boat...

-

- **CUMBERLAND FULL SCALE C & O CANAL BOAT REPLICA**: Located along the Trestle Walk at Canal Place, guides in period clothing discuss the history of the C&O Canal and daily life aboard a canal boat. Visitors can tour the mule shed, hay house, and furnished Captain's cabin. Stand at the tiller and picture yourself on the historic C&O Canal with a load of coal bound for Georgetown. See how families lived and worked on the canal.

- **SHOPS AT CANAL PLACE**: The Shops at Canal Place offer a unique shopping experience, featuring one-of-a-kind gifts and souvenirs, delectable treats, and fabulous dining. The Shops include Awesome Gifts & Collectibles, Arts at Canal Place, Queen City Creamery, The Crabby Pig, Timeless Treats, Tree House Toy Shop, Wild Mountain Cafe, and Simply Maryland. Hours of individual stores vary.

- **GEORGE WASHINGTON'S HEADQUARTERS**: Riverside Park at Greene Street. One room cabin used by a young George Washington while aiding General Braddock. Built in 1754-55, it is the only remaining structure of Fort Cumberland. (301)-777-5132.

CANALFEST / RAILFEST

Cumberland - CanalPlace. Events and activities for visitors of all ages, this festival celebrates the transportation history of the Queen City with many modern twists. Free entertainment. (second weekend in July)

GORDON-ROBERTS HOUSE

Cumberland - 218 Washington Street 21502. http://gordon-robertshouse.com/. Phone: (301) 777-8678.   Hours: Wednesday-Saturday 10:00am-5:00pm. Tours on the hour.   Note: The Allegheny County Historical Museum is also downtown and open every day but Monday and holidays. Best to visit during special events.

Visitors are welcomed by costumed tour docents that escort them along three floors of the home illustrating the lifestyle of an upper-middle class family of the late 1800's. During Tea Socials, enjoy a soothing cup of tea served by an elegantly costumed server. This 1867 home was built for Josiah Gordon, a President of the C&O Canal. The second family to live in the home was the W. Milnor Roberts family who lived in the home for sixty years and added modern conveniences such as indoor plumbing and an elevator which ran between the first and second floor.

A Museum-Explorer Tour is offered to school-age children. This tour offers children the opportunity to use clues to find specific items in the house and highlights how people lived, worked, and played in the 1800s. Victoria Mouse House Tour- young visitors will meet Victoria Mouse, The Gordon-Roberts House puppet, and help her gather items to pack for a trip. Items Victoria will need for her trip are pictured on a handout allowing young visitors to look for those items as they tour the museum. A small admission is charged.

WESTERN MARYLAND SCENIC RAILROAD

Cumberland - *13 Canal Street (2nd floor of Canal Place) 21502. Phone: (301) 759-4400 or (800) TRAIN 50. www.wmsr.com. Admission: Basic 3.5 hour tours cost around $45.00 for adults and about $30.00 for kids. Add $15.00-$30.00 for lunch option. Military discounts.*

The restored early 20th century train steams on a 32-mile round trip through the mountains between Cumberland and Frostburg. Enjoy three centuries of transportation history on scenic excursions or special events (Day out with Thomas week). The scenery is beautiful any time of year and they stop for a short layover in Frostburg to stretch and purchase a treat. We also recommend you purchase or bring coloring books/crayons; travel games and a deck of cards to do along the way (unless the excursion is a themed one with entertainment on board). The Western Maryland Scenic Railroad departs at 11:30am or 1:00pm, Thursday-Sunday (May-December).

NORTH POLE & SANTA'S EXPRESS TRAINS

Cumberland - *Canal Place depot. The North Pole Express departs Cumberland at 6:00pm (Santa's Express departs at 11:30am), and the round trip lasts approximately 3 1/2 hours. Jolly Santa meets the train at the Depot in Frostburg, where riders will be served cookies and hot chocolate or candy canes. Admission. (Thursday, Friday and Saturdays in December, up to weekend before Christmas)*

HERITAGE DAYS FESTIVAL

Cumberland - *Washington Street historic district. www.heritagedaysfestival.com. 250 arts and crafts and food booths; demos, entertainment, encampments, carnival, historic tours, steam train excursions. Some admission for select activity. FREE. (second weekend in June)*

HUSKY POWER DOGSLEDDING

Deep Creek Lake (Accident) - *2008 Bumble Bee Road (I-68 exit 14A to US 219 south 10 miles to McHenry. At Mosser Road, turn left bear right and then bear left onto Bumble Bee for 2-3 miles) 21520. Phone: (301) 746-7200. www.HuskyPowerDogsledding.com. Tours: Kennel visit: year round, reservations necessary, 1-2 hours, minimum $100.00 fee up to 5 people...$20.00 each person over 5 person minimum. Mushing Ride: $275.00 or $195.00 per person (two people) (includes Kennel tour). Minimum age for mushing rides and kennel tours is 8 years old.*

Dogsledding is a very popular recreational sport in many northern states, and now can be enjoyed in Maryland all year round! Depending on the time of year (cooler is better), make your arrangements with the enthusiastic and commanding couple who operate this unique business. Why do these dogs prefer cold temperatures? Siberian and Alaskan Huskies love the cold! As you pull down the driveway and they see visitors, they yelp, almost yelling with glee - showing you how excited they are to pull today! An adorable doggy playground! Equally exciting are the yelps and expressions of glee from your

Now here's a sign we don't see everyday...

kids when they see the beautiful dogs by their individual kennels. As everyone quickly stumbles out of the vehicle, Linda will begin to describe certain characteristics of the dogs, show you a video about the dogs and their love for mushing, and how they train them to obey commands. All done with the dogs yelping for more hugs, fresh water, or the first chance to be on the pull team! The dogs are so healthy and each is adorable with different colored fur, eyes, paws. Each and every dog is named, too. Often the names fit their personality. Zsa Zsa is the female dominant dog of the whole lot - a pampered queen, she gets attention first to show the rest of the team she's top dog. How do the dogs get chosen for lead, pull or wheel positions (clue: it has to do with how smart they are)? The command "Gee" means what? How about "straight on"?

Now, the most memorable part: dog sledding or carting. No Snow? - they still go out on the "Dogsled-on-Wheels" - a specialized cart mushers use to train their dogs when there's no snow. Once the dogs are tied onto the line, they can't wait to be released and pull. Once off, it is peacefully quiet, the only sounds are those of the snow or brush crunching under you, the panting of the dogs eager to run, and the musher's strong calls. You just hold on and relax. Once back at base, the dogs are anxious to be served hearty compliments, hugs and fresh water. What an unforgettable treat!

The dogs LOVE to run... hang on Jenny!

COVE RUN FARMS CORN MAZE

Deep Creek Lake (Accident) - *Cove-Run Farms (I-68 exit 14A, 3.5 mile south to right on Cove Run). www.coverunfarmscornmaze.com. Ten-acre educational corn maze, pumpkin patch, play area, pedal tractor track, barn tours of working dairy farm – milk or feed cows, snacks for purchase. Admission. (mostly Friday – Sunday afternoons/ evenings, other weekdays by appointment in September/October)*

SMILEY'S FUNZONE PIZZERIA

Deep Creek Lake (McHenry) - *(1/2 mile north of Deep creek Bridge on Rte. 219) 21541. Phone: (301) 387-0059. www.dclsmileys.com. Hours: Daily afternoons until 9:00pm or later. Schedule changes seasonally. Admission: FREE. All amusements operate on tickets ($4.00-$8.00 generally) or an all day wristband (miles of smiles, $34.50).*

Whether you're a kid or a kid at heart, you'll love Smiley's. Start outside with Frontier Adventure Golf with greens, traps and water hazards. Or, one of three go-cart tracks, batting cages or Splash & Crash bumper boats. We loved the fact that each activity is monitored by roaming managers and cameras for safety and prevention of rowdy youth acting up. Heading indoors, try Lazer Tag or Lazer Target (ex. Duck hunting), two arcade buildings (with the latest video and redemption games) or Old Time Photography (dress in old time western wear or contemporary magazine cover scenes). After you're exhausted from the activities, re-energize with a snack or a meal. Try Smile'n Supreme pizza. They have wings voted the best on the lake and for hot buffalo wings, we agree. Also, soups and salads, appetizers like cheese fries or onion rings or maybe some wonderful homemade spaghetti and meatballs. Sandwich and wraps, too. Their kid's menu has 10 items to select from - all under $5.00.

WISP RESORT AT DEEP CREEK LAKE

Deep Creek Lake (McHenry) - *290 Marsh Hill Road (US 219) 21541. Phone: (800) 462-9477. www.wispresort.com.   Admission: Rates as low as $99.00 per night. Adventure Packages as low as $59 per person (several activities included).*

This casual resort has almost too many activities to choose from. Most roomscome with continental breakfast which you need to fill up on to have energy for your day! With energy to burn, either take a dip, play or swim laps in the huge, warm indoor pool, hot tub (the deck has warming lights to keep you cozy and dry faster), fitness center and racquetball courts. Or, venture outside for some extreme sports....

Slippery Slope fun...

SUMMER: Wisp Outdoors - experience new adventures each day. Wisp offers water and land sports such as water skiing, paint ball (target or combat), whitewater rafting, rock climbing, golf, kayaking, fly fishing, and disc golf. They also now have a Canopy Tour (tree top ziplines) and Mountain Buggy rides. Oversized terrain vehicles bring a whole new dynamic to touring the mountain. Weekend and some evening sunset pontoon rides, bonfires, and concerts, too. You'll notice many disc golf holes on your way up the scenic chairlift ride - it's long and slow enough to take in the scenery. For another fun adventure, try taking mountain bikes up the lift and down the mountain! With your trail map in hand, try the beginner Possom Trail first. Your first ride will probably go slow and you'll use your brakes most of the time. After that, you'll know the trail and can coast more and ride faster (best for kids age 8+ with some bike riding skill). What fun, though! Grab

Ski slope mountain biking...

some lunch at Wispers and then head back out to cool off on the Summer Tubing ramp - a slippery wet slide. Not too extreme, the whole family can tube. Don't want as much adventure? Try a leisurely pontoon boat tour on the Lake (departs from the Discovery Center). Ask the captain to point out the various restaurants to try and folks who own some beautiful lakefront homes.

WINTER: 32 slopes and trails of ski-able terrain that includes a new super pipe, 2 RailParks, Terrain Trails and Gardens. Ski Carpet and Tow Ropes, Chairlifts. Cross-country snowshoe and snowmobile tours, snow tubing and snowboarding.

YEAR-ROUND: Popular in Europe, the Mountain Coaster at Wisp Resort is only the fourth one built in the United States, and the second on the East Coast. The Mountain Coaster is a hybrid of an alpine slide and a roller coaster. Riders travel 1,300 feet uphill before descending, twisting, turning, dipping and rolling for 3,500 feet downhill. The attraction is open year-round, and operates at night as well.

FLAG ON MOUNTAIN MARYLAND

McHenry - *Wisp Resort Hotel. A patriotic tribute to our country including music and a living American Flag. (Flag Day, June 14th).*

MCHENRY HIGHLAND FESTIVAL

Deep Creek Lake (McHenry) - *Garrett County Fairgrounds. Complimentary shortbread along with Celtic fun including athletic games, fiddlers, bagpipes, sheep dogs, concerts, dancing, craft and food. Admission. www.highlandfest.info. (first Saturday in June)*

DEEP CREEK LAKE FIREWORKS CELEBRATION

Deep Creek Lake (McHenry) - *Deep Creek Lake. Food music, games and spectacular fireworks display launched off the mountain overlooking the Lake. www. deepcreeklakeinfo.com. (July 4th)*

LAKESIDE CREAMERY

Deep Creek Lake (Oakland) - *20282 Garrett Hwy 21550. Rte. 219 or inside Smiley's Funzone. (301) 387-2580 or www.lakesidecreamery.com. Over 90 flavors are made on the premises including unique favorites like Cake Batter, Cantelope, Graham Cracker*

Swirl, PB&J or Cinnamon Bun flavors. Visit by car or boat.

TRADER'S COFFEE HOUSE

Deep Creek Lake (Oakland) - *21311 Garrett Hwy 1/2 mile south of Deep Creek Bridge on Rte. 219 south, 21550. www.traderscoffeehouse.com (301) 387-9246. On a rainy, foggy or chilly morning, this coffee house is a haven for locals and visitors. Freshly brewed coffee and cappuccinos or lattes and wonderful chai tea to start. Juices and smoothies for the kids (or hot cocoa). Need some carbs for an energy breakfast? Try fresh bagels, strudels, Belgian waffles, croissants, cinnamon rolls, doughnuts, quiches and muffins. They have many cozy tables and chairs to cuddle your cup. Before you leave, browse through shelves of books, mugs (we had to get one), local crafts and gift packages to take home.*

AUTUMN GLORY FESTIVAL

Deep Creek Lake (Oakland) - *County wide. www.autumngloryfestival.com. Fall foliage festival. Two parades, official Maryland state banjo and fiddle championships, crafts, Oktoberfest, square dancing, bagpipes, bluegrass, storytellers festival, and a fly-in. 40 events in all. Admission for some. (five days mid-October)*

DEEP CREEK LAKE STATE PARK & DISCOVERY CENTER

Deep Creek Lake (Swanton) - *898 State Park Road (off US 219 or US 495, follow signs) 21561. http://dnr2.maryland.gov/publiclands/ Pages/western/deepcreek.aspx or /discovery.aspx. Phone: (301) 387-4111 or (301) 387-7067 center. Hours: Park open 8:00am-sunset. Center open daily 10:00am-5:00pm (summers); weekends rest of year. Admission: FREE to Discovery Center. Day use charges are $3.00 per person (summertime) or $3.00 per vehicle (rest of year). Add $1.00 for out of state residents. Note: Feeding programs - "We've got Worms" or Critter Encounter; Scales and Tales outside in the Aviary.*

This park is home to black bear, wild turkey, bobcat and one mile of shoreline along the state's largest lake, with public boat access. Besides staying on the lake and loving the outdoor adventure, the park hosts a great kid-friendly Discovery Center. Children can put their hands in a black bear paw print, touch fossils, and sneak a peek under a microscope to learn about local underwater creatures along the shores of the lake. The huge center also displays cultural and historical items, a lighted geography map of the Lake, mounted specimens, an aviary, and children's interactive room. Daily, they show live feed video of a bird's nest or underwater fish pond. The Naturalists ("Ammo" and "Frog") love to catch creatures from the park and display them. Look for red-eye bass, American Toads, or a Monarch butterfly. The Aviary hosts raptors like hawks and the screech owl. The owl has beautiful, big eyes, doesn't he? Check their website to join a planned family hike during your visit. New - a forest canopy walkway!

turtle critter

FIRESIDE DELI

Deep Creek Lake (Swanton) *- 2205 Glendale Road, 2 miles past State Park Rd 21561. www.firesidedeli.com. (301) 387-0083. A place more for the moms and dads to enjoy (local and around-the-world wine and exotic party and dessert cheeses plus sparkling beverages are queen here), our kids found they loved the meatball sandwich and the Chicken Parmesan Panini. Their Cuban panini is wonderful as is all of their wraps - especially anything with MaryEllen's picky selection of cheeses on top. Fresh salads and various cheeses and gourmet chips fill the plate as sides. Specialty sauces and European packaged desserts or mixes are sold, too, to take home. Open daily for lunch and most days, dinner. Sandwiches run between $6.00-8.00 and are very large portioned. Smaller appetites may want to choose half portions with salad, side or soup for the same price.*

GREEN RIDGE STATE FOREST

Flintstone *- 28700 Headquarters Drive NE (I-68 exit 64) 21530. Phone: (301) 478-3124.http://dnr2.maryland.gov/forests/Pages/publiclands/western_ greenridgeforest.aspx*

Green Ridge is the second largest of Maryland's State Forests consisting of a 44,000-acre oak-hickory forest. The region's average annual precipitation is the lowest in the state - just 36 inches - creating pockets of desert-like habitats known as shale barrens. Unusual plants, like the Prickly Pear Cactus, Large Blazing Star and Kate's Mountain Clover are found here. Magnificent views of the surrounding landscape can be seen from Point Lookout, Banners, Logroll, Warrior Mountain and No Name Overlooks. Green Ridge offers a variety of camping and hiking experiences, as well as off-road recreation.

Most of the trails are too long to hike with kids in tow but you can begin one and turn around before too long. Rich in history, the forest was once the site for the Carroll Furnace, originally built as a 1830s steam powered saw mill.

FROSTBURG STATE UNIVERSITY PLANETARIUM

Frostburg - *Tawes Hall, Frostburg State University 21532. Phone: (301) 687-4270. www.frostburg.edu/planetarium. Hours: Sundays at 4:00 and 7:00pm (September - May). Admission: FREE.*

The hour-long presentation includes a look at current evening skies and a multi-media show that changes each month.

THRASHER CARRIAGE MUSEUM

Frostburg - *19 Depot Street (I-68 exit 34, Rte. 40 to Depot Street) 21532. Phone: (301) 689-3380. www.thethrashercarriagemuseum.com. Hours: Thursday-Sunday 12:30-2:30pm. Open weekends only (May, September, October, November, December). Closed January - April. Admission: $2.00-$4.00 per person (age 7+).*

Travel to a time when craftsmen practiced the art of carriage making. Visit a collection of horse-drawn vehicles representing all walks of life. Tours led by costumed docents offer a glimpse into the world of the elegant traveler. Imagine riding in a formal carriage or the Vanderbilt family sleigh. Stories of the clothing, activities, and lifestyles of Victorian Americans are interspersed with the fascinating details of these remarkable vehicles. Special weekends, kids can participate in hands-on activities such as scavenger hunts, carriage wheels and whirl-a-gigs.

SAVAGE RIVER STATE FOREST / NEW GERMANY & BIG RUN STATE PARKS

Grantsville - *349 Headquarters Lane (US 219 south to Glendale Road, east. Left on Rte. 495, follow signs) 21536. Phone: (301) 895-5453. http://dnr2.maryland. gov/publiclands/Pages/western/bigrun.aspx or /newgermany.aspx. Hours: Daily 8:00am-sunset. Admission: $2.00-$4.00 per person on summer weekends, ski weekends and holidays.*

This is the largest of the state forest and park system facilities. <u>**BIG RUN STATE PARK**</u> is situated on the mouth of the savage River Reservoir. With boat launches nearby, Big Run is a popular base camp for outdoor lovers intent on fishing, hiking or hunting. Big Run is the trailhead for a six-mile hiking trail, known as Monroe Run.

NEW GERMANY STATE PARK's lake was formed when Poplar Lick Run was dammed for, once-prosperous, mill operation. The lake offers a boat launch, non-motorized boat rentals, swimming, fishing, flatwater canoeing, hiking, a nature center and cross-country skiing (rentals available). CASSELMAN RIVER BRIDGE STATE PARK (Rte. 40) is the namesake for the centerpiece, often photographed, 80-foot stone arch bridge - the longest single-span stone arch bridge in the country when it was built in 1813. It was reportedly made longer than it needed to be in hopes that the planned Chesapeake and Ohio Canal would pass under it. A public celebration was held at the bridge on the day that workmen removed the supporting timbers. To the amazement of many, the bridge did not collapse. The railroad and then modern highways replaced the well-traveled path once used crossing the bridge.

SPRUCE FOREST ARTISAN VILLAGE

Grantsville - *177 Casselman Road (just off I-68, along the Old National Road) 21536. Phone: (301) 895-3332. www.spruceforest.org. Hours: Monday-Saturday 10:00am-5:00pm.*

Spruce Forest Artisan Village is a non-profit living museum, where nine contemporary artists, working in restored 19th century log cabins, open their studios to the public. Visitors may also shop in the eight craft galleries, picnic along the Casselman River, and explore other historic buildings, including Stanton's working grist mill, the Miller House, Village Church, and Compton School. Artists in Residence include: metalsmith, potters, bird sculpture; slate painter, weaver, stained glass; and metal sculptor. If you're in the area for a little while, plan ahead to attend art classes.

LIVING HISTORY PROGRAM

Grantsville - Spruce Forest. Step back in time to when George Washington traveled through Garrett County, both as a young surveyor and later as an officer in the French and Indian War. Period costumes, food and artifacts, as well as demonstrations to take you back in time. FREE. (third long weekend in May)

CHRISTMAS IN THE VILLAGE

Grantsville - Spruce Forest Artisan Village. Visit artisan studios as you stroll through candle-lit villages. Storytelling, complimentary refreshments, concerts. Admission. (first weekend in December)

ANTIETAM RECREATION

Hagerstown - *9745 Garis Shop Road (1-70 take Exit 29 (Route 65 - Sharpsburg Pike) past McDonalds, second left onto Wagaman Road. At the stop sign turn right onto Garis Shop Road) 21740. www.antietamrecreation.com. Phone: (301) 797-3733. Shows: Summer - every Saturday evening (June-August). Winter - almost every Thursday, Friday, Saturday (mid-November thru December). Admission: Chuckwagon & Show: $25.00-$35.00 per person. Water Activities open to the public are $8.00 per person. Note: Summer camp is a great place to enjoy swimming, riding, canoeing, kayaking, tennis, games, drama, arts and crafts, and much more. Groups rent the facility on Saturdays and school and home school groups utilize the facility during the month of May and September.*

At Antietam Recreation, they specialize in providing active and educational fun in a Christian environment. Summer comes to Maryland with guns a'blazin'! The Wild West Show, featuring World Champion Roper Andy Rotz, runs every Saturday (June-August). These shows include dinner (with fried chicken, potato salad, applesauce, baked beans, rolls, cake and lemonade), followed by outdoor activities like swimming, boating, cable ride, boat slide and other activities, plus the action-packed cowboy drama. You'll see galloping horses, swishing hoop skirts, lively song-and-dance numbers, thrilling stunts, exciting fight sequences, and incredible tricks by their resident cowboy, World Champion Roper Andy Rotz. It's a dinner theater like none other and great for kids cause they get to play around, too.

DISCOVERY STATION

Hagerstown - *101 West Washington St., downtown (across from the Washington County courthouse, metered parking on street) 21740. Phone: (301) 790-0076. www.discoverystation.org. Hours: Tuesday-Saturday 10:00am-4:00pm. Closed Mondays, Sundays and major holidays. Admission: $7.00 adult, $5.00 senior (55+) and military, $6.00 child (2-17). Active military FREE.*

This "hands on" learning museum includes exhibits that promote science, technology and local history through displays and programs that are both educational and entertaining. Included is Hagerstown's Aviation Museum, exhibits from Maryland's Science Center, and more.

Inside a GIANT safe...

Look for an actual model of a Triceratop skull, see the film "When Dinosaurs Roamed America" and wonder at the animatronics that recreate Tyrannosaurus Rex. Or, demonstrate how the eye focuses light, how we perceive motion and color, and how the brain processes visual information into a meaningful picture. Look for angels and Cheshire cats that appear and disappear; a solar powered spacecraft, the Titanic, or a farm exhibit where you can harvest corn or dig for veggies.

HAGERSTOWN SPEEDWAY

Hagerstown - *15112 National Pke (along US 40 near Clear Spring) 21740. Phone: (301) 582-0640. www.hagerstownspeedway.com.*

Hagerstown Speedway features several special events throughout its season including AMA Grand National Motorcycles, monster trucks, World of Outlaw Sprint Cars & Late Models, DIRT Modified and MACS late models. The 1/2 mile, semi-banked clay oval and quarter midget track are on location. Weather permitting, the racing season opens late March and continues until the last weekend of October. Mostly Saturday evening events. Admission charged and varies depending upon the event.

MARYLAND SYMPHONY ORCHESTRA (MSO)

Hagerstown - *13 South Potomac Street, downtown (most performances take place at the Maryland Theatre at 21 South Potomac) 21740. Phone: (301) 797-4000. www.marylandsymphony.org.*

The MSO provides high quality performances for the four-state region. Kids especially like the Symphony Saturdays, Annual Salute to Independence and the Holiday Concert.

PLAZA HOTEL

Hagerstown - 1718 Underpass Way (I-70 & I-81, I-81 north exit 5A Halfway Blvd) 21740. www.ramadaplazahotelhagerstown.com (301) 797-2500. A full service hotel that provides pleasing accommodations at reasonable cost. Tastefully decorated rooms with refrigerators, coffee makers, hair dryers, satellite TV, and more. Indoor heated pool, sauna, spa, fitness center, restaurant on premises.

SCHMANKERL-STUBE BAVARIAN RESTAURANT

Hagerstown - 58 South Potomac Street, downtown (US 40 west, left on Potomac, corner of Antietam St). 21740. (301) 797-3354 or www.schmankerlstube.com. Hagerstown's Bavarian Restaurant carries on the Old Bavarian and German traditions in a truly ethnic atmosphere: "Schmankerl" meaning a Bavarian culinary delicacy and "Stube" a cozy room. Often personally greeted by Charlie Sekula, the proprietor, or by attractively dressed waiters and waitresses in typical Bavarian dress, the guest quickly feels at home in an inviting, cozy environment. If you're not familiar with Schnitzel, Wurst and Strudels - try a sampling of each. Lunch and dinner served daily except Monday.

THE TRAIN ROOM

Hagerstown - *360 South Burhans Blvd. (US 11) (I-81 exit 5) 21740. Phone: (301) 745-6681. www.the-train-room.com. Hours: Monday & Friday 9:00am-6:00pm; Tuesday, Wednesday & Thursday 9:00am-5:00pm; Saturday 9:00am-5:00pm; Sunday Noon-5:00pm. Slightly reduced hours and no Sundays (summer). Admission: $5.00 adult, $1.00 child (3-12).*

The Train room offers model railroading enthusiasts, collectors and novice alike a completely unique experience. A large display of Lionel® model railroading items in 0.027 and standard gauge. A 20'x12' two level, four track model railroad layout which is the centerpiece. You will also see a large selection of other Lionel Products, Model planes, Geiger counters, science kits, fishing equipment, records, electric fans and hundreds of other items manufactured by Lionel® and its subsidiaries over the years. Although most of them are behind glass in showcases, everything is colorful and nostalgic. The Science kits are especially interesting (wish you could still get some of them). Bring the grandparents along for stories of toys they loved in their youth.

HAGAR HOUSE & HAGERSTOWN CITY PARK

Hagerstown - *110 Key Street (located in Hagerstown City Park) 21741. Phone: (301) 739-8393. www.hagerhouse.org. Hours: Friday-Saturday 10:00am-4:00pm (April-October). Admission: $5.00 adult, $3.00 senior (62+) and student (13-17), $2.00 youth (6-12).*

This is the original home of German colonist, Jonathan Hager, founder of Hagerstown. Hager was also known as the first German to make his mark in politics. Built with solid walls and foundation, it was uniquely erected over two springs, and is completely restored with period furnishings.

Look for giant wardrobes; pop goes the weasel; a horse's tail fly-swatter; a broom made from one piece of wood; and actually see the cool spring running right thru the house basement. Re-enactors are present for annual Easter, Christmas and Living History Festivals each year.

HAGERSTOWN CITY PARK - nestled in the city's South End, is considered one of America's Most Beautiful. 50 acres of trees, flowers and open spaces surround three man-made lakes that are home to hundreds of ducks, swans and geese. Park facilities include a concession stand, picnic areas, grills, playgrounds, sport courts, walking trails and a restored steam engine. Engine 202 was built by the Baldwin Locomotive Works in 1912. It is the only Western Maryland road-type steam locomotive in existence. Cabooses built in town are available to board and a small museum is open for a small admission. Do you know what a velocipede is? Ask the engineer at the museum to take you up in the Engine 202.

JONATHAN HAGAR FRONTIER CRAFT DAYS

Hagerstown - Jonathan Hagar House. 60 craftsmen, food, Hagar House tours & Appalachian-style music. (mid-September weekend)

HAGERSTOWN ROUNDHOUSE MUSEUM

Hagerstown - *300 S Burhans Blvd (US 11) 21741. www.roundhouse.org. Phone: (301) 739-4665. Hours: Friday, Saturday & Sunday 1:00-5:00pm. Admission: $0.50-$5.00 per person. FREEBIES: Kids Page with Puzzles & Trivia - /KidsPage.html.*

The Museum is filled with artifacts, photos, railroad art, model railroads, a library, a roster of Western Maryland employees, and a gift shop. There are trains for kids to run, and specials events include the Trains of Christmas and Railroad Heritage Days.

RAILROAD HERITAGE DAYS

Hagerstown - Hagerstown Roundhouse Museum. Historic railroad equipment artifacts and photos, trains for kids to run, HO and O model railroads to see. Admission. (second weekend in June)

THE TRAINS OF CHRISTMAS

Hagerstown - Hagerstown Roundhouse Museum. 300 S. Buthans Blvd (US 11). The visions, sounds, and snows of Christmas past and present on an "O" Gauge railroad. Admission (December, January & February, Friday-Sunday)

AUGUSTOBERFEST

Hagerstown - Central Parking Lot. Augustoberfest is a re-creation of the festivities found at traditional Oktoberfest celebrations – authentic German musicians, dancers, Bavarian food. A children's area features clowns, games, rides and more. www. augustoberfest.org. (last weekend in August)

WILSON COUNTRY STORE / ONE ROOM SCHOOLHOUSE

Hagerstown (Clear Spring) - *14921 Rufus Wilson Road (Route 40 west just past the Conococheague Creek on Rufus Wilson road) 21722. Phone: (301) 582-4718. www.facebook.com/Wilson-Store-117814391580134/ Hours: Store: Open most days 9:00am-5:00pm. Closed Tuesdays & Sundays. Admission: FREE. Shopping is tempting, though. Note: The schoolhouse looks as though the pupils just went to recess. Open by appointment and special events. Call ahead.*

Wilson Country Store, built in the 1850s, stocks stuff that you just don't see anymore. The store sells everything from seed potatoes to three brands of liniment salve (what is it? The kids ask?). They also carry a standard assortment of modern groceries. Try some of their cheese selections, too. Locals really love their white cheddar.

YOGI BEAR'S JELLYSTONE PARK

Hagerstown (Williamsport) - 16519 Lappans Rd (I-81 exit MD 63/68, turn east one mile) 21795. www.jellystonemaryland.com. (800) 421-7116. A fun and full day and night can be had here. They have almost hourly activities planned all day long each summer including bingo, treasure hunts, pool games, movies and such. Cabins and campsites are available huddled near attractions or off in secluded woods. Play Yogi mini-golf, pedal carts and the moon bounce. Cool off in one of two pool areas. One basic, the other Water Zone is full of interactive squirts and sprays and two new giant, twisting waterslides. Finish off the day with the Bear's Cave black light game room.

C & O CANAL VISITOR CENTER

Hancock - *326 E. Main Street 21750. Phone: (301) 678-5463. www.nps.gov/choh/. Hours: Daily 9:00am-4:30pm. Closed winter months. Admission: Voluntary donation.*

The Chesapeake and Ohio Canal had its beginning in 1828, when President John Quincy Adams broke ground for what was called "The Great NationalProject", a canal that would stretch from Georgetown, near DC and end in Pittsburgh.

The canal would be used to carry goods and supplies inland and aid with the migration of people heading west to settle beyond the original 13 colonies. The estimated cost: about $3 million and would take ten years. When the canal

> **THE C&O CANAL PAW PAW TUNNEL** - an engineering marvel is just south along Rte. 51, right at the Maryland/WV border, across the Potomac River. Thousands of men labored to build this dramatic portal through an entire mountain.

was completed in 1850, it had taken 22 years and $13 million to build, plus it fell short of the original destination of Pittsburgh and ended in Cumberland, Maryland. Worse yet, upon completion, the canal was obsolete because of the railroad. Despite all of this, the canal remained open 74 years. Boats pulled by mules floated tons of cargo, including coal, hay, hydraulic cement and fertilizer from Cumberland to Georgetown. Inside the Visitors Center, relive the canal era through models of canal boats, pictures and memorabilia. Giant trees shade a sandy towpath between the river and the old canal bed, visited by thousands of hikers, bikers, birders, and naturalists who enjoy the spectacular scenery of the park.

SIDELING HILL

Hancock - *(off I-68 exit Woodmount Rd. at the top of Sideling Hill Mtn. 5 miles west of Hancock) 21750. http://dnr2.maryland.gov/wildlife/Pages/publiclands/western/sidelinghill.aspx Phone: (301) 678-5442. Hours: Daylight hours, stop, park and view. Admission: FREE.*

More than one hundred thousand people annually visit what's been called a geological marvel - one of the best rock exposures in the NW United States. In the early 1980s, a massive project began to construct a roadway. To begin this monumental task, a V-shaped wedge was blasted out of Sideling Hill. More highway construction cut through the mountain exposing almost 850 vertical feet of a textbook example syncline (exposed sedimentary rock formations). There are fossils galore! It's much more interesting to study science "hands and view-on" (a giant science project). You can even touch a piece of the oldest Maryland rock! If weather permits, take a walk outside up the fenced walkway, to view the cut up close. Several geologic wayside stations help you interpret what you see.

A walk over the pedestrian bridge offers good photo opportunities from the middle of the bridge, as well as from the opposite side, south of the road. Why is water and rust seeping from the rock?

WESTERN MARYLAND RAIL TRAIL

Hancock - *(one mile off I-70 to Rte. 56 or parking lot one mile west of I-70 on Rte. 144 on Main street) 21750. Phone: (301) 842-2155. www.westernmarylandrailtrail. org/WMRT/ Hours: Open year round 8:00am-sunset, weather permitting. Admission: FREE.*

The Western Maryland Rail Trail provides a unique paved hiking and biking trail built on an abandoned railroad bed. Over 21 miles, the easy-to-access trail extends from Big Pool (near Fort Frederick) to Pearre (foot of Sideling Hill Mountain) paralleling the Potomac River and the C&O Canal. Traveling this trail, hikers, cyclists, joggers and in-line skaters experience the beauty of rolling farmland, abundant wildlife, and history of the surrounding area. Interpretive programs and special events are held throughout the year.

DANS MOUNTAIN STATE PARK

Lonaconing - *17410 Recreation Area Road (I-68 exit 34, Rte. 36 south to Midland) 21539. http://dnr2.maryland.gov/publiclands/Pages/western/dansmountain.aspx Phone: (301) 463-5487. Hours: Dawn - dusk. Miscellaneous: Dan's Rock is within the park. (left onto Paradise Street Extended, cross bridge and go to the second street (Paradise St) and turn left and go about three miles) LONACONING IRON FURNACE AND PARK is on Rte. 36. The furnace, erected in 1837, used coal and coke rather than charcoal to make iron. Day use admission is free.*

This day-use park has rugged mountain terrain, and an Olympic-size pool with a waterslide. Nearby, Dans Rock is a 2,898 foot rock structure that sprawls along the brow of Dan's Mountain overlooking the panoramic Potomac Valley that stretches for twenty miles. The viewer will be delighted with the colorful foliage and the surrounding rolling mountains from the new observation deck with gazebo. Dan's Mountain received its name after Daniel Cresap, one of the first settlers in the area, who was killed on the mountain.

CRANESVILLE SUBARTIC SWAMP

Oakland - *(Cranesville & Lake Ford Rds, just past Deep Creek Lake) 21550. Phone: (301) 387-4386. www.nature.org/ourinitiatives/regions/northamerica/ unitedstates/maryland_dc/placesweprotect/cranesville-swamp.xml. Hours: Daylight hours.*

A swamp in Maryland? Walk in the footsteps of prehistoric creatures in the small piece of forest and bog remaining after the Ice Age - wild and still home to a range of species of plants usually found in the extreme northern areas of Alaska and Canada. Home to a bog that contains peat more than three feet deep, plants that eat insects, a conifer that sheds its needles in fall, and an owl that fits in the palm of a hand. Listen for the saw-whet owl's strange, tooting call. A 1,500 foot boardwalk crosses the swamp, and six trails wind through this unusual tundra region. Although all trails are fewer than two miles and not difficult to walk, hiking boots are recommended as some trails may be muddy.

HERRINGTON MANOR STATE PARK

Oakland - 222 Herrington Lane (4 miles past entrance to Swallow Falls) 21550. http://dnr2.maryland.gov/publiclands/Pages/western/herrington.aspx   Phone: (301) 334-9180. Admission: $3.00 per vehicle, off peak and summer weekdays. $3.00 per person summer weekends and ski season weekends. Add $2.00 for non-state residents. Note: Summer Wednesday morning hayrides through the park into the outlying forest. $5.00 per person.

The park features a 53-acre lake and beach for swimming and non-motorized boating (canoe and paddle boat rentals). Other activities include hiking, biking trails, interpretive programs, groomed cross-country ski trails along with ski/ snowshoe rentals, and 20 log cabins available to rent.

APPLE BUTTER BOIL

Oakland - Herrington Manor/Swallow Falls State Park. Enjoy arts, crafts, and music while stirring the apple butter and feasting on a corn roast. Admission to State Park. (Labor Day weekend)

PLEASANT VALLEY DREAM RIDES

Oakland - 1689 Pleasant Valley Road (follow 219 3 Miles South of Oakland, Turn Left On Paul Friend Road) 21550. www.pleasantvalleydreamrides.com/sleigh.htm. Phone: (301) 334-1688. Tours: Carriage/Sleigh Rides: $12.00-$16.00 per person (age 3+) on the hour daily except Sundays 10:00am-10:00pm. Dairy Farm Tours Monday through Saturday 10:00am-5:00pm (on the hour). $5.00-$8.00 Per Person (Under 3 Free). Tours By Reservation Only. Milking at 4:00am and 4:00pm daily.

Looking for a great family or group activity near Deep Creek Lake Resort? The picturesque area known as Pleasant Valley is the backdrop for your horse drawn tour of the Miller Family Farm. Take a winter sleigh ride or a horse drawn carriage ride and enjoy the pastoral mountain beauty of this Amish community. Tour the agricultural facilities and learn about daily life on an

Amish dairy farm. Educational hands-on experiences are included.

Tour the Farm and learn about life on an Amish Dairy Farm. Hand feed cows grain or baby calves using a bottle. No matter what time of day, they will prep a cow and allow you to hand milk it, then put the cow on the milker to demonstrate how a cow is milked today.

POTOMAC-GARRETT STATE FOREST/ BACKBONE MOUNTAIN

Oakland - 222 Herrington Lane (US 219 south to Sand Flat Road, turn east past Rte. 135, through town of Deer Park) 21550. Phone: (301) 334-2038. http://dnr2. maryland.gov/forests/Pages/publiclands/western_potomacforest.aspx   Hours: Dawn to dusk.

Home to the highest point in any Maryland state forest, BACKBONE MOUNTAIN (3,220 feet). A densely forested and serene area, this is a favorite of hikers. This steep gradient has numerous fast falling brooks and streams which feed the river. Don't forget to pick up a certificate near the marker sign confirming that you made it to the highest point in Maryland. (easiest access is from WV Monongahela National Forest; head south on Rte. 219, sign will be on your left). The rest of the forest's public lands are for fishing, primitive camping, 3-D bow range, snowmobile trails and some hiking/biking trails. Tweens might really enjoy the fun and challenging shoots at 30 life-size dimensional targets on the archery range. Activities are of a more primitive nature and the hiking trails are 3+ miles long.

SWALLOW FALLS STATE PARK

Oakland - 222 Herrington Lane (six miles north of town) 21550. Phone: (301) 334-9180.   http://dnr2.maryland.gov/publiclands/Pages/western/swallowfalls.aspx

Hours: Daylight hours. Admission: $3.00 per person (summer). $3.00 per vehicle (rest of year). Out of state residents add $2.00 to all service charges. Note: Hiking, campground, fishing, picnic area, playground and nature programs (summer).

See some of Maryland's best waterfalls. This mountainous park contains some of the state's most breathtaking scenery. The Youghiogheny River flows along the park's borders, passing through shaded rocky gorges and creating rippling rapids.

Muddy Creek Falls is a vivacious 52-foot waterfall surrounded by tall hemlocks and an old forest (possibly over 300 years old). These falls are the tallest waterfalls in the state and are so accessible. Begin at the trailhead right by the small Visitors center. Walk a short distance on the path and then bear to your right for another short distance on a path lined with soaring hemlocks. Then, begin the boardwalk portion that leads you to many easy viewing platforms. You can hear the rush of the falls as you approach. The first one is near where Edison, Ford, Firestone and friends once camped in the early 1900s.

Another takes you to the top of the falls. Yet another, with wooden steps and platforms, takes you to the bottom of the falls. All observation decks have fantastic views. Once you're at the bottom, the adventure trail begins. Climb over rocks and under small cave overhangings while still on a trail. Remember to bring some water and first aid basics. Few falls are as impressive as locals will tell you - but these trails and falls are!

BROADFORD LAKE RECREATION AREA

Oakland (Mountain Lake Park) - *(Rte. 135, Mountain Lake Park & Recreation Lane) 21550. Phone: (301) 334-9222. www.mtnlakepark.com/pages/recandparks.html. Hours: Daily 9:00am-sunset. Closed mid-November thru March. Admission: a few dollars per vehicle or person.*

This popular family park has a lake, concession stand, picnic and beach area, volleyball, basketball, boat launch, and boat and pavilion rentals. The beach and swimming area is most popular for kids in the area.

EASTER EGG HUNT

Oakland - Broadford Lake Park. Hunt begins at Noon - sharp. A free event for area children ages 2-10 sponsored by local media. Three different age groups hunt for thousands of Easter eggs stuffed with candy, prizes and $50 savings bonds. (Saturday before Easter)

SIMON PEARCE GLASSBLOWING

Oakland (Mountain Lake Park) - *265 Glass Drive (Rte. 219 south to Oakland downtown. Then Rte 135 and turn left on Glass Drive) 21550. Phone: (301) 387-5277 or (877) 452-7763. www.simonpearce.com. Hours: Monday-Friday 10:00am-3:30pm, Weekends 10:00am-5:00pm. Admission: FREE.*

Visitors to the site can take self-guided tours to observe the glassblowers at work. The setup includes a catwalk viewing gallery above the factory floor providing a great "birds-eye" view. Explanatory process sheets and details along the way describe the glassblowing process. Glass vessels began hundreds of years ago in wide variety. Using similar old-world techniques, clear glass is formed by melting, gathering, blowing, shaping, finishing and annealing (cooling very slowly). Art in motion...we were mesmerized! We inquired about all the movements necessary to shape the molten glass. The manager said the artists call it "the dance" - all the twisting and tooling and blowing and cooling synchronized! Did you know the first piece new glass blowers work on is a glass ice cube? Once they've successfully made several hundred, they move on to napkin holders - then the big stuff.

Don't try this at home kids...

WASHINGTON COUNTY RURAL HERITAGE MUSEUM

Sharpsburg - *7313 Sharpsburg Pike (Rte. 65) (I-70 exit 29, five miles south on Rte. 65 at the Washington Cty. Agricultural Education Center) 21713. Phone: (240) 420-1714. www.ruralheritagemuseum.org. Hours: Weekends 1:00-4:00pm (Mid-January - early December). Admission: Free, donations accepted.*

The museum contains more than 2,000 items, most of which are on loan from or have been donated by local residents. Upon arrival, there is a short video to introduce visitors to the museum. Exhibits include: a typical General Store (on loan from the Washington County Historical Society); examples of Rural Living, such as a farm kitchen, parlor, and a country church; and examples of Modes of Travel, such as an original Conestoga wagon, sleighs and sleds. Other exhibits contain equipment and artifacts used by local farmers, and displays on butchering and dairying. Kids are often invited to watch crafting like broom making, grain grinding, milking and butter churning. Great time to visit is their Spring or Holiday Open House or the annual SpudFest. Ever harvested potatoes with the prize being homemade potato chips?

ANTIETAM BATTLEFIELD

Sharpsburg - *(along MD 34 & 65. Main entrance is off of MD 65, ten miles south of I-70) 21782. Phone: (301) 432-5124. www.nps.gov/anti/. Hours: Daily 8:30am-5:00pm. Open until 6:00pm summers. Closed only major winter holidays. Admission: $4.00 per person fee or $6.00 per family. Tours: The best way to view the battlefield is to take the self-guided driving tour. The tour road is 8½ miles long with 11 stops including Dunker Church, The Cornfield, Bloody Lane and Burnside Bridge. Most visitors drive the route, but walking and biking are encouraged. Audiotape or CD programs, which enhance the self-guided tour, may be purchased from the bookstore. Note: Be sure to visit the new Pry House Field Hospital Museum. This new museum is located in the historic Pry House which served as Union Commander General George B. McClellan's headquarters during the battle. The museum is sponsored by the National Museum of Civil War Medicine and is open daily 10:00am to 5:00pm. Educators: Curriculum Materials: www.nps.gov/anti/forteachers/curriculummaterials.htm. FREEBIES: Scavenger Hunts: www.nps.gov/anti/forteachers/upload/scavenger%20hunt%20general.pdf.*

The Battle of Antietam on September 17, 1862, climaxed the first of General Robert E. Lee's two attempts to extend the Confederate effort into the North. This peaceful family town was the place where the slow moving giant armies exploded, leaving 23,110 dead and wounded. More men were killed or wounded at Antietam than on any other single day of the Civil War. Visitors can still feel the profound stillness of the battlefields. Although neither side gained a decisive victory, Lee's failure to carry the effort effectively into the North produced two important results: Great Britain postponed the recognition of the Confederate government, and President Abraham Lincoln issued the Emancipation Proclamation on January 1, 1863. "Antietam Visit," an award-winning film,

Walk over the famous Burnside Bridge

is shown on the hour. This 26-minute movie recreates the battle as well as President Abraham Lincoln's visit to the Union commander General George B. McClellan. Every day at 12:00 noon a new one hour documentary about the battle of Antietam narrated by James Earl Jones is shown in the visitor center theater.

The driving tour can be a little long for kids but look for interesting tidbits found on these stops: Clara Barton's visit (angel); the Dunker Church where men from both sides chatted and had peace when not in battle; Bloody Lane where so many fell; and the famous walk out to the Burnside bridge.

Peace at this church...

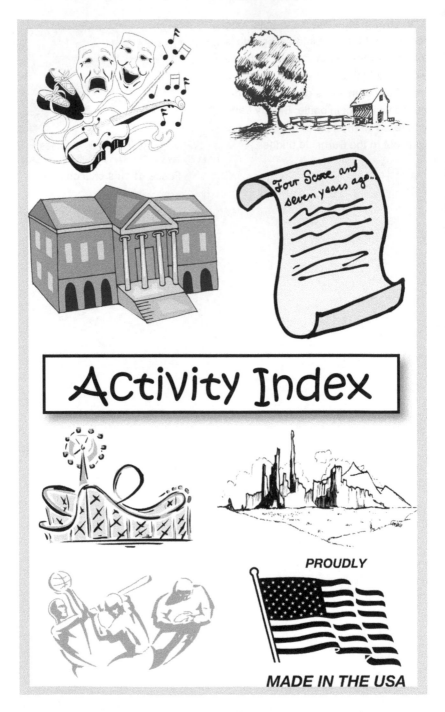

Activity Index

HISTORY (cont.)

SUGGESTED LODGING & DINING

CAPITAL *Frederick*, Sleep Inn, 14

CAPITAL *Frederick*, Hampton Inn & Suites, 14

CAPITAL *Largo*, Radisson Hotel Largo, 20

CAPITAL - DC *Washington*, Clyde's At The Gallery, 34

CENTRAL *Annapolis*, Annapolis Ice Cream Company, 60

CENTRAL *Annapolis*, Buddy's Crabs & Ribs, 61

CENTRAL *Annapolis (Eastport)*, Carrol's Creek Café, 71

CENTRAL *Annapolis*, Chick & Ruth's Delly, 61

CENTRAL *Baltimore*, Hyatt Regency Baltimore, 76

CENTRAL *Baltimore (Columbia)*, Doubletree Columbia, 87

CENTRAL *Friendship*, Herrington Harbour Inn, 98

CENTRAL *Galesville*, Pirate's Cove Restaurant, 99

CENTRAL *Havre de Grace*, Laurrapin Grille, 101

CENTRAL *Havre de Grace*, MacGregors Restaurant, 101

CENTRAL *Havre de Grace*, Vandiver Inn, 102

EASTERN SHORE *Cambridge*, Hyatt Regency Chesapeake Bay Resort, 119

EASTERN SHORE *Ocean City*, Princess Royale Resort Hotel, 133

EASTERN SHORE *Rock Hall*, Durdings Store, 136

EASTERN SHORE *Salisbury*, Quality Inn Salisbury, 137

EASTERN SHORE *Smith Island (Ewell)*, Bayside Inn, 125

SOUTHERN *Lexington Park*, Hampton Inn, 152

SOUTHERN *Lexington Park*, Linda's Café, 152

SOUTHERN *Solomon's Island*, Stoney's Kingfishers Seafood House, 161

WESTERN *Deep Creek Lake (Oakland)*, Lakeside Creamery, 180

WESTERN *Deep Creek Lake (Oakland)*, Trader's Coffee House, 180

WESTERN *Deep Creek Lake (Swanton)*, Fireside Deli, 182

WESTERN *Hagerstown*, Plaza Hotel, 186

WESTERN *Hagerstown*, Schmankerl-Stube Bavarian Restaurant, 187

WESTERN *Hagerstown (Williamsport)*, Yogi Bear's Jellystone Park, 189

TOURS

CAPITAL *Dickerson*, White's Ferry, 11

CAPITAL *Walkersville*, Walkersville Southern Railroad, 28

CAPITAL - DC *Washington*, Old Town Trolley Tours, 33

CAPITAL - DC *Washington*, DC Duck Tours, 38

CAPITAL - DC *Washington*, Tourmobile Sightseeing, 40

CAPITAL - DC *Washington*, Bureau Of Engraving & Printing Tour, 42

CAPITAL - DC *Washington*, White House, 45

CENTRAL *Annapolis*, Historic Annapolis Museum, 62

CENTRAL *Annapolis*, Schooner Woodwind, 65

CENTRAL *Annapolis*, Thomas Point Schoal Lighthouse Tour, 67

CENTRAL *Annapolis*, U.S. Naval Academy, 65

CENTRAL *Annapolis*, Discover Annapolis Trolley Tour, 68

CENTRAL *Annapolis*, Family Fishing Adventures, 69

CENTRAL *Annapolis*, Pirate Adventures On The Chesapeake, 68

CENTRAL *Annapolis*, Watermark Cruises & Walking Tours, 69

TOURS (cont.)